Public Banks

Public banks are banks located within the public sphere of a state. They are pervasive, with more than 900 institutions worldwide, and powerful, wielding tens of trillions in assets. Public banks are neither essentially good nor bad. Rather, they are dynamic institutions, made and remade by contentious social forces. As the first single-authored book on public banks, this timely intervention examines how these institutions can confront the crisis of climate finance and catalyse a green and just transition. The author explores six case studies across the globe, demonstrating that public banks have acquired the representative structures, financial capacity, institutional knowledge, collaborative networks and geographical reach to tackle decarbonisation, definancialisation and democratisation. These institutions are not without contradictions, torn as they are between contending public and private interests in class-divided society. Ultimately, social forces and struggles shape how – and if – public banks serve the public good.

THOMAS MAROIS is a Senior Lecturer at SOAS University of London and Senior Research Fellow in Patient Finance and Banking at the UCL Institute for Innovation and Public Purpose (IIPP). He sits on the Advisory Board of the Public Banking Institute, has authored the book *States, Banks and Crisis* (2012) and co-edited the book *Public Banks and Covid-19* (2020).

Public Banks

Decarbonisation, Definancialisation and Democratisation

THOMAS MAROIS

SOAS University of London and UCL Institute for Innovation and Public Purpose

CAMBRIDGE
UNIVERSITY PRESS

CAMBRIDGE
UNIVERSITY PRESS

University Printing House, Cambridge CB2 8BS, United Kingdom

One Liberty Plaza, 20th Floor, New York, NY 10006, USA

477 Williamstown Road, Port Melbourne, VIC 3207, Australia

314–321, 3rd Floor, Plot 3, Splendor Forum, Jasola District Centre, New Delhi – 110025, India

79 Anson Road, #06–04/06, Singapore 079906

Cambridge University Press is part of the University of Cambridge.

It furthers the University's mission by disseminating knowledge in the pursuit of education, learning, and research at the highest international levels of excellence.

www.cambridge.org
Information on this title: www.cambridge.org/9781108839150
DOI: 10.1017/9781108989381

First published 2021

A catalogue record for this publication is available from the British Library.

ISBN 978-1-108-83915-0 Hardback

For my family, and for the struggles to come.

Contents

Figures

Tables

Boxes

Abbreviations

AAAA	Addis Ababa Action Agenda
AIIB	Asian Infrastructure Investment Bank
ASEAN	Association of Southeast Asian Nations
ATB	Alberta Treasury Branch
BCE	Before the Common Era
BND	Bank of North Dakota
BNDES	Banco Nacional de Desenvolvimento Econômico e Social (National Bank for Economic and Social Development)
BPDC	Banco Popular y de Desarrollo Comunal
BRI	Belt and Road Initiate
CCB	China Construction Bank
CDB	China Development Bank
COP	Conference of the Parties
CPC	Communist Party of China
CPI	Climate Policy Initiative
CPRP	COVID-19 PACE Recovery Program
CRAFICARD	Committee to Review the Arrangements for Institutional Credit for Agriculture and Rural Development
CSOs	civil society organisations
DM	Deutsche Mark
EIB	European Investment Bank
ESG	environmental, social, and governance
FCL	Labour Capitalisation Fund
FfD	financing for development
FoEUS	Friends of the Earth United States
FX	foreign exchange
GCC	Gulf Cooperation Council

GHG	greenhouse gas
GLLR	Global Lenders of Last Resort
GNI	gross national income
GPI	Global Public Investor
GRI	Global Reporting Initiative
HELCOM	Helsinki Commission
HLM	high-level manager
IATF	Inter-Agency Task Force
ICBC	Industrial and Commercial Bank of China
IFI	International financial institution
IMF	International Monetary Fund
KfW	Kreditanstalt für Wiederaufbau
KPIs	key performance indicators
MENA	Middle East and North Africa
MSMEs	micro-, small- and medium-sized enterprises
NABARD	National Bank for Agriculture and Rural Development
NADB	North American Development Bank
NAFTA	North American Free Trade Agreement
NDEP	Northern Dimension Environmental Partnership
NGOs	non-governmental organisations
NHB	National Housing Bank
NIB	Nordic Investment Bank
OECD	Organisation for Economic Cooperation and Development
OMFIF	Official Monetary and Financial Institutions Forum
PBI	Public Banking Institute
PBOC	People's Bank of China
PFI	public financial institution
PPPs	public-private partnerships
RBI	Reserve Bank of India
RBS	Royal Bank of Scotland
RFC	Reconstruction Finance Corporation

RIDF	Rural Infrastructure Development Fund
RMB	renminbi
ROAAs	return on average assets
RRBs	Regional Rural Banks
SBA	Small Business Administration
SDGs	Sustainable Development Goals
SELF	Small Employer Loan Fund
SEO	senior environmental officer
SHG-BLP	Self-Help Group-Bank Linkage Programme
SIDBI	Small Industries Development Bank of India
SMEs	small- and medium-sized enterprises
SWF	Sovereign wealth fund
TNI	Transnational Institute
UNCTAD	United Nations Conference on Trade and Development
UNFCCC	United Nations Framework Convention on Climate Change
UNRISD	United Nations Research Institute for Social Development
UO	ultimate owner
WEF	World Economic Forum
WHO	World Health Organisation

Introduction

The impacts of climate change are worsening, even as greenhouse gas emissions continue to increase. Far more ambitious climate action – including climate finance – is critical, especially for the poorest and most vulnerable. Given these broad trends, it is clear that the world will not achieve the Sustainable Development Goals without a fundamental shift in the international financial system that enables us to address urgent global threats and restore trust in international cooperation. Action is needed at all levels.

UN Secretary General António Guterres, Preface to the UN Inter-Agency Task Force 2019 Financing for Sustainable Development Report, UN IATF (2019, iii)

For the Global Green New Deal, the task is more of a marathon than a sprint. Here public banks have another advantage, because they have a more diversified portfolio and broader geographic reach to underserved areas and segments of the economy and (especially development banks) take a longer-term approach. By contrast, private (and especially foreign) banks are known for avoiding such lending as they pick profitable cherries elsewhere.

UNCTAD (2019, XII)

For decades public banks were largely forgotten, considered anti-quated, and perceived as stagnant. Now they are *resurgent*, socially *contested*, and institutionally *dynamic*. In ways unimaginable just a few years ago, public banks have been catapulted to the centre of debate over sustainable, stable, and democratic development. This transpired as public banks were swept up in the events of three overlapping global crises – the crises of finance, of climate finance, and of Covid-19. As the 2008–09 financial crisis rocked the global economy, public banks lent into it. As it become apparent that private investors had failed to make good on a global green transition, public banks stepped in to help finance sustainable development. As emergency credits were urgently needed to face the impact of a global pandemic, public banks made them available. Through these crises public banks have emerged more prominent and powerful. But for

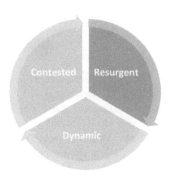

FIGURE I.I Contemporary public banks in class-divided society

whom? And what does their resurgence say about the ability of public banks to change and respond to societal challenges?

This book argues that public banks are resurgent not by virtue of being publicly owned but because of the institutional functions they have acquired over time and can perform within class-divided society (see Figure I.1). The functions of public banks, however, are far from neutral within neoliberalism, tending to favour private over public interests. This is not always or necessarily so. As contested institutions within global capitalism, public banks have also acquired pro-public functions able to catalyse decarbonisation, definancialisation, and democratisation. They too have the capacity to respond to emergencies like the Covid-19 pandemic. While never without contradiction, the dynamic functioning of public banks can and must be institutionally reinforced in ways that catalyse a global green and just transition.

This is not a commonly held position. For many international finance and development agencies, public banks are more and more seen as delivering a win-win solution that can smooth unstable financial markets, catalyse new green investments, and mask the immediate impact of a global pandemic *without* undermining long-held neoliberal marketisation logics, addressing social iniquities, or displacing the primacy of private accumulation interests. Chief among these agencies are the World Bank, Organisation for Economic Cooperation and Development (OECD), European Union, and the United Nations Finance for Development Office, which pitch their support as conditional on public banks' 'pro-market' orientation, time-limited interventions, and willingness to support risk-return preferences of private investors (see IMF/World Bank 2015; EPSC 2017; OECD 2017; UN IATF 2019). The rationale is couched in traditional 'market-failure' narratives: public banks can and should be market-fixing, not displacing, entities tasked with 'blending' public resources with private capital to provide longer-term, lower-risk, and ideally more stable and greener *private* investment opportunities (Stern 2007; Bhattacharya et al. 2016; Badré 2018). The raison d'être of public banks in this mainstream narrative is to support market-based and growth-oriented economic development by leveraging private capital.

However, the mainstream contradictions between unlimited carbonising growth strategies and limited decarbonising investment commitments, as well as between the class-divided preferences of investors for the sustainability of *financial capitalism* prior to the socially equitable financing of *sustainable development*, are never addressed. They have been instead reproduced within the United Nations 2030 Sustainable Development Goals (Martens 2017; Hickel 2019). This is despite the growing evidence questioning the efficacy of blended finance (Attridge and Engen 2019).

At the same time enduring problems of gender oppression, social inequality, eroded labour rights, weak democratic decision-making, and the ecological limits of capitalist growth have been by and large absent from academic research on the future of public banks in economic development, sustainable or otherwise (see Clark et al. 2005; Cull et al. 2017; Ferrari et al. 2017; Griffith-Jones and Ocampo 2018; Naqvi et al. 2018). This has not been the case elsewhere. Civil society and non-governmental organisations (CSOs and NGOs), trade unions, and critical scholars have criticised the financial blending strategy as a reworked form of public–private partnerships more concerned with profit maximisation than with addressing sustainable development and just transitions (see Sweeney and Treat 2017; Brown 2019; Murray and Spronk 2019; Steinfort and Kishimoto

2019). Therein public banks and finance are, not uncritically, seen as potentially viable alternatives.

The stakes over the future of public banks are high, though this is too often not well understood. Neoliberal common sense is that public banks are basically incapable of financing economic development effectively, let alone spearheading ambitions like a global green transition. As economist Yongzhong Wang notes in passing, '[o]bviously, the considerable demand for infrastructure investment cannot be satisfied by the public sector alone' (2016, 1; emphasis added). Economists trust that, at best, public banks can enable the private sector and maximise private finance for development through blending. UN data reinforces such neoliberal common sense, alleging that public banks have combined assets of but $5 trillion (UN IATF 2019, 143). What can $5 trillion do when we need $90 trillion in sustainable infrastructure investment by 2030? In this narrative, public banks can only leverage and catalyse private investment.

What if common sense is not good sense? What if the neoliberal narrative of public banking *incapacity* is more myth than fact? And if this were so, what if public banks could democratically catalyse an environmentally green and socially just transformation wherein the public interest took precedence over those of private investors?

The evidence suggests that these questions are anything but rhetorical. There are today 910 public banks worldwide that command $49 trillion in assets, a mass of capital nearly ten times greater than official UN estimates (see Chapter 1). And public banks are on the rise. Not only have bank privatisations stalled but governing authorities, north and south, are creating new public banks in Canada, Nigeria, France, American Samoa, Germany, Indonesia, the UK, and elsewhere. The US may soon follow suit with the 2019 passage of the Public Banks Bill (AB-857) in California, the fifth largest economy in the world, and as other US states and municipalities pursue similar action. This is not to mention the two new China-backed multilateral banks, the New Development Bank and Asian Infrastructure Investment Bank.

While this public banking resurgence is seemingly against all neoliberal odds, it needs emphasising that public banks are not inherently contrary to private interests or neoliberal aspirations. Much of what public banks did in the late nineteenth and early twentieth century transitions to capitalism was to subsidise private capital formation within national borders (Gerschenkron 1962). Today private investors support the financial blending agenda featuring public banks in order to protect and magnify their own prospects of capital accumulation. Yet public banks are complex entities and have also developed enduring public interest and collective good legacies that can be built upon, including public service support, knowledge and capacity building, providing for essential infrastructure, social and cultural lending, directed support for farmers and trades, environmental financing, municipality financing, and more. In certain public banks, these legacies will not be easily subordinated to private interests as pro-public social forces defend them and even advance a more democratic, green, and equity-oriented agenda.

Be they pulled to the private or to the public interest by contending social forces, indications are that public banks will have a materially significant place in the future of global finance for sustainable development. It is thus a major failing of scholars concerned with finance and development that there has been no theoretical rethinking of public banks as powerful and contested, and therefore *dynamic*, institutions within global financialised capitalism (Marois 2021).[1] Quite the opposite. While the economics literature lists off possible new market-expanding tasks for public banks, it continues to depend upon fixed, opposing, and ideologically charged tropes of public versus private ownership with scholars constantly striving to produce the

---

[1] While a more 'positive' literature on public 'development' banks has emerged in recent years, it is largely atheoretical and narrowly focused on development banks alone, offering no wider framework on public banks within capitalism. The exception to this tendency has been the longstanding research of Kurt von Mettenheim and Olivier Butzbach (see the Bibliography for a list of relevant works). The work of Natalya Naqvi (2019) notably draws out some of the social and political forces influencing decisions on public banks.

final say on the ultimate benefits of one form of bank ownership over another (see Chapter 2). This book makes no attempt to bridge these polarised economic divides. It instead reverses causality by focusing on how socially contested institutional *functions* give meaning to a bank's public ownership form.

The timing could not be more urgent as we confront the extinction-level crisis of climate change and need to find ways of building forward better in the wake of a global pandemic. Policymakers have struggled to have private banks look beyond their bottom lines as Covid-19 wrought economic paralysis. Public banks, by contrast, have made time available for communities to adjust (see Epilogue). Neither have private banks been pulling their relative weight in climate finance. Public banks have but one-fifth the resources yet channel nearly as much capital as private banks into green investments. Contrary to neoliberal idealism, the short-term, return-maximising horizons of private finance have failed to generate a global *green* transition at the speed or scale needed. Private finance has also failed to prioritise a socially just transition. Amidst financialisation most people face stagnating or falling wages, rising job insecurity and anti-labour practices, the retreat of public provisioning of essential services, skyrocketing inequality of wealth and opportunity, and persistent racism and sexism (Stockhammer 2012; Storm 2018). Recurrent crises are being resolved according to a neoliberal logic, that is, by letting the costs of recovery fall disproportionately onto workers, women, racialised communities, and the most marginalised in society while the benefits accrue to the already capital rich – either through the direct bailouts of large corporations and private banks or through the knock-on socio-economic impacts of austerity (Marois 2014; Tooze 2018). These injustices prevail as marketised and consumerist human activities feed climate change and global warming. Societies will have to face rising sea levels and extreme weather conditions that will foster recurrent waves of mass migration and economic hardship. There will be increased burden on our natural environment, from the coral reefs to the carbon sinks of vast forests and wetlands. In response, low carbon and accessible infrastructure needs constructing, local jobs need protecting, fossil fuels need to remain in the ground, the planet needs cooling, and universal social equity needs action. The already-built environment will come under new and growing threats as we struggle collectively to refurbish existing stocks while maintaining and upgrading public services and infrastructure as we transition to a net zero-carbon emissions future.

All of this will require massive financial investments, and a sea change in how we reproduce humanity. This will be subject to class-divided struggles over who benefits disproportionately from what public banks can do in response. Private interests are pushing to have public banks first protect their financial returns by absorbing the risks of climate finance. Public interests have secured gains, making public banks open to funding decarbonisation and climate change mitigation projects, as well as mandating them to provide longer-term and stable financing for development, often in support of jobs in micro-, small-, and medium-sized enterprises (MSMEs). Governance frameworks have enabled public authorities to activate public banking capacity at the height of a global pandemic. But there is the risk that public banks will fall victim to private interests and capital accumulation imperatives within neoliberalism and to potential abuse by corrupt political elites and oligarchs even in democratic and accountable societies. Powerful material interests will fight to entrench pre-existing and class-divided structures of inequality. Strategic pro-public and democratised responses will need to provide a socially equitable and materially significant financial alternative. Existing public banks offer the most viable platform.

A political confrontation over the future of public banks is unavoidable. Yet it would be naïve to presume that there ever was a time when public banks were *not* subject to class-divided and politically coordinated contestation among social forces (von Mettenheim 2010; Marois 2012; McNally 2020). Who will get what from the accumulated capital and institutional knowledge of public banks? From a pro-public and social equity vantage point, there is little hope

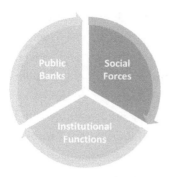

FIGURE I.2 Public banks being made and remade

of a green and just transition without powerful public banks that can be democratically commanded to function in the public interest. Put otherwise, democratised public banks are a necessary, if by no means sufficient, condition of a green and just transition (Marois 2015). To be sure, none of what public banks do is natural or neutral, for public banks and their functions *are made and remade* by contending social forces in time- and place-bound class-divided societies struggling over the future of those same banks and functions (see Figure I.2). There is evidence, nevertheless, of existing public banks being made to work towards a pro-public green and just transition. The cases studied in the book show that public banks have acquired the geographical scale, financial resources, institutional knowledge and experience, and democratic credentials to lead a pro-public response. None of these public banks are without contradictions. There is the need to press for the 'public' in banks to be 'pro-public' and for that to be democratically armoured.

I.I RESURGENT PUBLIC BANKS AND THE CRISES OF FINANCE, OF CLIMATE FINANCE, AND OF COVID-19

To understand the resurgence of and potential for public banks is to question what public banks are. For many observers, the simple answer is that public banks are financial institutions owned publicly by a state or government authority (De Luna-Martínez and Vicente 2012). There is truth in this no doubt, but it is limited. My view is that ownership on its own tells us little. Yet much of the finance for development literature fundamentally relies on ownership as *the* harbinger of inherent institutional characteristics (La Porta et al. 2002). For Keynesian 'development' approaches, public banks are stereotypically meant only to provide additional finance to the private sector, driving growth in the capital stock (Skidelsky et al. 2011; Griffith-Jones et al. 2018). For neoclassical 'political' approaches, public banks are meant only to serve politicians' self-interests, causing market inefficiencies and economic underdevelopment (Barth et al. 2006). In these economic narratives a bank's public ownership form determines its intended institutional functions, albeit with different conclusions. Confusion and uncertainty abound as empirical evidence substantiates competing claims both for and against public banks (see Chapter 2). The underlying conceptual essentialism impoverishes our understandings of otherwise diverse and complex public banks around the world (Butzbach et al. 2020). Nowhere is this dynamism more striking than where public banks tackle decarbonisation, definancialisation, and democratisation in compelling *and* contradictory ways.

An alternative dynamic approach to public banks in contemporary capitalism is therefore needed, an approach that does not permit essentialised tropes of public versus private ownership to predetermine what it is to be a public bank. Such an alternative must allow for historical and institutional change within capitalism, itself a global system of social reproduction driven by intra- and inter-class competition, conflict, and resistance (Coates 2014, 27). Rooted in political economy, the historical institutional and materialist approach of this book is to theorise public banks as socially contested and evolving entities, made and remade in time- and place-bound contexts within the wider structures of global financialised capitalism (Marois and Güngen 2016). To do so, institutional functions logically precede ownership form (Figure I.3; cf. Ho 2017, 2020). Such functions are not taken as timeless or fixed but rather as evolving and subject to the pull of contending public and private interests in class-divided

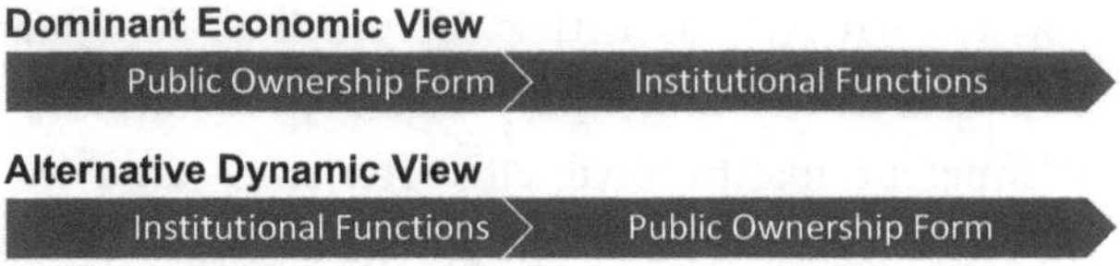

FIGURE 1.3 Ownership form and institutional functions

society. What social forces have public banks *do* make them what they *are*. This *dynamic* view of public banks offers a unique interpretation capable of accounting for the different institutional types and divergent practices of all public banks, as well as for their potential transformation.[2] Whereas existing economics scholarship has not moved past static views of ownership, a dynamic view offers a pathway to understanding the resurgence of public banks vis-à-vis the crises of finance, of climate finance, and of Covid-19 in non-essentialist and socially contested terms. To stress the point, a dynamic view of public banks, be they development, commercial, or universal types of public banks, does not accept that their public ownership form equates to any teleological purpose.

To eschew an ultimate purpose, however, is not to suggest that there are no such things as 'public banks' or that 'being public' is of no material consequence. Not at all. But it does complicate what it is,

---

[2] Chapter 1 goes into detail on the different types of public banks (from central banks to savings banks), how they fit into the credit system, and how they work with other financial institutions. Chapter 3 situates public banks historically. When referring to 'public banks' in this book, I focus on public commercial/retail banks (first tier), development or investment banks (second tier), and universal banks (combining commercial and development/investment functions). In brief, commercial banks are typically deposit-taking institutions with branch networks that provide regular banking services for individuals, households, SMEs, corporations, and governments. Development banks do not typically accept personal deposits or offer personal banking services (although there are exceptions) but instead specialise in accessing cheaper sources of capital, supporting long-term investments, and providing technical expertise to commercial banks, other institutions, firms, and governments. Universal banks combine both these functions, taking deposits and offering regular banking services while providing funds, investment strategies, and expertise for longer-term development.

then, that qualifies a bank as a public bank. In the dynamic view of this book, a public bank has four dimensions:

- It is located within the public sphere.
- It performs financial intermediation and banking functions but with no innate purpose or policy orientation.
- It can function in public and private interests.
- It persists as a credible, contested, and evolving institution.

Those familiar with the literature on public banks will note that this dynamic view makes no mention of an essential public policy orientation, no mention of any necessary mandate- versus profit-driven purpose, no mention of dominant public ownership, no mention of an underlying private sector orientation, and no mention of any specific institutional type of public bank (development, commercial, and so on). Typically the finance and development literature lifts at least one of these aspects to a place of functional determinacy: public banks are *50 per cent plus* government owned; (public) *development* banks are meant to promote private enterprises; public banks are *public policy instruments*; and so on (cf. Scott 2007; World Bank 2012a; Xu et al. 2019, 62–64). So while in recent years there has been a proliferation of empirical research charting the operational resurgence of public banks, it has been accompanied by remarkably little conceptual progress on public banks as changeable institutions within capitalism.

The four dimensions of a dynamic view of public banks, however, allow for change and for institutional variety to persist in and among public banks. More is said on this in Chapter 2. In brief, however, the first dimension of a public bank means that it is located within the public sphere of a state and society. This can be realised in myriad ways: by virtue of controlling public ownership (by a government, public authority, or other public enterprise); or according to a legally binding public interest mandate; or as set out in public law[3]; or

---

[3] By public law I mean laws that specifically govern relationships between the government and institutions in society. The German KfW and Costa Rican Banco Popular, for example, are banks founded and governed by public law.

by meaningful public representation and control; or by a combination of these factors. That is, any one of several concrete factors can objectively situate a bank within the public sphere, with ownership being but one possibility. It is also a dimension of public banks that they perform financial intermediation and banking functions. Again history shows that they have no essential orientation to what they do. Some public banks focus on mobilising money for industrialisation, others do not or not so much. Some have social development at their core while others are profit-oriented banks. Public banks have no manifest destiny. They can be (re)made in many ways. There is evidence of very inefficient and efficient public banks just as there are public banks that provide additional financing to the private sector and ones that almost exclusively target the public sector. It follows that public banks are not ultimately good or bad, pro-private or pro-public, institutions. They can and do function in both public and private interests, though not necessarily in balance. In reality public banks have multiple functions that are in no way reducible to being essentially this or that. Public banks are what contending social forces make them to be, if subject to changing relationships of power within global capitalism. So long as public banks are supported by social forces, even if they are contested, they persist as credible if evolving institutions.

This dynamic view allows for a different way of understanding why public banks have been catapulted to the heights of debate over sustainable, stable, and democratic development. Far from fulfilling some ultimate purpose, the resurgence of public banks has to do with the pull of public and private interests in class-divided society over how public banks function and for whom. In a dynamic view, what public banks do holds the key to understanding why and in whose interests they persist and are resurgent. This occurs in historical context. Today that means neoliberal financialisation.

Since the 1980s neoliberalism has evolved as an international strategy of development that suggests all social, political, economic, and environmental problems can be best resolved by more direct exposure to market imperatives (or 'marketisation') (Harvey 2005; Pradella and Marois 2015; Carroll et al. 2019). Financialisation emerged alongside and out of neoliberalism, gaining force since the 1990s (Fine and Saad-Filho 2017). Financialisation refers not only to the greater influence of financial actors and markets in capitalist society but also to the fusion of the interests of domestic and foreign financial capital in the state apparatus as the institutionalised priorities guiding the actions of state managers and government elites, often to the detriment of labour (Epstein 2005; Marois 2012; cf. Yalman et al. 2019). Neither neoliberalism nor financialisation is very amenable, in theory, to the continued presence of public banks. Yet against all odds, public banks persist. They do so because in different contexts both public and private interests, sometimes in tandem, sometimes not, have lent their often-contentious support to these contradictory public financial institutions. Public banks persist because they fulfil credible, if contested, functions within class-divided capitalism.

So while the persistence of public banks within neoliberal financialisation is beyond question, it no doubt involves a great deal of historical specificity. Different societies can and will (re)make their public banks in ways that reflect their own histories, domestic production, industrialisation, and export orientation strategies, cultures of public service provisioning, means of regional and global integration, domestic labour relations, responses to environmental degradation, democratic and despotic traditions, and so on. Power struggles within class-divided capitalist society shape whether public or private interests gain disproportionately or not from the operations and functions of public banks. Pro-public priorities for investing in healthy communities, equity-oriented and sustainable development, democratisation, public services for all, economic stability, and decent jobs recurrently confront private interest demands to maximise returns, subsidise industrial growth, constrain democratic decision-making, and support the needs of private investors and multinational corporations. Communities, civil society, organised labour, and environmental activists will often champion the public interest, whereas domestic and foreign capital, the World Bank, OECD, and investors champion the private interest. But not always. There is a grey area between what are public and private interests within capitalist social reproduction. This is true of what public banks do, why, and for whom, with the benefits not always being predictable or the consequences as intended.

Critical conjunctures, moments of systemic crisis, and even violent fissures in established interstate relations can play an important hand in the making and remaking of public banks. Some of the oldest and most stable public banks today were forged at times of crisis when governing authorities intervened to provide stability or to underwrite future economic and political might. The Bank of England (established in 1694) was founded in order to wage imperial war on France and Spain while profiteering from the Atlantic slave trade (McNally 2020). In France, the French Caisse des Dépôts et Consignations (established in 1816) was created to deal with the accumulated weight of colonial and imperial war debts. By contrast, the US Bank of North Dakota (established in 1919) was created to support drought-devastated farmers and the Canadian Alberta Treasury Branch (established in 1938) to respond to the impact of the 1930s Great Depression on farmers. The Turkish public banks Sümerbank, Belediyeler Bank, Etibank, Denizbank, and Halkbank were all founded between 1933 and 1938 to help finance state-owned enterprises and industrialisation, support municipal infrastructure and planning, fund power generation and mineral extraction, develop maritime capacity, and to back cooperatives, artisans, tradespeople, and small-scale producers, respectively, in an emerging peripheral capitalist economy. Distinctly, the German KfW (established in 1948) was designed to lead post–World War II reconstruction efforts and the Nordic Investment Bank (established in 1975) to address the region's recurrent balance of payments crisis. Public banks have long and diverse histories and rationales, even in countries typically more suspicious of state-led economic interventions.

The contemporary crises of finance, of climate finance, and of Covid-19 promise to remake dozens, if not hundreds, of public banks in the search for sources of sustainable and stable finance, and for potentially green and just transitions. The 2008–09 global financial crisis was an important first trigger. As global financial markets neared the precipice of collapse, governing authorities stepped in to rescue the 'too-big-to-fail' private banks, like Citigroup in the US and the Royal Bank of Scotland in the UK, effectively nationalising them. In places with existing public banks, like China, Germany, Brazil, France, Turkey, India, North Dakota, and so on, authorities responded 'counter-cyclically' by extending credits and making new investments as public banks simultaneously provided a safe haven for household savings amidst the financial crisis (Marois 2012; Scherrer 2017).[4] Public banks proved so adept at managing aspects of the global financial crisis that even longstanding neoliberal advocates of bank privatisation, like the World Bank, itself a (self-hating?) public bank, had to take notice and make policy space for public banks for the stable functioning of financialised markets (see World Bank 2012a).

On its own the 2008–09 global financial crisis probably would not have been enough to underwrite the public banking resurgence. Since then, however, diverse social forces, scholars, and governing elites have come to realise that we must urgently face the extinction-level threat of unmitigated climate change (Newell and Paterson 2010; Bhattacharya et al. 2016; Magdoff and Williams 2017; UNCTAD 2019). The scale of structural change required needs to be financed, and this in turn exposed the global crisis of climate finance – the second major trigger behind the resurgence of public banks.

---

[4] Clifton et al. (2021b) make the insightful point that in Europe the resurgence in public banking is also related to the rise of China, and its powerful public banks, as a strategy for European policymakers to work around the state-aid and industrial policy restrictions of the European Union.

Private investors and the promise of carbon markets have failed to fund a global green transition by proactively financing technological advancements, low-carbon infrastructure, and climate change mitigation and adaptation strategies at either the scale or pace needed despite having all the necessary financial resources (EPSC 2017). The tipping point was reached in 2015, several years after the global financial crisis had hit. It was first playing out in the lead up to the December 2015 United Nations (UN) Conference of the Parties (COP) 21 climate conference held in Paris. In July 2015, the UN Financing for Development (FfD) Office held a preparatory conference in Addis Ababa. The official UN document that resulted, the FfD Addis Ababa Action Agenda (AAAA), was remarkable for two related reasons (see AAAA 2015). First, it demanded that private finance do more to solve the climate crisis (clearly, it had not been doing enough), especially given the collapse of neoliberal carbon markets.[5] Second, the AAAA called on public financial institutions to play a more central role in tackling climate change (clearly, they could do more). The December Paris meeting then hammered home the necessity of action. A flood of reports, action strategies, criticisms, and calls to action followed. The high-level consensus reached was that private finance would not and could not alone fund the sustainable technologies and low-carbon infrastructures needed to achieve the 2030 UN Sustainable Development Goals (SDGs).

The reasons are not complicated. The necessary green investments do not meet private investors' risk–return preferences (IMF/ World Bank 2015; Spratt 2015; EPSC 2017; Xu et al. 2019). The longer-term, higher-risk, lower-return profiles of most sustainable development projects contradict the profit-maximising imperatives of private investors. Thanks, moreover, to four decades of neoliberal financialisation reforms, private finance has an entire 'financialised' world market of other investment opportunities from which to

---

[5] On the failure of carbon markets to address climate change or spearhead decarbonisation, see Lohmann 2006; Ervine 2018; Michaelowa et al. 2019.

choose. Not to be put off, however, high-level policymakers and financial economists reasoned that public banks could shift private investors' sentiments towards tackling the crisis of climate finance by *socialising* the risks incurred, thus allowing investors to maximise returns. This blending and mixing of public money with private capital should whet investors' appetites for climate finance, unleashing otherwise reticent animal spirits. The underlying normative claim is that only in this way can we hope to confront the global climate crisis, fund the UN 2030 Sustainable Development Goals, and raise the estimated $90 trillion in green investment funds by 2030 to hold down global warming (Bhattacharya et al. 2016; Badré 2018; cf. WEF 2006). The OECD (2017) was soon onside, probably for the first time in its history positioning 'innovative public financial institutions' as *catalytic* for a global green transition by helping to unleash unlimited pools of private capital. A 'pro-market additionality' consensus has since taken shape wherein neoliberal advocates and neo-developmental economists find common ground in having public banks bridge the failures of marketised investment strategies within neoliberalism (IMF/World Bank 2015; Abraham and Schmukler 2017; Griffith-Jones et al. 2018). Public banks must only do what private banks will not (additionality) and only in ways that promote capital growth without undermining market imperatives (pro-market).

It is not an uncontested strategy, either in high-level policy-making forums or on the ground. Powerful counter-narratives around financing alternative green new deals, just transitions, and pro-public solutions have found broad-based support within unions, NGOs and CSOs, and certain branches of the United Nations (for example, UNCTAD and UNRISD). Individual public banks, of course, provide financial additionality to the private sector but in practice they also fund much more, and often according to pro-public rationales that have little resemblance to the neoliberal ideals canonised within some high-level UN forums and World Bank finance for development strategies. The tensions between the theory and practice of climate finance remains a constant thread running through each of the book's public bank case studies, and it constitutes the focus of the book's proposal for a democratised public bank that is green and just (Chapter 7).

If the climate crisis was not enough of a global catastrophe, then the Covid-19 global pandemic would push enshrined neoliberal marketisation logics past the brink. The pandemic struck with unprecedented speed in early 2020, eclipsing the economic impact of the 2008–09 global financial crisis (OECD 2020). Market solutions were nowhere to be found, with even the über laissez-faire US-based Ayn Rand Institute begging for a government handout.[6] As country after country triggered lockdowns restricting work, travel, and leisure, national governments unveiled colossal emergency stimulus packages in response. The Covid-19 crisis simultaneously hit finance, industry, households, SMEs, governments, and essential services. Whereas bank bailouts and nationalisations sufficed in 2008–09, a more coordinated, broad-based, state-led, and rapidly executed strategy was required to stem the immediate effects of lost income, skyrocketing health expenditures, and mounting pandemic mitigation costs. Immediate responses had to be soon followed up with longer-term support measures to get people, businesses, and public services back on their feet. Policymakers needed banks to play a critical role in distributing programme funds and in financing economic recovery. In places like the United States and UK, however, authorities struggled to deliver support programmes through unwilling private banks (which were criticised for demanding far too restrictive conditions, regardless of government backing, and for profiting excessively). In places with existing public banks, though, many were able to quickly execute coordinated plans with the government and develop specific in-house measures that often went beyond what was officially requested (Mertens et al. 2020; McDonald et al. 2020; cf. AADFI

---

[6] H. Coster, 'In Sign of the Times, Ayn Rand Institute Approved for PPP Loan', *Reuters*, 7 July 2020. Available at www.reuters.com/article/us-health-coronavirus-ppp-ayn-rand/in-sign-of-the-times-ayn-rand-institute-approved-for-ppp-loan-idUSKBN248026. Accessed 10 August 2020.

2020; ALIDE 2020; EAPB 2020). Existing public banks leveraged their accumulated masses of capital, geographic networks, and financial expertise in response (see Epilogue).

Almost immediately international commentators urged the marrying of Covid-19 recovery actions with climate transition strategies in order to 'build back (or forward) better'. Speaking on Earth Day, 22 April 2020, UN Climate Chief Patricia Espinosa implored that with this 'restart a window of hope and opportunity opens ... an opportunity for nations to green their recovery packages and shape the twenty-first century economy in ways that are clean, green, healthy, safe and more resilient'.[7] Even the World Economic Forum (WEF) put this critical moment in unambiguous terms (WEF 2020, 19):

> COVID-19 is a stark reminder of how ignoring biophysical risks can have catastrophic health and economic impacts at the global scale. If recovery efforts do not address the looming planetary crises – climate change and nature loss – a critical window of opportunity to avoid their worst impact will be irreversibly lost.

Yet the WEF intervention should serve as a sharp reminder that public responses to Covid-19 and the climate crisis are open to new vectors of class-divided struggle. Social forces will seek to bend the resources of public banks towards contending public and private interests, with private interests enjoying a running start (cf. OECD 2020). The future *may* result in collaborative strategies towards a green and just transition, but it may *also* result in profitability priorities leading the way (notably via the World Bank's blending agenda). Neoliberalism remains the dominant ideological and economic framework shaping the logics of crisis responses. The 2020 IMF Fiscal Monitor, for example, acknowledges the need for public banks to support Covid-19 recovery while at the same time criticising public banks as a whole for underperforming relative to their private sector

---

[7] See www.un.org/en/un-coronavirus-communications-team/un-urges-countries-%E2%80%98build-back-better%E2%80%99. Accessed 20 May 2020.

peers (*as if* maximising returns is a necessary concern for public banks) (see IMF 2020; Chapter 3). Who benefits disproportionately from how public banks function remains contested within class-divided capitalism.

The question remains whether or not public banks *will* offer substantive green and just financial alternatives. The answer is that it fully depends on whether social forces in society make it so, with contradictions inevitably arising. Societies can do so, insofar as there are public banks that have long-practiced longer-term, well-governed, and even greener lending practices well before today's crises of finance, climate, and Covid-19. The Nordic Investment Bank and the German KfW, for example, had environmental mandates fifteen to twenty years in advance of the Addis Ababa Action Agenda. In 2002 Costa Rica's Banco Popular passed a 'Democratisation Law' that affirmed its 290-member Workers' Assembly as the highest decision-making body and mandated gender parity across all core decision-making forums, institutionalising a form of governance distinct from market-based models. In response to the 2008–09 global financial crisis Turkey's nation-wide Ziraat Bank increased domestic lending as a matter of 'social responsibility' (Ziraat Bank 2010, 15) – well before the World Bank (2012a) acknowledged and legitimated this practice of 'counter-cyclical' lending. In the American Midwest the Bank of North Dakota has earned nationwide praise for rapidly and effectively lending into the Covid-19 crisis to support local businesses, students, and families. In Brazil, the Caixa Econômica Federal has unveiled an extensive public banking Covid-19 response, providing targeted credit supports to small and large businesses, municipalities and states, students and households, as well as to Brazil's public services and farmers.

Societies also may not make them so. Public banks do not necessarily entail any green and just alternative at all to neoliberal financialised business as usual. The financial blending agenda of the World Bank to 'maximise finance for development' is setting renewed neoliberal terms of reference and logics for what public banks can and should do, which is to support private accumulation one way or another. While public banks have long interacted with the private sector and financed industrialisation, the single-minded bending of public banks into 'alignment' with private sector needs and priorities is more pernicious, reflecting the structural power of neoliberal and financialised rationalities (Marois 2012; Scherrer 2017). Green transformation in neoliberal terms is seen as but a new opportunity for private accumulation.

There is no shortage of public banks taking a neoliberal financialised path. Take, for example, the pro-neoliberal orientation of the new Canada Infrastructure Bank, founded in 2017 and made to be geared towards co-investing with the private sector – as a means of realising the public interest such that, for example, municipal water provisioning is best realised by the bank *facilitating* privatisation. The New Development Bank and Asian Infrastructure Investment Bank likewise frame the public interest as maximising private investments. In Brazil, the large development bank, BNDES, has aggressively supported private sector investments in ethanol expansion, eroding environmental sustainability but driving accumulation (see Vergara-Camus 2014). The pro-market strategy of mobilising persistent public banks for private accumulation goes back to the first waves of neoliberal transformation. Established in 1983 by South Africa, the Development Bank of Southern Africa was first staffed by neoliberal technocrats and backed by the World Bank in its promotion of market-based restructuring. In Turkey governing authorities used the country's large public universal banks throughout the 1990s to absorb and smooth the social costs of neoliberal transformation in ways that have increased social inequality (Yalman et al. 2019). The underlying point is that there is no necessary connection between a public bank's ownership form and its institutional functions. Social forces make them so, with good versus bad, green and just, being subject to one's social location of power and reproduction within class-divided society. However, by addressing the historical and material conditions of their reproduction, we can better grasp their contradictions, the social forces at work and how power and politics are internalised within them, and what might be the possibilities for resistance and change (cf. Soederberg 2010, 12). Pitched in this light, issues of economic growth, financial stability, environmental sustainability, democratic accountability, and pandemic recovery can take on quite distinct meanings and practices, reflecting the pull of public and private interests.

I.2   A NOTE ON METHODOLOGY

It is worth pausing to note that the book's research methodology is organised around multi-sited case studies, drawn from the global south and north, with the evidence base being largely qualitative in orientation and drawn from multiple sources. The case study approach allows me to excavate otherwise invisible information on causal relationships between different institutional types of public banks, sources of funding, and governance structures in relation to how specific public banks have faced the crises of finance, of climate finance, and of Covid-19. That is, case studies help us to understand the time- and place-bound experiences of specific institutions in their own socio-economic settings (George and Bennett 2005; Peck and Theodore 2012; Yin 2014; Ho 2017). The analytical approach involves iterative stages of familiarisation, thematic identification, mapping, and interpretation. None of this work is oriented towards deducing the ultimate economic benefits of public versus private bank ownership.

Case study evidence draws on secondary sources from across the social science disciplines, making the book an interdisciplinary project. As available and appropriate, I use primary documents and grey literature, including official communications, policy papers, propagated laws, annual reports, the media, and issue papers. In certain cases, semi-structured interviews with public bank staff and officials, government and industry representatives, and civil society advocates enrich the book's interpretation. Larger-scale empirical data (global and institutional level) is sourced from primary documents and from online databases (specifically from Orbis BankFocus). The incorporation of multiple interdisciplinary sources of information and data, qualitative and quantitative, aids the triangulation (or perhaps better said, 'multi-angulation'; Ho 2017, 12) of evidence – the principle that case study phenomena should be explored from multiple, and sometimes conflicting, perspectives to enhance the reliability of its evidence-based claims. This interdisciplinary approach has helped to draw out the internal contradictions of each public bank case study. The case study approach, moreover, facilitates the building of the book's theoretical and conceptual innovations (cf. Feagin et al. 1991; Meyer 2001; George and Bennett 2005). It has allowed me to challenge the 'siloed' disciplinary boundaries in economics and the finance for development literature. Finally, the case studies are purposively selected as representative of different types of public banks, including commercial/universal and national developmental/multi-lateral ones. Consequently, the book can speak about public banks in general.

The book purposively traverses the global north–south divide by selecting public bank cases studies from both political regions. This is theoretically justified by positioning individual public banks within states that reproduce themselves within global financialised capitalism. Practically, there are existing relationships between public banks in the north and the south. It makes little sense to reproduce a false north–south divide and there is no reason that scholars and practitioners in the north should not learn from the promising practices and pitfalls of the south (and vice versa).

It needs emphasising that it is neither the intent nor the orientation of this book to defend any specific public bank, to promote some idealisation of public banking in general, or to make the case for any ultimate form of ownership (be it public, private, or mixed). Nor does the book attempt to resolve the operational differences between or superiority of any specific institutional type of bank – be it universal, development, or commercial. Not at all. The aim is instead to draw on diverse historical contexts to document the existence and persistence of dynamic public banks in practice. This contributes to understandings of what their functions are, who benefits, and why. This should help us rethink what the realm of the possible is for public banking for a green and just transition.

I.3   THE ARGUMENT RESTATED AND STRUCTURE OF THE BOOK

From a historical institutional and materialist theoretical approach, I argue that public banks are resurgent within financialised capitalism *because of* the institutional functions acquired and performed in class-divided society. Their functions are *contested*. What public banks do and why is subject to the pull of public and private interests in time- and place-bound contexts within global financialised capitalism. In short, public banks are made and remade by contentious social forces. This leads to an understanding of public banks not as essentially good or bad by virtue of their ownership form but as historically *dynamic* institutions. Public banks will therefore always struggle with navigating the tumultuous and contradictory waters of capitalist society. Nevertheless, I also argue that pro-public social forces *should make* public banks capable of democratically financing a green and just transition. Case study evidence shows that public banks can acquire the representative structures, financial capacity, institutional knowledge, non-competitive and collaborative networks, and geographical reach needed to do so in the public interest.

Five premises, developed in eight chapters, substantiate the book's arguments. The first premise is that public banks persist globally and do so with substantially more financial firepower than is commonly recognised in the literature. The second premise is that a dynamic view of public banks is better able to explain the resurgence of public banks than the dominant 'political' and 'development' economic views, which rely on fixed notions of public versus private ownership. The third premise is that public banks have a historical legacy of performing a wider array of political and economic functions than allowed for in most economic theory. The fourth premise, built on in the case study chapters, is that public banks have acquired functions in the public interest and operate in 'pro-public' ways, if never independently of contending public and private interests. To be sure, public banks have also acquired functions in the private interest. These contending orientations can generate contradictions in what public banks do and for whom, for example, by funding both carbonising industrial development and decarbonising energy transitions. A dynamic view is needed to disaggregate such institutional complexity. The fifth premise is that there are sufficient existing pro-public functions to synthesise what a democratised green and just public bank can and should look like, thus providing a floor for debate over the future of public banks.

Following this introduction, Chapters 1 through 3 expand on the empirical, conceptual, and historical framing of the book. Chapter 1, 'The World of Public Banks', locates public banks within the credit system and empirically maps out the extent of contemporary public banks globally, evidencing that their combined capacity is exponentially greater than what is typically reported. Chapter 2, 'Contrasting Evidence, Contending Views: Towards a Dynamic Alternative', surveys the economic evidence and theory for and against public banks, arguing instead for an alternative dynamic view of public banks. Chapter 3, 'Credible Legacies, Neoliberal Transition', provides a historical overview of public banks, of their acquired institutional functions, and of the post-1980s neoliberal transition.

Chapters 4 through 6 are case studies illustrating the constitutive and contradictory elements of the public banking resurgence. Chapter 4, 'Decarbonisation', looks at the China Development Bank and the Nordic Investment Bank. These two public development banks have clear decarbonisation strategies with public interest objectives. How public banks actually finance decarbonisation, however, is subject to intense power struggles and class contradictions. The World Bank and UN have intensified the contradictions by advocating that public banks essentially absorb private investors' financial risks to catalyse new green investments. Chapter 5,

'Definancialisation', looks at the Indian National Bank for Agriculture and Rural Development (NABARD) and the American Bank of North Dakota. The former is a national 'apex' development bank and the latter a state-level commercial bank. Both public banks function to mediate and 'fix' flows of mobile financial capital within identified spatial regions. Neither banks' definancialisation operations, however, are unaffected by the class divide of capitalist social reproduction. Chapter 6, 'Democratisation', looks at Germany's KfW and Costa Rica's Banco Popular y de Desarrollo Comunal. The KfW is among the world's largest public development banks while the Banco Popular is a nationwide universal public bank. These two banks stand out for having acquired contrasting governance structures that democratically connect popular demands to how the bank functions, if unevenly so. Democratisation has not erased the pull of private interests within capitalism, but it has enabled the banks to pursue a more public interest trajectory.

Taken as a whole, the case study lessons are substantial. The China Development Bank illustrates the ability to scale up and direct finance rapidly; the Nordic Investment Bank the practice of implementing an accountable 'green' investment floor; the Bank of North Dakota how local social forces can create and sustain a public bank even within otherwise hostile territory; the NABARD how national authorities can institutionally direct domestic financial flows from capital rich to poor regions; the Banco Popular how workers can substantively democratise a bank; and the KfW how representative governance can translate national political priorities into mandated banking practice. Each case also illustrates the contradictions that need to be confronted in order to better make public banks green and just.

The final two chapters conclude the book. Chapter 7, 'A Democratised Public Bank for a Green and Just Transition: A Proposal', synthesises the complex and concrete functions performed by real public banks in a proposal of how to finance a socially just, sustainable, stable, and democratic green transition in the public interest. The chapter does not imply that any society can seamlessly create a public bank free of class-divided conflict and contradictions. I hardly imagine that to be possible. Rather, the synthesis stands as an evidence-based corrective to today's narrow 'market failure' and 'pro-market additionality' finance for development narratives. It is meant to spur debate and action on the future of public banks for a pro-public green and just transition.

The last chapter is an epilogue, titled 'Public Banks in a Time of Covid-19'. The contribution was not, indeed could not, have been conceived of when the book was first planned or even mainly written. But the Covid-19 crisis and the emergency responses of public banks could not be left out of a book on contemporary public banks. The event reinforces the argument. That said, the Epilogue was written very much 'within' the pandemic, in May 2020, while most of the world was in lockdown and the actions of public banks were still a moving target. It narrates the Covid-19 responses of each of the six public banks explored in Chapters 4–6. The Epilogue does not, however, assess their impact, which is impossible to do as many programmes were announced within days or weeks of 'putting pen to paper', so to speak. It tentatively illustrates, nonetheless, that public banks can respond rapidly to societal challenges in ways typically not possible within private banks – if *made* to do so.

As a final word, I would like to add that the chapters of the book need not be read in strict order. I have tried to signpost the main conclusions of each chapter and cross-reference as appropriate. The introduction has oriented you to the book's overall thrust. That said, *the book is an argument*. It is an interdependent whole, not an edited collection of independent contributions. What is written in one place may well depend on evidence and reasoning elaborated elsewhere. Keep this in mind as you explore *Public Banks*.

I   The World of Public Banks

> The trend towards partnerships with the private sector is based on a
> number of assumptions, not least the belief that global problems are too
> big and the public sector is too weak to solve them alone.
>
> J. Martens (2017, 12)

It is not uncommon for most to be caught unawares of the world of
public banks. Academics, policymakers, and civil society organisations often believe that four decades of neoliberal financialisation
has either eradicated public banks altogether or terminally neutered
their capacity. Those familiar with the financing for development
(FfD) literature will no doubt admit to some important exceptions,
such as Brazil's Banco Nacional de Desenvolvimento Econômico e
Social (BNDES), Germany's Kreditanstalt für Wiederaufbau (KfW), the
State Bank of India, and, of course, all of the Chinese juggernauts.
Most will know of little beyond. As a result, the FfD debate lacks an
accurate empirical appreciation of the sheer number, diversity, distribution, and assets of existing public banks worldwide.

This chapter aims to correct this misconception. I argue that
global public banking capacity is exponentially greater than what
tends to be reported. Two premises support the argument. First, the
FfD literature provides an inconsistent and inaccurate empirical
account. The forcefulness of this premise depends on the second
premise, namely that national and subnational public banks persist
in significant institutional numbers and size. Understanding the
actual capacity of (sub)national public banks is a precondition
for having an informed debate on the future of public banks
and for whom they might catalyse a global green and just transition.
To open this discussion, I first locate public banks within the
wider credit system and in relation to other types of public
financial institutions.

1.1   LOCATING PUBLIC BANKS WITHIN CREDIT SYSTEMS

Contemporary credit and financial systems are not natural or trans-historical structures but dynamic products of history, social relations, and the general development of capitalism (Harvey 1999; Itoh and Lapavitsas 1999; Spratt 2009). The institutions constituting credit systems have tended to evolve in ways that accelerate and magnify the amounts of credit available to the economy, which have in turn enabled greater concentrations of capital and the intensification of capital accumulation. Three functions of credit systems in contemporary capitalist development stand out. First, credit systems function to mobilise and magnify money savings *as capital*. Unlike in pre-capitalist epochs, no sum of money need be unproductive as all money, from households, corporations, and governments, can be transformed into investable capital through financial institutions and credit systems (Mandel 1968, 222–23). Second, credit systems tend to reduce barriers to capital moving between different spheres of production and circulation. Modern credit systems enable the transfer of capital from auto manufacturing to solar-panel production and then from solar-panel production to pharmaceutical engineering and so on. Such transfers often depend on the perceived risk-return profiles of investments. In this way credit systems function to eliminate barriers to the equalisation of the rate of profit. Market competition and accumulation imperatives drive capital from areas of investment with lower rates of return to ones with higher rates, a process facilitated by credit systems. Third, credit systems enable the creation of fixed capital (the 'built' environment) now in anticipation of future value creation and extraction. The building of highways and bridges can be paid for over time, as can expensive and intensive capital investments that magnify productive capacities. Modern credit systems are thus specialists in making *time* available (buy now, pay later) (see Konings 2018). In doing so, credit systems go some way to reconfiguring space, both in terms of the built environment and in terms of shaping political spaces like states (Harvey 1999).

FIGURE I.I Interconnected elements of a modern credit system
Sources: Itoh and Lapavitsas (1999); Spratt (2009)

As such, credit systems are interconnected with capitalist development and social reproduction. Figure 1.1 helps to illustrate the basic point, and to locate public banks therein. At base processes of industrial and commercial capital accumulation (that is, the labouring, making and building, and selling of things for capital accumulation and social reproduction) demand forms of credit to function efficiently. One of the simplest forms of credit facilitating this involves inter-firm trade and credit. That a cloth manufacturer allows a chairmaker to take delivery of fabric now but pay later is a time-tested credit practice that persists. But it can be a bit clumsy and not always the most efficient method. Individual financial institutions emerged to provide more rapid, efficient, and larger amounts of credit by combining, mobilising, and augmenting savings as credit (that is, by providing 'intermediation' between the capital rich and poor). Public and private (sub)national banks (commercial, universal, and development), savings institutions, and similar such financial institutions are some examples (discussed later). Credit systems also provide more direct forms of financing through capital and money markets. Capital markets offer more one-to-one forms of financing through bond markets (where you borrow directly from an investor) and equity markets (where investors take on an ownership or 'equity' stake). Alongside these there are the international derivative markets (hedging against future uncertainty in asset prices) and foreign exchange (FX) markets for the trading of national currencies. Money markets provide a space for very short-term borrowing. Banks make regular use of 'overnight' loans here to meet their daily reserve requirements.

Central banks are national financial institutions that control the issuance of paper money and support the credit system within their borders. Most central banks are typically publicly owned and controlled, but not all. They function as the bank of individual banks, disciplining domestic financial institutions and instilling day-to-day confidence in the credit system by providing liquidity and by acting as the lender of last resort in times of uncertainty, crisis, and war. Central banks help to guarantee the creditworthiness and quality of the banks and money within its remit to underwrite economic expansion. In doing so, they may undertake financial supervisory duties over the national payments system and financial institutions and decide or influence national monetary and exchange rate policies. Central banks have an international role in balancing payments between different nation states. As part of more state-led development strategies, central banks have created and channelled money reserves into national developmental priorities.

Within global capitalism, however, individual states and central banks need to be disciplined from time to time (Harvey 1999, 250). For this reason, a set of global lenders of last resort (GLLR) emerged in the early twentieth century. These GLLR include the international financial institutions (IFIs), specifically the Bank for International Settlements (established in 1930) and the World Bank and the International Monetary Fund (established out of the 1944 Bretton Woods Conference). Realistically, one must also include the US Federal Reserve as a GLLR, as it is often the linchpin for any IFI rescue packages by virtue of the US government having veto-level voting rights at both the IMF and World Bank and by virtue of US dollars typically topping up emergency bailout packages (from which US authorities extract conditionalities) as the pre-eminent form of world money.

1.1.1 The Types of Public Banks

This book focuses on public banks that, like private banks, mobilise and magnify different sources of capital to make loans, thereby providing a form of financial intermediation – the pooling, augmenting, and transferring of money, capital, and credit from one agent with surplus funds and who wishes to save (capital rich) to those who are short on funds and wish to borrow (capital poor). Funds are transferred via financial contracts and securities, which become an asset for the lender and a liability for the borrower, forming a legal claim to future cash flows. Banks, of course, are much more than this function as what they *do* and for *whom* have vast social, economic, ecological, and political implications. Historian David McNally (2020) traces the origins of money and the earliest central banks to slave-based and war-oriented economies. Economist Jan Toporowski observes that the origins of capitalist banking systems can be traced back to intra-class tensions among European aristocrats and nascent capitalists, with the latter demanding that the idle wealth of aristocrats be put in the service of industrialisation through banks (1994, 20). Over time, a credit system developed where all money savings can be made 'productive'. With the global consolidation of industrial capitalism, both public and private banks multiplied, creating and channelling money into accelerating circuits of capital.

In the Introduction, I specified that a 'public bank' is one that is located within the public sphere and performs financial intermediation and banking functions but according to no innate purpose or policy orientation. It can function in public and private interests and persists as a credible, contested, and evolving institution. These public banks come in different institutional types and sizes, from small subnational municipal and state-level banks to nationwide and central banks. Three types of (sub)national public banks make up most of the numbers and assets, however (see Section 1.3). These include public commercial, development, and universal types of banks.

Public commercial banks (also referred to as first-tier and retail banks) accept short-term personal, corporate, and public sector deposits and then transform and magnify these sources of capital into short- and long-term loans and credits for individuals, corporations, and governments. Commercial banks will, in addition, offer a full range of day-to-day banking services (from chequing and savings to insurance and mortgage services) and have extensive branch and instant teller networks, as well as online services. Public commercial banks operate at local/municipal, national, and even international scales. There are other types of public banks that perform functions similar to, but not the same as, commercial banks. For example, public savings banks tend to offer a more bottom-up version of public commercial banks, which are shaped by public interest mandates and local stakeholder engagement processes (see Butzbach 2012, 36–37; von Mettenheim 2012, 9–10). Postal banks accept deposits and offer more limited, albeit accessible, personal financial services via their post office networks. Through the public sphere, postal bank deposits can be converted into government financing instruments, public infrastructure investments, or channelled into other public banks as a source of capital.

Public development banks (also referred to as second-tier, investment, policy, or promotional banks) typically do not provide day-to-day financial services. This type of public bank often specialises in structured finance and bond issuances, supporting larger and longer-term investments and infrastructure projects, providing on-lending to commercial banks, financing government programmes and the public sector, and supporting SMEs and large corporations. As the names suggests, these banks specialise in financing 'development', which is often equated with accelerating economic growth.

Development banks may also provide guarantees and subsidies to targeted sectors and can contribute technical expertise. Their funding base typically is not from short-term deposits but from government and commercial bank transfers, international development agencies, or from bond issuances.

Public universal banks combine the day-to-day financial services of commercial banks (savings, chequing, mortgages, and so on) with the investment services of development banks. Universal banks can use the deposits held as savings for local, regional, and national developmental projects. Universal banks are less common within the advanced capitalisms but are much more so within the developing and emerging capitalisms. This is because historically universal banks could draw savings from across a country and then channel them into development projects and capitalist industrial transformation in otherwise 'capital poor' territories.

There are other types of public banks and financial institutions to note. Public multilateral banks function are like (sub)national development banks (that is, not deposit-taking but investment oriented) but they are owned by multiple countries and may perform functions akin to the international financial institutions. In many ways, a public multilateral bank is both an individual financial institution and a lender of last resort. Sovereign wealth funds (SWFs) are public investors, likewise traversing the national and international scales of operations. SWFs are often capitalised from government commodity exports and state-owned enterprise revenues and tend to finance long-term national development initiatives (Barrowclough and Gottschalk 2018, 6). Other types of public financial institutions can include public pension funds and mutual funds, which manage households' future savings and retirement plans, as well as insurance companies. That these financial institutions exist and reproduce themselves within the public sphere means that there is scope for solidarity-based inter-institutional collaborations. There is no innate reason for such collaborations to occur, yet public financial institutions can be made to do so given the public mandate.

I.2 THE IMPOVERISHMENT OF PUBLIC BANKS IN INTERNATIONAL DEVELOPMENT

The impoverishment of data on public commercial, development, and universal banks is rife in the FfD literature. Despite having access to substantial research budgets and economic expertise, the chief architects of this problem include the World Bank, IMF, OECD, as well as the United Nations. The World Bank, a public multilateral bank, is ironically the most culpable. Having failed to provide reliable and substantive data on public banks for decades, it decided to do so in the wake of the 2008–09 global financial crisis. The World Bank has since authored two quite non-comprehensive public banking surveys. The first came in 2012, optimistically titled the *Global Survey of Development Banks* (de Luna-Martínez and Vicente 2012) and the second came five years later, titled the *2017 Survey of National Development Banks* (de Luna-Martínez et al. 2018).

The 2012 survey opens by acknowledging that 'little is known' about existing public banks' operations, mandates, services, clientele, regulatory and governance frameworks, and challenges (de Luna-Martínez and Vicente 2012, 2). The data provided begins to offer a much-needed empirical corrective, though it is hampered by the fact that it could garner responses from just ninety public banks in sixty-one countries. The follow-up 2017 survey fared worse, receiving only sixty-four responses. The 2012 survey also applied very loose ownership-based criteria: a bank is public if it has 'at least 30 per cent state-owned equity' (de Luna-Martínez and Vicente 2012, 4). This level of ownership better reflects 'public influence' than control (see Schmit et al. 2011; Table 1.2). The 2017 survey slips much further by defining a public development bank as having *any* level of government ownership at all (de Luna-Martínez et al. 2018, 12). This makes for a thin evidentiary cocktail (and hardly comparable results between surveys). More telling is the ontological worldview implication that any form of 'public' ownership at all, in and of itself, constitutes a priori institutional determinacy. For most social scientists, this is an unacceptable leap of neoliberal faith.

The World Bank survey's data on public banks has subsequently proven to be misleading and inconsistent. For one, both surveys misrepresent the *types* of public banks included. They were not just 'development' banks as the titles indicate. The surveys also include commercial and universal public banks, such as the Banco Nacional de Costa Rica, Ziraat Bank in Turkey, and the Land Bank in the Philippines. To be fair both surveys make note that different types of banks are captured. But this raises questions – why target *only* development banks in the first place and why mistitle the surveys, as such, twice? There are also problems in terms of estimating public bank assets. The 2012 survey estimates that the ninety public banks included have assets totalling $2.01 trillion (at the end of 2009). For the ninety banks, this is probably accurate. Yet the 2012 survey also notes that 25 per cent of all banking assets globally are publicly owned without saying how they arrived at this figure or what this 25 per cent represents monetarily (de Luna-Martínez and Vicente 2012, 2). The 25 per cent ratio is closer to the estimates provided later in the chapter but also implies that there are trillions of dollars more in combined public banking assets worldwide (Table 1.2). Yet you will not find any mention of this 25 per cent figure in subsequent World Bank or UN reports. For example, the World Bank's follow-up *Global Financial Development Report 2013 (GFDR 2013)* reproduces the $2 trillion in assets figure (World Bank 2012a, 120) while stating that public banks 'account for less than 10 percent of banking system assets in developed economies and double that share in developing economies' (2012a, 103) – figures that do not match its 2012 survey. For the sixty-four banks in the 2017 survey, total assets are less than half that reported in 2012 at a mere $940 billion (de Luna-Martínez et al. 2018, 21). None of the World Bank's reports, moreover, try to indicate total public banking institutional numbers. World Bank data thus presents an underwhelming and inconsistent picture of global public bank capacity that, in turn, reinforces neoliberal 'common-sense' strategies to maximise private finance for development: public banks persist but they are financially too weak to do anything but leverage private finance.

Other international institutions do not resolve the knowledge gap. A 2017 IMF working paper on bank ownership estimates that public banks, measured at 50 per cent or more 'government' ownership, account for 18 per cent of total public and private banking assets in 2010 (Cull et al. 2017, 6). This is a dated but realistic estimate. Yet the IMF, like the World Bank, does not convert this ratio of assets into monetary terms and fails to indicate the total institutional numbers. In contrast, a 2017 OECD report on climate finance indicates that there are 'more than 250' national development banks with assets of over $5 trillion (2017b, 273) based on research by Studart and Gallagher (2016). While more precise, the picture remains inaccurate. The problem of impoverished data bleeds into the United Nations Inter-Agency Task Force (IATF) on Financing for Sustainable Development. The IATF is the body tasked with responding to the 2015 UN Financing for Development Addis Ababa Action Agenda (AAAA) on financing the 2030 Sustainable Development Goals (SDGs). Since the IATF annual reports began in 2016, they have reproduced a narrative of public banks only having the capacity to support private investors (UN IATF 2017–19). This advice is presumably evidence based: the IATF holds that 'national development banks' have assets not exceeding $5 trillion (UN IATF 2017–19, 143). What good is $5 trillion when the world needs $90 trillion to confront the 2030 SDGs (see Bhattacharya et al. 2016)? Presumptively little more than a supporting role, hence the recurrent IATF calls to also align public banks with private investors' aspirations.

The World Bank, IMF, OECD, and UN – each well-funded and influential knowledge producers and shapers in the international community – have thus provided inaccurate, incomplete, and/or misleading data on public banks, systematically underestimating existing public banks worldwide, their over 900 institutions, and their combined assets nearing $50 trillion (see Table 1.2). This evidentiary

failure is plausibly connected to the long-standing neoliberal orientation of the World Bank and IMF, which remain committed to the
preferential expansion of privately owned financial institutions and
marketisation (Cammack 2003; Babb and Kentikelenis 2018).
Reinforcing seemingly insatiable neoliberal 'no alternative' narratives, the debate on the potential (and pitfalls) of public banks for
financing a green and just transition has been impoverished in ways
that bolster private interest strategies.

Heterodox development views have also contributed in ways that
can limit understandings of public banks. These often more positive
accounts tend to only consider, empirically and theoretically, public
development and investment banks at the national and multilateral
scale (for example, see Minsky et al. 1993; Culpeper 2012; Barone and
Spratt 2015; Scherrer 2017; Griffith-Jones and Ocampo 2018;
Macfarlane and Mazzucato 2018; UNCTAD 2018). This is usually to
the exclusion of public commercial and universal banks, which have
greater total assets, far greater institutional numbers and geographical
reach, and often work collaboratively with their public development
bank peers. Therein, there are quite divergent empirical accounts and
categorizations, even within the narrow 'development' bank type. For
example, Studart and Gallagher (2016) identify 'more than 250' national
development banks with assets of over $5 trillion. Xu et al. (2019)
identify 539 development finance institutions worldwide (no estimate
of combined assets given). The Finance in Common (FiC) preparatory
booklet for the first global conference of public development banks in
November 2020 (organised by heterodox economists) states there are
'about 450' public development banks with $11.2 trillion (FiC 2020).

The reasoning for this narrowing to development types is left
unstated, but the preference to exclude other types of public banks is
clear (see Griffith-Jones et al. 2018). Such exclusion cannot be for lack
of the empirical tools needed to deal with the different types of public
banks, as undoubtedly economists have these (cf. Levy Yeyati et al.
2007). It also cannot be for being unaware of commercial or universal
public banks, for these institutional types are acknowledged and, at

times, even subsumed to a development bank categorisation (not unlike in some neoclassical studies) (Xu et al. 2019). The preference must be theoretical. This is fine, but it nonetheless demands justification that has, as yet, not been forthcoming. To be clear, this does not refer to justifications *for* development banking, which are made in the literature. (Aghion 1999; Griffith-Jones et al. 2018). This refers to a theoretical justification for singling out public development banks, conceptually and empirically, from all other types of public banks. This has been absent, and it creates a noticeable gap in heterodox thought regarding public banking in general. Heterodox research need not always deal with commercial, development, and universal banks. That is not the point. But heterodox development views should be able to position public development banks within a more general conceptualisation of public banks and their diverse functions within capitalism, and then by extension specify why it is important to focus on this particular development type of public bank to the exclusion of other types (particularly given the wider institutional capacity and operational interconnections). It appears that the narrow focus on development banks seems to derive from worldviews based on the preferred functioning of public banks being limited to providing additionality to private investors to spur capital growth and market expansion, notably without competing with or displacing the private sector (Chapter 2). Public commercial and universal banks, however, typically do directly compete in financial markets (as do some development banks), a fact that might be hard to square within heterodox frameworks. Hence, the exclusion of all but development banks on average, as well as the relative underestimates of the world of public bank institutions and assets.

1.3 THE WORLD OF PUBLIC BANKS: INSTITUTIONS AND ASSETS

As of mid-2020 there are around 32,000 active public and private banking and financial institutions globally. Combined they hold over $281 trillion in assets (Table 1.1), an amount double the total global

Table 1.1. *Total public and private banks,*[1] *numbers and assets, 2018 and 2020*

	Number of institutions	Total assets
2018	33,992	$269.5 trillion
2020	31,971	$281.6 trillion

Sources: Orbis (May 2018); Orbis (June 2020)

GDP of $142 trillion (in 2019).[2] To disaggregate the world of public banking, I use a comprehensive online database specialising in global banking and financial institutions – the Orbis BankFocus (Bureau VanDijk) database. I offer four caveats on my use of the Orbis data on public banks. First, Orbis lists a total of eighteen different financial institution specialisations, from central banks to commercial banks to microfinance institutions. I use sixteen of the eighteen specialisations as 'public banks', typically excluding central banks and multilateral institutions (see the Table 1.1 footnote for the list of the sixteen specialisations I include). Not all of these are 'banks' proper, but most are – in fact, over 90 per cent of institutional numbers and financial assets are 'bank'-based institutions (Table 1.3). Therefore, for ease of narrative, I simply refer to the full array of institutional types generally as public 'banks'.

Second, to distinguish between public and private banks it is necessary to use the Orbis 'ultimate owner' (UO) search category.[3]

---

[1] Excluding central banks and multilateral banks, the data includes the following sixteen Orbis-designated institutional specialisations: commercial banks; savings banks; cooperative banks; real estate and mortgage banks; investment banks; Islamic banks; other non-banking credit institutions; specialised governmental credit institutions; bank holdings and holding companies; microfinancing institutions; securities firms; private banking/asset management companies; investment and trust corporations; finance companies; clearing and custody institutions; and group finance companies.

[2] International Monetary Fund, World Economic Outlook Database, April 2020. Accessed 29 June 2020.

[3] I acknowledge the problems and limits of employing an empirical ownership marker to define the world of public banks. As Butzbach et al. (2020) argue, there is a difference between ownership and effective control. Indeed, this book rejects using

The UO category includes all the distinct legal entities of banking institutions from around the world. So, if a bank has one or more legal entities within its overall corporate identity, Orbis will count each one individually (that is, the parent and its legal subsidiaries). For example, the State Bank of India has two listings, one for its headquarters in Mumbai and another for its Los Angeles, California, headquarters. The Agricultural Bank of China has separate headquarters in Beijing, London, and Moscow. These are all counted as separate banks. While empirically and legally accurate, it adds to the overall institutional count in ways that, qualitatively speaking, one might question ('padding' the numbers, so to speak). That said, there are very, very few public banks that have multiple headquarters around the world, so overall numbers are little magnified. Importantly, however, each bank's assets stay tied to each separate legal entity (so, for example, the Agricultural Bank of China's total assets are not counted three times over).

Third, the Orbis database does not distinguish between once-private-but-now-state-rescued public banks and public banks that have always-been or at least long-been publicly owned. Public ownership by 'UO' is a purely quantitative measure. Examples of once-private-now-state-rescued banks from the 2008–09 global financial crisis include the Royal Bank of Scotland, ABM Amro, NatWest, Belfius, and Dexia. Not dissimilarly, long-standing Turkish public banks absorbed failed private banks during its 2001 financial crisis, thus making private banks 'public'. Such institutional variations are important. But they can only be understood through qualitative case study research and, as such, are not captured by the Orbis data and not the focus of this chapter. Disaggregating and disentangling such cases, while of importance, is beyond the scope of this book and in need of further research in their own right.

'ownership' as a determinant of what the meaning of being public is. Nevertheless, to achieve a reasonable empirical estimate of assets and numbers, I have to employ the Orbis Ultimate Owner category.

Fourth, the Orbis database sometimes misses ostensibly public banks for technical reasons around a bank's legal classification or due to sometimes complex ownership structures. Some public banks are simply not captured. Take again the case of Turkey (Marois and Güngen 2019a; Marois 2019b). In early 2017, the ruling Justice and Development Party government placed two large public banks, Ziraat Bank and Halkbank, within a newly created sovereign wealth fund, the Turkey Wealth Fund (Türkiye Varlık Fonu). As a result, neither of the two 'public' banks nor their over \$200 billion in assets are counted in the Orbis database as 'public' banks – even though they effectively remain banks within Turkey's public sphere. Likewise, the Banco Popular y de Desarrollo Comunal in Costa Rica (see Chapter 6) will not appear in a public banking search because of its particular ownership structure. While founded under public law and with government representatives on the board, it is legally 'worker-owned' and hence classified in Orbis as a 'private' bank, despite its governance structure and senior staff describing it as 'public' (Marois 2017). A similar issue occurs with the German Savings Banks Association, the Sparkassen. Orbis locates its \$2.6 trillion in assets as 'private' in origin despite decidedly strong foundations within the German public sphere (Butzbach and von Mettenheim 2015). Undoubtedly, other such examples exist given the thousands of cooperative and community banks worldwide that are classified as 'private' even if they are substantively within a society's public sphere. Such cases deserve further research. For these reasons, therefore, the Orbis data on public banks should be taken as indicative rather than as definitive. Only case by case, country by country, research that compares the results of global databases like Orbis with institution-level data can yield a definitive account.[4]

---

[4] A 2019 mapping study of 'development finance institutions' (DFIs) by Xu et al. is a recent attempt to create a new comprehensive database by matching quantitative and qualitative data. This independent research identifies 539 DFIs worldwide. The research forms part of a larger China-based project on DFIs.

Table 1.2. *Public banks, dominant and influencing ownership, numbers and assets, 2018 and 2020*

Year	Number of institutions	Total assets	% of all public and private bank assets*
Dominant public ownership (UO 50.01% plus)			
2018	808	$41.76 trillion	16
2020	910	$48.71 trillion	17
Influencing public ownership (UO 25.01% plus)			
2018	1,037	$48.13 trillion	18
2020	1,181	$58.01 trillion	21

* Table 1.1.

Sources: Orbis (10 May 2018); Orbis (25 June 2020)

Table 1.2 provides data on total public bank institutional numbers and assets for 2018 and 2020. The top half refers to 'dominant' public ownership of Ultimate Owner (UO) 50.01 per cent or more, the bottom half to 'influencing' ownership of UO 25.01 per cent or more. The data includes the same sixteen Orbis-designated specialisations specified in Table 1.1, which excludes central banks and multilaterals (these are discussed later).

The results are strikingly different from those circulating in current financing for development debates. Under dominant public *ownership* in 2020, there are 910 public banks with combined financial assets of $48.71 trillion. This equals to 17 per cent of all banking assets worldwide, public and private combined. The data for 2020, moreover, represents an increase of $7 trillion in assets and an increase of over 100 public banks since 2018.[5] While I do not often refer to the influencing public ownership of banks category in the

---

[5] As always, the empirical data must be treated cautiously. I cannot say why there is an increase in institutional numbers here, just that there is an increase. It could be from the creation of new banks or from changes in relative ownership levels or from legal classification changes, each of which need to be explored at the institutional level.

book, it is nevertheless useful to see what it looks like. For some observers, this 25 per cent plus level of ownership is enough to exert control over an institution or, at a minimum, allow for substantive institutional influence (see Schmit et al. 2011; cf. de Luna-Martínez and Vicente 2012). In 2020, there are 1,181 such public banks with combined assets of $58 trillion, which is equal to 21 per cent of total public and private bank assets. This is an increase of 144 banks and $10 trillion in assets since 2018.

In this book, I will refer to there being 910 public banks with $49 trillion in assets (rounding up) as my empirical marker. Evidently, this estimate far exceeds the $2 trillion to $5 trillion in assets and the 250 or so in institutional numbers circulated by the World Bank, OECD, and UN. It also exposes neoliberal narratives of public banking incapacity as more myth than reality.

Having a fair global figure is but one part of the puzzle of public banks. Another part is China, whose fifteen largest public banks alone have assets totalling just over $23 trillion – nearly half of total global public banking assets (Orbis, June 2020). Three of China's public commercial banks are the largest banks in the world, public or private, period. These include the Industrial and Commercial Bank of China (ICBC), the China Construction Bank (CCB), and the Agricultural Bank of China with combined assets of $15 trillion.

There are, of course, other sizable public banks outside of China that count among the largest twenty-five public banks in the world. For example, there are Germany's KfW Group with $569 billion in assets and India's State Bank of India with $557 billion in assets. The failed-private-but-then-state-rescued banks, the UK-based Royal Bank of Scotland with $949 billion in assets and the Netherlands-based ABN AMRO with $421 billion in assets, fall into this same elite grouping. Qualitatively, however, RBS and ABN AMRO tend to be more private than public in their corporatised operations (although there are domestic social movements aiming to change this to make them more publicly-oriented; see Vanaerschot 2019). Other large, long-held public banks include Italy's Cassa Depositi e Prestiti ($504 billion), Russia's Sberbank ($484 billion), and the Banco do Brasil ($360 billion) – the twenty-fifth largest public bank. It is worth noting that these national scale public banks each have assets exceeding those of the largest multilateral public banks, including the World Bank's $283 billion.

The 26th to 100th largest public banks have combined assets of $9.74 trillion dollars, with most public banks in this range having assets of $50 billion to $200 billion. The 101st to 300th largest public banks have combined assets worth $4.51 trillion, with most institutions having between $7.5 to $50 billion in assets. Many of the 600 or so remaining smaller public banks have assets of $500 million to $5 billion, with the smallest public banks having less than $100 million in assets. While the largest public banks capture our attention, it would be a mistake to think that only large size matters. Smaller public banks can do important local and regional work and function as important conduits of capital and knowledge. For example, a 2016 Roosevelt Institute study, *The Municipal Bank*, shows how local banks can provide needed investments for affordable housing, infrastructure, and community economic development (Beitel 2016). Smaller public banks may also prove to be game-changers in global efforts to confront the crisis of climate finance linked, as they often are, to municipal and regional water and energy infrastructure projects as well as to households and possible refurbishment strategies.

1.3.1 Public Banks by Institutional Type: More than Just Development

The impressive efforts to explore development banking have failed to capture the institutional diversity or inter-connectedness of development, retail/commercial, universal, postal, savings, and other types of public banks within credit systems. Clarifying the diversity of institutional types can help to avoid unwarranted perceptions that developmental banks are the only public banks that matter and that there is otherwise limited public banking capacity. Table 1.3 provides data

Table 1.3. *Public banks by institutional type, numbers and assets, 2018 and 2020*

Type of bank	2018				2020			
	No. of Insts.	% of Insts.	Assets $bn	% of Assets	No. of Insts.	% of Insts.	Assets $bn	% of Assets
1. Commercial banks	390	48.6	22,817	60.2	435	47.8	27,850	57.2
2. Savings banks	31	3.7	1,930	5.1	34	3.7	1,823	3.7
3. Cooperative banks	25	3.1	22	0.06	32	3.5	23	0.05
4. Real estate and mortgage banks	26	3.2	428	1.1	30	3.3	451	0.9
5. Investment banks	41	5.1	355	0.9	42	4.6	1,409	2.9
6. Islamic banks	21	2.6	291	0.8	24	2.6	286	0.6
7. Other non-banking credit institutions	5	0.6	87	0.2	7	0.8	190	0.4
8. Specialised governmental credit institutions	135	16.8	8,122	21.5	159	17.5	9,044	18.6
9. Bank holdings and holding companies	22	2.7	1,837	4.9	20	2.2	5,019	10.3
10. Microfinancing institutions	2	0.3	0.4	0.001	3	0.3	1.1	0.002
11. Securities firms	14	1.8	53	0.1	20	2.2	185	0.4
12. Private banking/asset management companies	13	1.6	277	0.7	13	1.4	452	0.9
13. Investment and trust corporations	8	1.0	64	0.2	10	1.1	72	0.2
14. Finance companies	69	8.6	1,589	4.2	78	8.6	1,858	3.8
15. Clearing and custody institutions	–	–	–	–	3	0.3	34	0.07
16. Group finance companies	–	–	–	–	Nil	Nil	Nil	Nil

Sources: Orbis (January 2018); Orbis (June 2020)

on dominant publicly owned banks according to the sixteen different Orbis-designated institutional types, including their institutional numbers and assets. It also shows the relative percentage of numbers and assets compared to the other types of public banks included in the table.

Three broad and significant observations can be drawn from the data. First, there is existing public capacity across many types of banking institutions. Second, the bulk of public bank numbers and assets are nonetheless in commercial and retail-type tier 1 institutions. Commercial, savings, cooperative, and mortgage banks account for nearly 60 per cent of public bank numbers and over 60 per cent of assets in 2020. An important implication is that retail/commercial and savings banks will often have extensive branch networks and geographical reach. For example, the Vietnam Bank for Social Policies, the State Bank of India, the Banco de la República Oriental del Uruguay, and the Caixa Econômica Federal of Brazil all have nationwide branch networks. These can translate into effective financial access and provide a means of mobilising domestic savings (von Mettenheim and Del Tedesco Lins 2008; von Mettenheim 2010; Marois 2012). Retail/commercial and savings banks can also serve as very practical partners with development banks (which typically lack branch networks). For example, the French Postal Bank channels domestic savings from around the country into national developmental programmes, as do the public commercial banks in India (see Chapter 5). Third, tier 2 public development banks, notably specialised governmental credit institutions, investment banks, and finance companies, also have significant combined public financial assets. Yet at just over 25 per cent of assets and just over 30 per cent of institutional numbers, the near exclusive focus on them in the economics literature and within the UN finance for sustainable development debate needs to be rethought. The strategic linking of developmental and retail/commercial public banks is a time-tested strategy that is common to the developmental experiences through much of the global south, from China to Costa Rica, and in the global north, notably in European countries like Germany and France. These collaborative public–public financial relationships need to figure far more centrally within contemporary finance for development debates.

1.3.2   The Spaces of Public Banks: Geographical and Political

The data on public banks' numbers and assets under dominant public ownership can also be organised in the Orbis database according to different spatial groupings differentiated by geographical and political boundaries. Table 1.4 illustrates the regional distribution of public banks spread across eight Orbis-designated regions for 2018 and 2020. These include Africa, North America (Canada and the United States only), Eastern Europe, Western Europe, Far East and Central Asia, Middle East, South and Central America, and Oceania. There are six matters of note. First, the Far East and Central Asia stands out, both in institutional numbers and assets. This is of course led by China, but with significant contributions from Japan and India. Second, Europe, east and west, retains significant public banking capacity with combined numbers exceeding 300 and assets of over $10.5 trillion. The 2008–09 global financial crisis led to a spike in Western Europe's total assets due to the state-led rescues of failed private banks (Cull et al. 2017, 47). The largest rescued private banks include the Royal Bank of Scotland, ABN AMRO, Dexia, and NatWest, which account for over a third of the region's total assets. Europe is followed by South and Central America with 116 institutions and $1.3 trillion in assets – although the lion's share of assets is held in Brazil. This region's assets, like Oceania's, have exceptionally shrunk over the last two years. Third, all other regional assets have expanded, including a relatively significant expansion in Africa in both numbers and assets. Fourth, in North America (where Orbis erroneously excludes Mexico), only five of the twenty-eight listed public banks report their assets, with most of these being tiny institutions in the United States. For reasons unknown, moreover, neither the publicly owned Bank of

Table 1.4. *Regional distribution of public banks, 2018 and 2020*

Region	2018		2020		Notable public banks[6]
	No. of Insts.	Assets ($bn)	No. of Insts.	Assets ($bn)	
Africa	67	412	99	533	National Bank of Egypt; Banque Misr (Egypt)
North America*	25	305	28	326	Canada Mortgage and Housing Corporation
Eastern Europe	116	1,135	110	1,236	Sberbank and VTB Bank (Russia)
Western Europe	196	8,906	215	9,365	Royal Bank of Scotland (UK); ABN AMRO (Netherlands); KfW (Germany); Belfius (Belgium); Cassa Depositi e Prestiti (Italy); La Banque Postal (France)
Far East and Central Asia	236	24,420	280	34,756	ICBC China; Japan Post; State Bank of India; Chunghwa Post (Taiwan); Industrial Bank of Korea

North Dakota nor the Territorial Bank of American Samoa are listed as public banks, despite being so. Fifth, in Eastern Europe the Russian public banks dominate the region as Chinese banks do in East Asia.

---

[6] These public banks are merely illustrative, with each having their own complex dynamics, ways of institutional reproduction, and contradictions. For example, while the Emirates NBD and Abu Dhabi Commercial Bank are state-owned public banks, within the GCC these banks are closely connected to the region's large private conglomerates, which in turn include conglomerates owned and controlled by ruling families in a private capacity. For an analysis of the complex family and state ownership and control patterns within the GCC region, including the financial institutions, see Hanieh (2018).

Table 1.4. (*cont.*)

Region	2018		2020		Notable public banks[6]
	No. of Insts.	Assets ($bn)	No. of Insts.	Assets ($bn)	
Middle East	38	650	51	905	Emirates NBD (Dubai) National Commercial Bank (Saudi Arabia); Abu Dhabi Commercial Bank; Bank Melli Iran
South and Central America	116	1,783	116	1,299	Banco do Brasil; Banobras (Mexico); Banco de la Nación (Argentina); Banco Internacional de Comercio (Cuba)
Oceania (Australia)	7	262	8	259	Queensland Treasury Corporation; Tonga Development Bank

* The United States and Canada only.
Sources: Orbis (January 2018); Orbis (June 2020)

Finally, in the Middle East the largest three public banks, with about half of all assets, are in the Gulf Cooperation Council (GCC), followed by three others located in Iran.

Table 1.5 shows the distribution of public banks by Orbis-designated political regions, specifically the G8, ASEAN, EU28, GCC, MENA, NAFTA, and OECD. This data offers another useful vantage point for public banks globally. Notably, China is not a member of any of the political groupings, which helps us gain insight into the 'rest of the world'. For example, without China the ASEAN region has relatively few public banks and a much smaller portion of total assets. Likewise, the Middle East, Gulf, and North Africa regions have only a small percentage of public banks. Most strikingly, by excluding China we see that most public banking assets are within

Table 1.5. *Distribution of public banks by political region, 2018 and 2020*

Political region	2018		2020	
	No. of Insts.	Assets ($bn)	No. of Insts.	Assets ($bn)
OECD	269	10,578	287	15,940
EU28	183	8,090	175	8,105
G8	185	7,782	195	13,181
MENA	83	1,011	115	1,365
ASEAN	50	633	59	885
GCC	23	451	32	653
NAFTA	30	360	35	425

Sources: Orbis (January 2018); Dominant public ownership (50.01 per cent). The political region includes the countries as defined by the organisation itself

regions dominated by the advanced capitalisms in Europe (the OECD, EU28, or G8).

Even as public banks are ubiquitous around the world, the presence of public banks at the (sub)national level varies dramatically in numbers and asset control from country to country, requiring further research. The only relatively recent data is provided in a 2012 Word Bank report (World Bank 2012b). We can glean the following from the report. One, there is no necessary link between a country's wealth and levels of public banking relative to private banking. In Germany, public banks account for 31.5 per cent of public and private banking assets in 2010. In Turkey, it is 31.6 per cent. In Portugal, it is 22.6 per cent and in Pakistan 21 per cent. The advanced capitalisms may or may not have significant public bank ownership levels just as poorer developing and emerging capitalisms may or may not. The macroeconomic evidence is inconclusive at best.[7] Second,

---

[7] See Chapter 2 for a review of the contrasting and inconclusive empirical evidence correlating public bank ownership to levels of national development.

such national variety reinforces the need to be cautious on questions of size and scale. It is rather more of interest that 61 per cent of banking assets are public in Ethiopia, or 22 per cent in Poland, or 12.5 per cent in the Philippines, than whether those public banks are the largest public banks in the world. As the World Bank's follow-up 2017 survey confirms, public banks 'are highly diverse in terms of their size, financial performance, development objectives, business models, funding arrangements, and governance practices' (2018, 6). It is all too easy to tunnel our vision towards the goliath Chinese, German, Indian, French, and Brazilian public banks. Yet for smaller countries (and their provinces, states, and municipalities) large-scale public banks may neither be necessary nor desirable as local projects are less costly and massive banks can easily overwhelm the development process while undermining local decision-making capacity (Romero 2017; cf. Ray et al. 2020). Equally important is the need to develop supportive research and collaborative opportunities for public banks to improve their operational efficiencies and capacities at all scales of operation, small and large, local and national (cf. Hanna 2018a, 37–38). Third, as always, there is a need to be cautious with aggregate data, opting always for further in-depth case study analysis to best inform policy and practice. For example, the 2012 World Bank data records Canada and the United States at 0 per cent public bank control even though there are existing public banks in both countries.

1.3.3   The Multilaterals, Central Banks, and Public Pension Funds

The focus of this book is on (sub)national scale public banks. With the exception of the Nordic Investment Bank (itself an under-studied multinational public development bank, see Chapter 4), I do not dwell on multilateral banks, central banks, and public pension funds. These public financial institutions are, of course, massively important to domestic politics and the global political economy. The multilaterals control significant financial resources and have real sway over knowledge production and discourse setting (Humphrey 2016). Central banks are core financial institutions, sitting at the peak of national credit systems with diverse histories of funding imperial expansion, wars, national economic development, and neoliberal restructuring (Congdon 2012; Epstein 2015; McNally 2020). Public pension funds are responsible for millions of households' future savings while being powerful enough financially to discipline local, national, and foreign politics as well as multinational firms' investment strategies (Clark 2000; Soederberg 2010). As with public banks, these public financial institutions are *made* and *remade* in historical context – subject to the pull of public and private interests within class-divided society and global capitalism.

Here I provide estimates of their relative assets and numbers. As of mid-2020 there are seventy-seven public multilateral banks with combined assets of $4.0 trillion (Orbis, June 2020). The largest entity is the European Stability Mechanism (ESM) with assets of $921 billion. The sixth largest entity is the European Financial Stability Facility (EFSF) with assets of $222 billion. These two financial institutions are not your usual multilateral-type banks but serve as rather special purpose institutions for dealing with financial instability and crisis. The largest multilateral bank proper is the European Investment Bank (EIB) with assets of $692 billion. The Bank for International Settlements (which is more a bank of central banks) holds the third spot with assets of $404 billion (cf. Seabrooke 2006). It is followed by the World Bank with $283 billion in assets. The much-discussed Asian Infrastructure Investment Bank (AIIB) and New Development Bank fall within the multilateral category but with assets of just $22.6 billion and $11.8 billion respectively.

For data on central banks and public pension funds worldwide, I turn to the UK-based Official Monetary and Financial Institutions

Forum (OMFIF).[8] Its 2019 *Global Public Investor* (GPI) report identifies 173 central banks with assets worth $13.55 trillion. In addition, the 2019 GPI report identifies 491 pension funds with assets worth $15.69 trillion. Table 1.6 situates public banks within a wider panorama of public financial institutions (PFIs) that includes the multilaterals, central banks, and public pension funds. It is important to perceive the wider whole as PFIs can and do work together collaboratively within states and across borders (see Barrowclough and Gottschalk 2018 on solidarity finance among PFIs).[9] These institutions can also cooperate to provide catalytic financing for a global green and just transition (UNCTAD 2019). According to Dennis Lockhart, former president and CEO of the Federal Reserve Bank of Atlanta (2000–17), public investors like pension funds will become 'a natural market for long-term infrastructure investments' (OMFIF 2017, 12). These same public investors can also play vital roles in providing emergency financing, as done in response to the Covid-19 pandemic (see the Epilogue). Table 1.6 adds public banks' assets to the multilaterals, which equates to $53 trillion. If you then add in central banks, then the combined assets come to $66 trillion. Finally, if you include public pension funds then contemporary PFIs command $82 trillion in combined assets, totaling some 58 per cent of global GDP. There is truly massive and already existing public financial institutional and material capacity.

---

[8] OMFIF describes itself as 'an independent think tank for central banking, economic policy and public investment – a neutral platform for best practice in worldwide public-private sector exchanges' (www.omfif.org/about/). According to OMFIF, institutions are *public* financial institutions 'if they fulfil at least one of the following characteristics: they are owned or financed by the state; they serve public employees; or they are constituted as public institutions under public law' (OMFIF 2019, 201). OMFIF does not specify any specific minimum level of ownership to qualify as public.

[9] I do not address sovereign wealth funds (SWFs) separately here. The GPI 2019 report identifies eighty-six SWFs with $8.58 trillion in assets. However, a number of the SWF institutions, but not all, named in the GPI 2019 report have been included within Orbis data on public banks discussed earlier.

Table 1.6. *Situating public banks among public financial institutions, numbers, assets, and percentage of global GDP*

Categories	No. of Insts.	Assets ($tn)	Assets as % of global GDP (2019)*
Public banks	910	48.71	34
Public banks plus multilaterals	987	52.71	37
Public banks plus multilaterals plus central banks	1,160	66.26	47
Public banks plus multilaterals plus central banks plus public pension funds	1,651	81.95	58

* $142 trillion according to 2020 IMF data.

However, the international development community, led by the World Bank, has tended to impoverish our empirical knowledge of public banking numbers and financial capacity, reinforcing and reproducing inaccurate mythologies of public bank incapacity, which intentionally or not reinforce neoliberal narratives of public sector powerlessness. The ideological objective seems to be underscoring that there is no alternative to public banks courting private finance. Yet the world of public banking is exponentially greater than commonly understood, and there appears to be no imminent convergence towards private and market-based finance (cf. Megginson 2005b; Maxfield et al. 2017). Public banks persist as credible institutions within neoliberalism, pulled as they are between contending public and private interests. The class-divide of this persistence is taken up in the chapters that follow.

2 Contrasting Evidence, Contending Views

Towards a Dynamic Alternative

It perhaps comes as no surprise, but the economics literature is anything but conclusive on public banking. Reliant on fixed yet polarised tenets of public versus private ownership, its scholars offer contrasting evidence on and contending theories of public banks in economic development. For observers outside the discipline, they would be right to surmise that there is no general case for or against public banking and no economic consensus on the ultimate superiority of public or private banks. This division within economics occurs along ideological lines. For heterodox 'development' views, there is good theory and evidence for public banks. For orthodox 'political' ones, the opposite. The aim of this chapter is not to resolve these antinomies but to illustrate them in order to move past them. The economics literature is too preoccupied with fixed notions of public and private ownership, and this impedes understanding of how and why public banks evolve. By contrast, I argue for a dynamic political economy view of public banks. In this view, what public banks are depends instead on how social forces in class-divided societies make and remake them over time. That is, contested institutional functions are logically prior and give meaning to the public ownership form.

The chapter proceeds as follows. The first section details the contrasting evidence claims of neoclassical and heterodox economics on public banks. The second section then explains the theoretical divide behind these two contending views. The third section develops the book's alternative dynamic view of public banks.

2.1 THE CONTRASTING EMPIRICAL EVIDENCE

Since the 1980s market advocates have sought to undermine the past legacies and future potential of public banks in development in favour of private, profit-maximising banks. Critics of public banks point to poorly run institutions and cases of abuse by state elites, adding weight to the neoliberal 'government failure' narrative. Neoclassical economists, in particular, feared market atrophy as large industrial groups were seen to be overly reliant on preferential loans, raising concerns of moral hazard, economic disequilibria, and costly bailouts of public banks and their tied-in clients (Marcelin and Mathur 2015). Economists were not alone in their criticisms. Civil society organisations have long documented the impact of development bank–funded large-scale infrastructure projects on indigenous peoples' lands and communities and, more recently, exposed the difficulty of bringing sustainability criteria to bear on public banks' decision-making processes. Researchers have questioned the lack of community voice and popular representation within the more centralised national development banks that are 'distant from the bottom up forces of firms and individuals as potential borrowers' (von Mettenheim 2012, 14). To be sure, public banks have exhibited their fair share of problems. This includes each of the case studies presented in this book. Each public bank embodies contradictions between the progress made on decarbonisation, definancialisation, and democratisation and other operations that undermine these same processes. Yet the potential, as opposed to just the pitfalls, of public banks has been little explored until recently: 'In the literatures to be addressed, it may be said that critical and positive literatures exist on private banking; but only critical literatures exist on state banking.'[1]

Orthodox economists and political view advocates have narrowly focused on the pitfalls of public banks and championed bank privatisation as the solution (Caprio et al. 2004; Megginson 2005b; Cull et al. 2017). The theoretical case for privatisation was bolstered by the material interests of domestic and foreign finance capital who understood the opportunity, wanting to profit from the concurrent

---

[1] A comment made by one confidential reviewer on the book's manuscript, which is worth being reproduced here.

opening up of global financial markets and the promised sell-offs of public enterprises, including banks, in the late 1980 and during the 1990s (Guillén Romo 2005; Bayliss and Fine 2008; Marois 2008). All of this was backed ideologically by 'public choice' liberal political economists and monetarily by northern development agencies like USAID, as well as by the World Bank (Buchanan 1999; Marois 2005; Fine 2008). During this early phase of neoliberal transformation relatively little was heard or written about public banks, except by advocates of privatisation. Convinced of an imminent market-driven, global convergence of development in the south towards that of the north, neoliberals and orthodox economists had not really presaged any real future for public banks in global capitalist markets (cf. Barth et al. 2006). Yet public banks persisted, and so the empirical evidence against them needed to be built up.

Thus for those orthodox economists who discouraged public banks on ideological grounds they had to demonstrate the relative economic and developmental inefficiencies of them versus private banks (Andrews 2005). The World Bank was at the forefront of this pessimistic research programme. Its 2001 *Finance for Growth* report argues that '[w]hatever its original objectives, state ownership tends to stunt financial sector development, thereby contributing to slower growth' (2001, 123). This despite acknowledging a few pages later that the 'primary evidence' against public banks had been 'anecdotal' since the 1980s (World Bank 2001, 127).

The World Bank has since reinforced this same conclusion in the inaugural *Global Financial Development Report 2013*, stating that the 'empirical evidence largely suggests that government bank ownership is associated with lower levels of financial development and slower economic growth' (World Bank 2012a, 101). This time, however, the World Bank had to recognise that public banks play a role in counter-cyclical lending at times of economic downturn – that is, public banks can effectively lend into a crisis to overcome the crisis, such as what occurred in 2008–09 (World Bank 2012a, 2). Most recently the IMF Fiscal Monitor reproduced this hedged orthodox message: public banks can be of counter-cyclical use at times of crisis (like during the global finance crisis and the Covid-19 pandemic), but such interventions are at best a time-limited and narrowly-applicable second best option (IMF 2020, 62).

Large-scale empirical studies have helped to substantiate the neoclassical political view against public banks, typically designed to test their efficiency, profitability, and growth effects. The study by La Porta et al. (2002) is the literature's benchmark (also see Section 2.2). The study explores the data on public or 'government-owned' banks in ninety-two countries between 1970 and 1995. The study concludes that where public banks persisted, this correlated with slower financial and economic development. While the authors note that as 'with most growth regressions, these results are not conclusive evidence of causality' (La Porta et al. 2002, 290), the neoclassical consensus based around this research is that 'bureaucrats make bad bankers' (see World Bank 2001, 123; Demirgüç-Kunt and Servén 2010, 98–99). Subsequent empirical work confirms that '[o]verall, there is little evidence that government bank ownership provides substantial benefits (relative to other types of ownership) to the banking sector, the real economy, or users of banking services, especially in developing countries' (Cull et al. 2017, 30). Here public banks are nested within wider research claims that state-owned enterprises 'generally have low productivity, distort competition, and can be plagued by corruption' (IMF 2020, 66). An enduring feature of orthodox research is the direct application of private banking assessment criteria, such as financialised profitability and efficiency criteria, to public banking performance as a method of extracting relative performance differences. For example, a 2010 study by Cornett et al. concludes that public banks were less profitable than private banks during the East Asian financial crisis. This is perhaps a foregone, if irrelevant, result for public banks that were lending into a crisis and bailing out failed private banks.

Country-based neoclassical case studies mirror the large-scale empirical assessments, with research homing in on the negative impacts of public versus private bank ownership within individual countries. Empirical evidence attests to lower growth rates and developmental inefficiencies linked to bank nationalisation (as a violation of contract and private property rights), political manipulation, or related lending tied to government elites (Calomiris and Haber 2014). Solutions invariably involve intensifying market discipline and the privatisation of public banks. This was evident in a series of case studies produced in the early 2000s on developing countries, each pointing to government failures, political corruption, and economic inefficiencies in public banking (see Caprio et al. 2004; del Ángel-Mobarak et al. 2005; Haber 2005). Correlations between increased lending and greater central government electoral success in Turkey likewise suggest evidence of political manipulation of the country's public banks (Bircan and Saka 2018). In general, the neoclassical case against public banks appears watertight.

However, heterodox economists and development view proponents offer a contrasting empirical account. Researchers often premise their work by challenging orthodox methodologies that graft private sector performance criteria onto public institutions. Heterodox economists contend that this approach generates unacceptable selection biases and distorts results around potentially positive efficiency, productivity, and developmental gains of public banks (see Levy Yeyati et al. 2007; cf. Mühlenkamp 2015). One industry report on European public banks puts the criticism sharply (Schmit et al. 2011, 104):

> This wide range of underlying economic rationales [of public financial institutions in Europe] renders meaningless most performance-based analyses of public sector banks, since all that such analyses measure is financial performance (which presupposes the overriding aim of profit maximisation), neglecting all other kinds of objectives pursued by public financial institutions.

Heterodox scholars then put orthodox evidentiary claims to the test. A 2007 study by economists Levy Yeyati et al., written in response to conclusions drawn by La Porta et al. (2002), provides the benchmark.

The authors empirically examine both firm-level research on public bank performance and macroeconomic research on cross-country comparisons. At a macroeconomic level, Levy Yeyati et al. (2007) replicate and update the La Porta et al. (2002) dataset, concluding that 'the results demonstrating that state ownership inhibits financial development and growth are far less robust than previously thought', arguing instead that public banks can help to smooth out recurrent boom/bust credit cycles (2007, 245). A subsequent 2012 large-scale regression study by Andrianova et al. casts further doubt on the neoclassical study of La Porta et al. (2002). Andrianova et al. instead show that between 1995 and 2007 'government ownership of banks has been associated with *higher* average growth rates' (2012, 449; emphasis added).

Heterodox researchers have also provided empirical evidence that contrasts with neoclassical conclusions on corruption. Levy Yeyati et al. for example, acknowledge that there is some evidence of increased lending during elections years but emphasise that much depends on context. More recently, a 2020 Europe-based study of public development banks from 2002 to 2015 concludes, in contrast to La Porta et al. (2002), that the evidence for the 'political view' of development banks is largely inconclusive even if in 'flawed democracies' large development banks tend to increase lending activity during election periods (Frigerio and Vandone 2020). Heterodox empirical work further undermines orthodox claims that public institutions struggle to meet policy mandates (for example, see IMF 2020, 51). A 2018 study by Mazzucato and Semieniuk assessed global investments in renewable energy power plants from 2004 to 2014, assessing ten different types of public and private financial actors, including, but not limited to, public banks. The results on public banks were unambiguous, showing significant capacity to provide supportive long-term, mission-oriented financial resources geared to increasing renewable energy capacity (cf. Mazzucato 2015).

Heterodox studies, moreover, offer contrasting assessments at the level of country case studies. An edited collection looking at

Brazil, Germany, and India highlights the stabilising and developmental benefits of public banks, particularly amidst wider patterns of global financialisation (Scherrer 2017). Similar conclusions are drawn in Griffith-Jones and Ocampo's (2018) edited book, which further highlights the positive contributions of public development banks, north and south, to infrastructure development, market growth, and counter-cyclical lending capacity. Ray et al.'s (2020) contribution recognises the environmental and governance challenges of public development banks but also illustrates cases where governments, civil society in the Amazon, and development banks have worked to create frameworks to help mitigate infrastructure risks to ecosystems and communities. In the prominent case of Germany, multiple case studies point to how its public banks have assisted policymakers positively respond to economic challenges, including sustainable transitions (Deeg 1999; Chakravarty and Williams 2006; Moslener et al. 2018; Naqvi et al. 2018). A study of the Brazilian public banking giant, the BNDES, positions it as a repository of domestic technical expertise that helps to deliver national policy and financial capacity, especially in terms of offering long-term investments (Doctor 2015). Arora and Wondemu (2018) point to India's public banks contributing to higher rates of regional growth. So too in Turkey, where public banks have advanced regional development strategies (Öztürk et al. 2010). In Canada, research points to the Alberta Treasury Branch providing stable credits and accessible banking services to local farmers and rural communities for over eighty years (Anielski and Ascah 2018). In France, its system of public banks effectively mobilises domestic savings and channels them into national, regional, and municipal infrastructural priorities (Cochran et al. 2014). In general, the heterodox case *for* public banks also appears watertight.

What conclusions can be drawn from the contrasting orthodox and heterodox large-scale empirical and country case study evidence? Both approaches are confident that the evidence points to a general trend of public bank ownership, albeit in totally opposing and polarised directions – as either for or against. The inference to be drawn from the economics evidence, then, is not on the ultimate advantages or disadvantages of public banks. Rather, it should be that no universal conclusion at all can be attached to the 'public' ownership of banks as a general and homogenous object of analysis. There is no conclusive evidence of public banks being ultimately good or bad. Contending theories tend to reinforce, rather than overcome, the evidentiary divide.

2.2 THE CONTENDING THEORETICAL VIEWS

In the financing for development literature, orthodox neoclassical and heterodox Keynesian economic approaches often correspond to 'political' and 'development' views on public banks. The orthodox political view tends to depict public banks in monochrome, seeing the public or 'government' ownership of banks as ultimately undesirable in both economic and social justice terms. Moreover, public ownership is pitched as an inherently second-best option to what are otherwise naturally private firms. Economist William Megginson writes, 'It is important to realize that state ownership must always be a deliberate act that *preempts or replaces private ownership'* (2005a, 34; emphasis added). Theoretically, the political view is justified by liberal economic theory wherein the maximum extension of market-based exchange relations is taken as the surest way to maximise human happiness. The extension of the market is thought to allow for the satisfaction of needs, progress, and the optimal distribution of goods. Liberalism as embodied in neoclassical economics is a theoretical worldview committed to the 'market-based coordination' of human reproduction. This economic 'truth' was expressed by Alan Greenspan, former chair of the US Federal Reserve, who said that 'markets are an expression of the deepest truths about human nature and ... as a result, they will ultimately be correct' (quoted in Wade 2002). By theoretical (and ideological) necessity, state-led 'extra-market coordination' and public sector provisioning is socially regressive and economically suboptimal.

Notwithstanding public banks have prevailed and continue to serve significant roles in economic development in different places and at different times. This historical fact is hard to explain away. 'Market failure' emerged as a neoclassical conceptual tool to address the gap. One of the earliest definitions sees it as a 'failure of a more or less idealized system of price-market institutions to sustain "desirable" [consumption and production] activities or to stop "undesirable" activities' (Bator 1958, 351). Put otherwise, markets fail when the idealised individual pursuit of self-interest in a price-market system generates systemic inefficiencies in the allocation of goods and services. The notion of 'market failure' thus theoretically allows for some form of limited government intervention, public policy, or public provisioning within neoclassical assumptions and without sacrificing the preferred system of self-interested market-based exchange. Therein public banks can be acceptable, time-limited, expressions of otherwise exceptional market failures. But this conceptual opening is not acceptable to all neoclassical economists.

More radical neoclassical economists and libertarian political economists maintain that government interventions into 'market failures' will lead to even worse inefficiencies, violations of private property, and threats to individual economic liberty due to the more serious problem of 'government failures' (Buchanan 1999; Tullock et al. 2002). This radical right response to the market failure paradigm dealing with persistent public ownership and extra-market coordination was championed by the Virginia school of political economy and formalised as 'public choice' economics. The approach has been heavily backed by American corporate capitalists, notably the Koch family, that financed its institutionalisation within George Mason University, the Cato Institute, the Institute for Humane Studies, and the Mont Pelerin Society (MacLean 2017). While more extreme in their market fundamentalism, protection of capitalist prosperity over labour rights, and scepticism for democratic politics, public choice economists share hardcore theoretical agreement within neoclassical economics and liberal political economy around individual self-interest, human nature, egoism, and so on (Shleifer and Vishny 1994; Arnsperger and Varoufakis 2006). Orthodox libertarians just take these postulates to the political extreme, building on and moving beyond the works of Friedman and Hayek in their defence of hyper-market determination and individual liberty at any social or democratic cost.

This radicalised branch of neoclassical orthodoxy is connected to the 'political' view of public banks. The 'political' in this school of thought refers to the liberal view of the inherent nature of self-interested individuals to use and abuse government, state, and public resources for their own good and at the expense of other individuals' economic liberty and wealth accumulation, rejecting even time-limited government interventions into 'market-failures', understanding all such interventions as politically motivated forms of corruption that distort otherwise self-correcting (but ultimately correct and just) market processes (Shleifer 1998; Dinç 2005; Vanberg 2005). Political, public, or government control over economic resources like public banks necessarily leads to corruption, economic inefficiencies, and underdevelopment (La Porta et al. 2002; Caprio et al. 2004; Barth et al. 2006; Cull et al. 2017). La Porta et al. explain that according to a political view 'governments acquire control of enterprises and banks in order to provide employment, subsidies, and other benefits to supporters, who return the favor in the form of votes, political contributions, and bribes' (2002, 266).

Economists working with a political view of public banks emphasise 'government failure' and employ narratives like the 'crowding-out' of private investors by public banks. Invariably, calls for bank privatisation follow. The political view has found an institutional home within important World Bank policy and practice forums (see World Bank 2001, 2012a; Demirgüç-Kunt and Servén 2010). Political view scholars are warmly received by 'government failure' thinktanks and advocacy hubs like the Cato Institute (Haber 2005; Megginson 2005b; Calomiris and Haber 2014). There is a shared belief that attributing anything progressive or positive to public banking is idealistic, naïve, or both (Barth et al. 2006, 34–35). Again

La Porta et al. provide the benchmark, themselves also regular World Bank contributors. The authors summarise the political view and its fundamental difference with heterodox 'development' views, and it is worth quoting at length (2002, 266–67):

> A government can participate in the financing of firms in a variety of ways: it can provide subsidies directly, it can encourage private banks through regulation and suasion to lend to politically desirable projects, or it can own financial institutions, completely or partially, itself. The advantage of owning banks – as opposed to regulating banks or owning all projects outright – is that ownership allows the government extensive control over the choice of projects being financed while leaving the implementation of these projects to the private sector. Ownership of banks thus promotes the government's goals in both the 'development' and the 'political' theories. In the former, ownership of banks enables the government both to collect savings and to direct them toward strategic long-term projects. Through such project finance, the government overcomes institutional failures undermining private capital markets, and generates aggregate demand and other externalities fostering growth. In the political theories, ownership of banks enables the government to finance the inefficient but politically desirable projects. In both theories, the government finances projects that would not get privately financed. In the development theories, these projects are socially desirable. In the political theories, they are not.

Indeed the differences are stark in significant ways between the contending economic views. In contrast to political views, heterodox Keynesian development views tend to argue *for* extra-market coordination of the economy, seeing government action and forms of public ownership as essential for managing the ebbs and flows of inherently unstable capitalist economies (Minsky 2008[1986]; Thirlwall 2011). Stable growth and development are seen to depend on the active role of state and the 'machinery of government' (Gerschenkron 1962;

Shonfield 1969). But there are limits to extra-market coordination in capitalist economies. According to John Maynard Keynes, 'The important thing for government is *not* to do things which individuals are doing already, and to do them a little better or a little worse; but to do those things which at present are *not done at all*' (1926, 46; emphasis added). In theorising public banks, heterodox economists tend to place this tenet of Keynes at the forefront.

With the contemporary resurgence of public banks in global capitalism, the concept of 'additionality' has become the heterodox sine qua non of why public banks should exist. That is, public banks are best when they exist *in addition to* private banks and when they support market growth, stability, and capital accumulation (Skidelsky et al. 2011; Mazzucato 2015; Griffith-Jones et al. 2018). Additionality is the impact beyond that which would have occurred *without* a public bank intervening or participating (cf. Spratt and Ryan-Collins 2012, 1). And, additionality involves crowding in, rather than crowding out, private investments (Griffith-Jones et al. 2011; Griffith-Jones and te Velde 2020). A key feature of heterodox additionality involves public banks socialising private investment risks to stimulate or crowd-in the private sector and encourage market development (Di John 2016). Development views often extend the concept of additionality to the provisioning of support for helping to develop underdeveloped financial markets in poorer countries (Levy Yeyati et al. 2007, 224). Public banks are conceptualised as functional substitutes for private banks and market-based finance, capable of offering long-term and stable investment capital (Gerschenkron 1962). Where private banks are unwilling or unable to finance development, it is the task of public banks to do so instead (Bennett and Sharpe 1980). Given these preferences, heterodox and development view research into public banks has tended towards largely focusing studies of public 'development' banks, often to the exclusion of other public banking types (for example, Griffith-Jones and Ocampo 2018).

While more radical political views have now largely jettisoned the 'market failure' paradigm, heterodox development views have bent it towards an extra-market coordination framework (Stiglitz 1994; Griffith-Jones et al. 2018). For example, former World Bank chief economist, Joseph Stiglitz, specifies three reasons for governments intervening in financial 'market failures', including (1994, 20) 'that financial markets are markedly different from other markets; that market failures are likely to be more pervasive in these markets; and that there exist forms of government intervention that will not only make these markets function better but will also improve the performance of the economy'. That is, enduring market instability and financial uncertainty justifies public banks, which by virtue of not being private banks can improve overall economic performance. A recent report on public development finance institutions (DFIs) reinforces the message of 'fixing market failures', pointing to how DFIs can overcome problems of information asymmetries, generate positive externalities, combat financial short-termism, and engage in pro-cyclical lending (Xu et al. 2019, 6–8). The report also points to how these public banks can be market creating.

In the wake of the 2008–09 global financial crisis, the development view has undergone more theoretical innovation than orthodox political views. Notably, heterodox economists have broadened their thinking on public (development) banks, adding a more proactive 'market creating' justification to the more reactive 'market failure' paradigm (see Mazzucato and Penna 2016, 2018; cf. Xu et al. 2019). Notably, Marianna Mazzucato's (2015) entrepreneurial state theorisation (which is largely based in a US model and on military spending) marries Schumpeterian creative destruction and Keynesian interventionism to provide the conceptual foundation. Mazzucato argues that the state has played a necessary role in making, not just fixing, capitalist markets and this has involved directing innovation. So too for public investment and development banks. They can fix market failures, yes, but public banks can also be involved in shaping and creating capitalist markets in creative ways. Four corrective and creative roles stand out: (a) counter-cyclical; (b) developmental; (c) new venture support; and (d) challenge-led

(Mazzucato and Penna 2016, 320). Aside from the counter-cyclical role, Mazzucato contends that orthodox fears of crowding-out do not apply to public bank interventions because 'in all other cases NDBs [national development banks] are doing precisely what the private sector is not' (Mazzucato and Penna 2018, 271). Public banks can instead 'crowd in' investments through their venture capital, economic dynamism, and mission-oriented roles. In this, Mazzucato's work captures some of what public investment banks do and, moreover, forwards an argument about what public banks can and should do. While making an important contribution in this direction, particularly by challenging the poverty of neoclassical views on the state, public banks, and value creation, her approach does not break with the heterodox methodology of placing ownership form ahead of institutional function (Mazzucato 2018, 229–69). This method has an enduring influence over the literature. As economists Levy Yeyati et al. explain, when evaluating what public banks should do and how well they do it, this 'requires a clear idea of what public banks are expected to do *a priori*' (Levy Yeyati et al. 2007, 223; emphasis added). The heterodox development view expects publicly owned banks to perform additionality, market failure, and market creating roles. The view has gained remarkable policy traction in the wake of the crises of finance, of climate finance, and of Covid-19 for the more positive roles of the state and public sector. But it has also gained credibility among private investors as it accepts a less contentious win-win scenario for public–private partnerships within capitalist economies and in ways that pose no challenge to the reproduction of class-divided society (much as Keynes himself accepted).

Another public banking policy innovation has taken form, that of pro-market additionality. It represents a theoretically uncomfortable convergence of orthodox and heterodox thinking on the potential of public banks in contemporary capitalism. It gained momentum with the overlapping crises of finance and of climate finance, which brought together those economists thinking about how to overcome these crises without crowding-out market forces and private investors. The resulting pro-market additionality narrative advocates a melange of market- and growth-oriented orthodox and heterodox policies that are, importantly, warmly welcomed in World Bank, IMF, and OECD circles (see Abraham and Schmukler 2017; Griffith-Jones et al. 2018). It provides a more restrictive narrative for what public banks are meant to do, wherein the public interest and social equity play little role beyond traditional market-based distributional mechanisms that are best achieved by public banks catalysing private sector growth and market expansion. Through this convergence, pro-market additionality logics retain hardcore ideological commitments to linear and top-down processes of economic expansionism that place public banks in a subordinate economic relation to private interests (OECD 2017).

Whether for, against, or convergent, heterodox development and orthodox political views share a common methodological grounding. In both schools of economic thought, a bank's public ownership form determines its legitimate institutional functions. This method, derived from ownership, tends to create fixed barriers to interpretation, building from a priori (or pre-scientific) tenets of ownership (cf. Butzbach et al. 2020). In this way, the method obscures the contentious and class-divided power struggles over public banks and, as significantly, overly constrains the realm of the possible, hindering our ability to see a much wider spectrum of how public banks already do offer viable, innovative, and practical solutions for a green and just transition.

2.3   TOWARDS AN ALTERNATIVE DYNAMIC VIEW

How else can we think about public banks without essentialising them or what they must do according to fixed and polarised notions of public versus private ownership? My approach is to turn current economic explanations on their heads. Rather than ownership form determining institutional functions, I argue the reverse. Institutional *functions* inform the meaning of being a *public* bank. What a public bank does and how it functions are, however, contested and changing, never simply grasping for some ideal form but always churning within the muck of class-divided society. Institutional functions are instead time- and place-bound, made and remade by individual and collective agents within capitalism (cf. Lefebvre 2016[1972], 63).

This focus on 'function' is not to revert to Parsonian theories of structural functionalism wherein institutions are seen, from some Archimedean and elitist point of view, to fulfil established purposes functional to the stable reproduction of society (Parsons 1971). Whereas structural functionalism accepts consensus and equilibrium an 'institutional function before ownership form' approach emphasises recurrent conflict and change (Ho 2017, 7; 241–42). Neither does this alternative approach separate power from the exploitative structures of capitalist social reproduction, as in mainstream economic views (Palermo 2019). Public banks are understood as pulled between contending and conflicting public and private interests, whose powerful influence can be more direct (as in legal governance frameworks) and more indirect (as with the pressures of capitalist competition). Power is not static but relational and exercised across individual, institutional, societal, and structural scales of social reproduction. The influencing effects of power can sometimes be quite visible and at others quite invisible, acting more behind the backs of individual and collective agents shaping their rationalities and choices. The functions of public banks are thus rather more contested and evolving, often in unintentional ways, than typically understood or expressed within the economics literature. This gives rise to the need for an alternative, non-essentialist, and dynamic view of public banks.

In a dynamic view, public banks are institutions. There are many types of institutions in society, differentially constituted by relatively persistent sociological patterns of behaviour, customs, established laws, sets of rules, and societal norms. In this book, 'institution' refers to variously owned and controlled entities and organisations that perform rule-defined functions (so, a bank is an institution that intermediates financial transactions and that can create money). In the social sciences and in development, institutions are of course much more complicated (Przeworski 2004). Institutions crystallise and formalise gendered, racialised, and class-based power relations. Institutions are as such historically co-constituted entities that take on significance and evolve within a larger socio-political whole. For development scholar Peter Ho, institutions are thus defined as 'endogenously shaped, context-determined social rules' (2017, 9–10). Far from being pre-social black boxes with fixed characteristics or natural meanings, institutions are dynamic and historical, being 'the *resultant* of social actors' and 'economic agents' interaction' (Ho 2013, 1091–92; emphasis added). Political economist Adam Hanieh offers a not dissimilar understanding (2018, 15): institutions are not 'self-contained, preexisting, independent, or autonomous things' but rather *relational social forms* that emerge, evolve, and persist through the production and reproduction of often conflictual interactions internal to global capitalism.

Institutions are thus both social and historically contextual entities. In this line of thinking, the social relations of global capitalism signify the contemporary context and conditions for the existence of specific institutions, rather than institutions being determinant relations in and of themselves (Albo 2005; Lefebvre 2016[1972]). Hanieh refers to this wider context as 'totality' whereas for Ho it is 'endogeneity'. Both scholars reject the explanatory potential of 'exogenous' factors central to mainstream economics methodologies. Rather, there is a shared ontological understanding of human existence and social interaction that refuses to place anything outside of these interactions, including institutional entities. History, society, and institutions are internally connected and hence co-constituted social processes. Institutions are not natural but complex, evolving, and malleable social constructs that provide some contribution to securing, however temporary or persistent, the economic, political, and social coordination challenges involved in historical social orders. Institutions are therefore partly constituted by and of this order, resting on an 'unstable equilibrium of compromise' (Jessop 2016, 25). According to political economist Martyn Konings, differences in

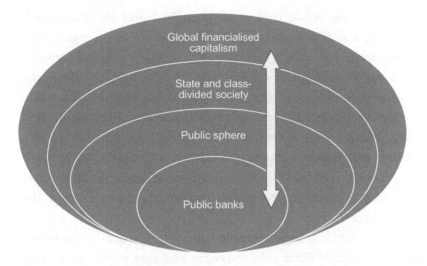

FIGURE 2.1 Public banks within global financialised capitalism
Source: Author

institutions, that is, their variegations across capitalist societies, occur because institutions are themselves crystallisations of associative relationships that involve 'continuous mutual observation, anticipation, and projection' (Konings 2018, 43–44). Through the shared logic of these mutual associations, constituent elements of society, like institutions, can 'come to perceive their own prospects of security as best served by performing certain functions in a wider pattern'. Institutions, and the individual and collective agents within them, are both influenced by and constitutive of the *shadow* of global capitalism (Jessop 2016; Palermo 2019). So too for public banking institutions.

This historical materialist conceptualisation internally (or 'endogenously') connects public banks through the public sphere to the state and class-divided society within global financialised capitalism (cf. von Braunmühl 1978; Alavi 1982; Harvey 1999; Marois 2012; Jessop 2016; Konings 2018). Figure 2.1 illustrates this conceptualisation, with the two-directional vertical arrow implying the co-constitution of institutions and structures. At the most immediate scale, there are 'public banks'.[2] Most public banks are commercial, universal, and development types of banks – the institutional types focused on in this book. A bank is legally 'publicly' owned if a government, public authority, or other public enterprise holds dominant ownership of 50 per cent plus (as employed in Chapter 1). There are other ways to position a bank as 'public', including by legally binding public mandates, by being founded in public law, or by having substantive public representation and control in the banks (or by some combination therein).[3] There are, therefore, multiple dimensions by which a bank can be situated as an institution within the public sphere.

The public sphere within a state is the space where public banks, as well as other public services and enterprises, are located and reproduced.[4] Here governing authorities can exercise power, control, influence, and privilege through the creation or management or mandating of economic and social institutions. According to Henri Lefebvre, the services performed in the public sphere 'are essential to a society and make up that society ... [t]hese include such things as schools and universities, transportation, health care and hospitals ...' (2016[1972], 114)

---

[2] It is worth restating from the Introduction that a 'public bank' is located within the public sphere; performs financial intermediation and banking functions, but with no innate purpose or policy orientation; can function in public and private interests; and persists as a credible, contested, and evolving institution.

[3] There is a literature discussing alternative forms of ownership that reasonably qualify an institution or entity as being public or public-like. Political economist Andrew Cumbers has developed a typology of such public ownership forms, which includes full or partial state ownership; local or municipal ownership; employee-owned firms; producer cooperatives; and consumer cooperatives (2012, 165; cf. Hanna 2018a, 72–82; McDonald forthcoming). These kinds of ownership variations are widespread among alternative banks, even if they remain largely unrecognised (see Butzbach and von Mettenheim 2014). So too are there important limits to pure 'ownership' categorisations of banks if taken in the absence of 'control' (Butzbach et al. 2020).

[4] I do not employ 'public sphere' in the sense developed by Jürgen Habermas (1991 [1962]), that is, as a theatre within modern society in which political participation is enacted through discourses (cf. Fraser 1990), although elements of the deliberative and democratic realm are nonetheless important to my usage and advocacy of democratised public banks.

The constitution of a public sphere within a state can affect how public banks reproduce themselves, but it does not do so in a priori or static ways. In the public sphere public banks can be enabled to function and operate according to reproductive logics and rationalities different from those of private banks directly exposed to market competition. Through the public sphere social forces can also make public banks function as if they were private, profit-seeking banks (Marois 2012).[5] Neither path is predetermined or necessarily stable. Yet as much as public banks can be made profit driven in the public sphere so too can they be made mandate driven, equity oriented, or green and just (or otherwise). This is important because for non-market and public interest orientations to prevail, public banks need to be shielded in the public sphere from the powerful coordinating influence of neoliberal marketisation imperatives.

The public sphere can provide that shielding. There are instances of more direct public sphere shielding, as when public banks are governed under public law, backed by sovereign guarantees, mandated to support public interests, run cooperatively with other public authorities and enterprises, in receipt of government transfers, operationally supported by other public institutions, or democratically run. Public shielding can also be more distant or even near non-existent in advanced cases of corporatisation, as when public banks are governed under private law, subjected to 'public choice' and new public management logics, re-regulated to operate at arm's length from public oversight, or mandated to maximise profits.[6] In other

---

[5] There is an extensive literature on the 'corporatisation' of public enterprises, or when publicly owned services and enterprises operate at arm's length from governing authorities and according to market-oriented, financialised performance indicators (Shirley 1999; McDonald 2014). While corporatisation is not inherently good or bad, under neoliberalism it has been used to 'depoliticise' and make independent public firms function in ways that typically privilege private interests and capital accumulation over public interests and social equity *within* the public sphere (McDonald 2016).

[6] Clifton et al. (2021b), for example, narrate how the turn of the Spanish public development bank, Instituto de Crédito Oficial, to capital markets for sources of funds also saw the bank turn towards more marketised and corporatised functions.

words, while situating a bank within the public sphere can enable a public interest orientation, it hardly guarantees it. Public banks can and do privilege their own self-interests or those of private interests and variations therein. There is no universal scenario that can be read off from the 'public' ownership form. Instead, what a public bank *does* and *is* depends on how contending social forces struggle to make public banks in time- and place-bound contexts within capitalism.

Public banks are thus further connected to the 'state and class-divided society'. Those authorities who control public banks (but which may differ from those who own the bank) decide whether and how a public bank will be shielded from profit and competitive impera-tives. This occurs in relation to contending public and private interests and political and economic imperatives. And it is an ongoing process that shapes and reshapes how, why, and for whom a public bank functions in society. Here states are understood as evolving social formations that, under capitalism, condense and crystallise historically specific, contested, and class-divided power relations (Jessop 1990; Harvey 2010, 55–56). Far from being static black boxes, states are malleable if at once 'momentarily fixed and formative' (Marois 2012, 27). While under capitalism states can appear as relatively separate from markets, in practice states (and their public spheres and public banks) are interwoven with markets and society at large (Poulantzas 2000[1978], 17–19). While tending to facilitate capital accumulation, states in capitalism are thus never independent of social contestation and power struggles, meaning that states are susceptible to social forces and pressure both from above and from below (Lefebvre 2016[1972], 130). States can otherwise be seen as a 'variable field of compromises' in the management of the contradictory conditions of capital accumu-lation and of social harmony (Poulantzas 2000[1978], 184; cf. O'Connor 2009[1979], 7; Soederberg 2010, 15). Because states are social and thus relational, they are sites of strategic struggle over the institutions and resources within them and their public spheres.

States exist within the world market and contemporary struc-tures of 'global financialised capitalism' (cf. von Braunmühl 1978;

Soederberg 2010). Capitalism itself is a historically specific but class-based system of economic development and exploitative social reproduction. Structurally unequal capital–labour relationships predominate across conflictual competitive markets, which are made possible by the predominant reality of private ownership and control over the means and social products of social production (Fine and Saad-Filho 2004; Hanieh 2013; Carroll et al. 2019). This system of social reproduction has not always existed, but it has consolidated as a global system of intertwined states and a competitive world market since the late-nineteenth and early twentieth centuries (Beaud 2001). Since the 1990s capitalism has assumed a more financialised trajectory. More is said on this in Chapter 5, but suffice it here to say that financialisation reflects the growing influence of financial imperatives over economic and social reproduction in ways that have driven the systematic transformation of capitalist economies and social reproduction (Epstein 2005; Lapavitsas 2011; Chesnais 2016; Fine and Saad-Filho 2017). Therein, the interests of finance capital have been systematically internalised within the state apparatus via central bank independence, inflation targeting, and state-led bailouts of private finance at times of crisis (Marois 2012; Tooze 2018). In these ways, the state is the one institution that global financialised capitalism cannot do without.

Capitalist social relations are understood in this framework as all-encompassing but not as all-determining. There is neither unhindered global convergence towards neoliberal and financialised capitalism nor unending national divergences. Instead, contemporary financialised capitalism involves both universalisation and differentiation (cf. Albo 2005; Marois 2012; Carroll et al. 2019). Universalisation insofar as unequal class structures, neoliberal financial logics, and marketisation processes are preserved, renewed, and intensified globally. Differentiation insofar as universalisation assumes institutional forms specific to and variegated by historically specific states and their class-divided societies. How states are integrated into the world market, moreover, is affected by where they are within the international hierarchy of states. The United States, other advanced capitalisms, and China are at the zenith, followed by emerging and developing capitalisms like Brazil, India, and South Africa. These are followed by the world's poorest low-income countries. Public banks in Algeria and Azerbaijan are qualitatively distinct from public banks in China, France, and Germany by virtue of where their states are in the international hierarchy.

In this holistic framework, public banks are historical, co-constituted, relational, and ultimately dynamic social forms within capitalism – a view that is fundamentally distinct from the fixed and monochrome political and development economic views. What public banks are and do cannot be read off from their ownership form. To do so is tantamount to ripping them out of historical time and geographical place – thus making public banks ahistorical and pre-social entities, that is, the very opposite of a dynamic view. Instead, understanding needs to move reflexively through interconnected scales of existence, going back and forth between how a public bank functions and what this means to be a public bank in a state in global financialised capitalism. This no doubt makes it more difficult to say why any particular public bank exists and persists, but it does make for more accurate assessments.

This 'function before form' conceptualisation draws on a theory of institutional credibility advanced by development scholar Peter Ho (2013, 2016, 2017). According to Ho, the concept of 'credibility' can help us to understand institutional persistence. The concept builds on the premise that 'institutions that exist and persist, fulfill a function, and are credible; otherwise they would have fallen into disuse or shifted into other types' (2016, 1126). 'Credibility' is therefore not about grafting a timeless judgement onto public banking in general or onto any public bank in particular. A credible institution is not essentially good or bad, it is simply one that persists for reasons located within society. Credibility thus refers to 'the collective expression of the functionality of institutions, or, more specifically, the reflection of actors' cumulative perceptions of endogenously emerged institutions as a common arrangement' (Ho 2016, 1125).

Credibility is a necessarily time- and place-bound concept that reflects perceived social support for how institutions function (Ho 2020). That is, institutions persist for reasons connected to what they do and for how they function in society. The key point is that social support, or not, for an institution takes analytical precedence over methodological and ideological attempts to dehistoricise and decontextualise institutions by elevating public or private ownership form to a place of universal determinacy (Ho 2014, 14). Social contestation, not stasis, shapes institutional persistence, or change, or possible dissolution.

This makes intuitive sense. If there are no social forces backing an institution, like a public bank, then it will fall into disuse, be closed, or be sold off. By contrast, if social forces have sufficient interest, power, and leverage to back an institution, like a public bank, then it will persist. It will be a credible institution, if not socially uncontested. The dynamic view of this book directly connects institutional credibility to class in the reproduction of public banks within global financialised capitalism (Marois and Güngen 2016).[7] A public bank persists and is credible within the current historical context of class-divided society and in accordance with how its functions are shaped and pulled by contending private and public interests. The momentarily fixed and formative, if inevitably evolving, institutionalised functions that result are complex and contradictory. This is concretely evident in the decarbonisation, definancialisation, and democratisation functions of public banks.

For radical libertarians, liberal political economists, and neoclassical economists, self-maximising private interests are primordial and unbendable motivators in individuals. Consequently, the pursuit of individual private interests can, does, and should shape society. Institutions in society should only enable such individual self-maximisation and the amassing of personal wealth as a societal

---

[7] In this article, we referred to a 'social content' view of public banks, which I here develop as a 'dynamic' view.

Table 2.1. *Contending views on public banks in development*

Issue at hand	Orthodox political view	Heterodox development view	Critical dynamic view
Relationship between ownership form and institutional functions	Ownership determines institutional functions	Ownership determines institutional functions	Institutional functions shape meaning of ownership
Views on public banks	Public banks are a priori shaped by private interests and for political gain; corruptible and inefficient	Public banks are a priori meant to support public goods, growth, welfare, stability, and development; meant to function in addition to private banks	Public banks are dynamic, historically specific, and institutionalised relational social forms; functions change according to pull of public and private interests within class-divided society
Preferred policy orientation	Privatisation; corporatisation; marketisation	Market additionality	Pro-public; economic democratisation
Market failures	Best overcome via extending 'free' markets or via limited government supervision, excluding public ownership;	Government can manage/ overcome via appropriate institutional interventions, including public ownership;	Specific to capitalist social reproduction, resulting in recurrent crises; costs of failures mostly fall on

	government failures more problematic	Justify government intervention to boost capital growth	workers, poor, women, and marginalised in society (socialisation)
Core theoretical paradigms	Neoclassical economics; libertarian and liberal political economy; public choice economics; neoliberalism	Heterodox economics; Keynesian and developmental economics; institutional political economy; Weberian elitism	Historical materialism and Marxism; historical institutionalism
Central actors in society	Individuals	Institutions and elites	Socially located individual and collective agents
Core problematic in contemporary capitalism	Minimise political interference in individual exchange relations (corruption); maximise extension of the market (freedom)	Stabilising unstable capitalist development; re-embedding of the economy due to neoliberal policy errors; reducing inequality	Exploitation of workers, women, and marginalised by capital; reclaiming and democratising the public sphere; public versus private interests
Preferred form of governance	Corporatised, market-based discipline and private monitoring	State elites (strong state or representative democratic)	Participatory democratic

Table 2.1. (cont.)

Issue at hand	Orthodox political view	Heterodox development view	Critical dynamic view
Views on states and public institutions	Composed of self-interested individuals and bureaucrats; must be constrained to ensure market contestability and individual liberty	Elite institutions able to manage the ebbs and flows of market; subject to power relations (but not class based)	Institutionalised social relationships of power endogenous to class-divided global capitalism
Views on markets	Neutral spheres of individual exchange; should be separate from politics and protected from government interference	Inherently unstable but manageable by state institutions and political will	Unequal social spheres of competition and class exploitation under capitalism
Mechanisms driving social change	Individual exchange and reciprocity; unintended consequences	Elite restructuring of institutions; societal counter-movements	Individual and collective agency; class struggle; conjunctural crises
Theoretical influences	Adam Smith, Jeremy Bentham, Friedrich Hayek, Edward Kane, James Buchanan, Milton Friedman	John Stuart Mill, Max Weber, John Maynard Keynes, Karl Polanyi, Hyman Minsky	Karl Marx, Rudolf Hilferding, Nicos Poulantzas, David Harvey

Source: Prepared by author

expression of social justice (Friedman 1962; Hayek 1984[1967]; Buchanan 1999). Critics, however, point out that private interests are rarely, if ever, purely individual or private. Collectives of capitalists and associated academics actively pursue political and economic strategies through the state's public sphere that are supportive of their combined collective interests in private capital accumulation, often at the expense of workers, the environment, democracy, and the public interest (Pringle 2011; Cumbers 2012; MacLean 2017; Ervine 2018; Konings 2018; Zaifer 2020). When referring to 'private interests', then, this means the privileging of capital accumulation, of the amassing of personal wealth, of the 'free' market, and of the primacy of private property rights over all else, even democracy.

The public interest, by contrast, is about privileging democratic economic redistribution, attending to the common needs of the many, and equitable social reproduction. Feminist scholar-activist Hilary Wainwright frames the public interest as involving the potential to socially value mutual dependence, collaboration, care, and an ethic of stewardship (Wainwright 2014, 4). In terms of socio-economic development, the public interest embodies a normative orientation towards the common good, human coexistence and social cohesion, environmental sustainability, democratic decision-making and management of economic processes, and equity and stability in social reproduction. It means protecting the needs of the most marginalized, including workers, women, the poor, and the structurally disadvantaged. It has aspects in common with the 'commons' movement, which espouses a not dissimilar normative orientation, if maintaining a clearer focus on the state and public sphere (cf. Felber 2015; Stavrides 2016; Bauwens et al. 2017). Of course, the public interest is not a homogenous 'thing' but a contested historical and social process inextricably inscribed with unequal power relations and collective aspirations within capitalism, transpiring in institutions, through the public sphere, across the state, and as inseparable from class-divided society. A starting point for political economists working with this conceptualisation, however, is that the public interest can be served by reclaiming the public sphere and state from the intensification and acceleration of exploitative capitalist social relations of reproduction in order to privilege equitable social reproduction in lieu of amassing of unnecessary quantities of personal wealth (cf. Cumbers 2012, 7; cf. McDonald and Ruiters 2012; Spronk and Miraglia 2015; Hanna 2018c; McDonald forthcoming). A dynamic view of public banks accounts for the influence of both public and private interests in the making and remaking of these institutions.

3   Credible Legacies, Neoliberal Transition

Contemporary studies have tended to bypass the historical dynamism of public banking institutions, focusing instead on recent manifestations or overly stylised representations of the past. These mostly economics works prefer to see the diverse legacies of public banks through narrow concepts like 'market failure' or 'additionality'. While using concepts is necessary for understanding, if concepts are employed to replace rather than enrich history, this can impoverish how we think of contemporary public banks and constrain how we imagine their future. This chapter aims to prise open the past of public banks so that we can reconsider the credible legacies of public banks in order to creatively rethink how public banks might confront the current crises of finance, of climate finance, and of Covid-19.

My argument is straightforward: the histories of public banks are more diverse than typically recognised within mainstream economics. Nevertheless, the transition to neoliberalism has tended to narrow the reproductive options for public banks towards more corporatised and marketised logics. Three sections substantiate the argument. The first section provides a brief history of public banks that, despite its brevity, cracks open the dominant economic narrative that public banks are essentially responses to market failures. The second section expands on this claim by illustrating the diversity of public banks' historical functions. The third section positions public banks within the global transition to neoliberalism and the new structural forces at play.

3.1   A BRIEF HISTORY OF PUBLIC BANKING INSTITUTIONS

The theory and evidence of contending economic views on public banks have already been elaborated. Suffice it to say that the commitments of mainstream economists to fixed conceptualisations of public ownership and to functions geared to the market and private capital formation disproportionately shape their understandings. It is in this worldview that the dominant 'market failure' rationale makes sense. Economists first imagine a world where 'the market' resolves all economic problems, enables human reproduction, and is the basis of wealth creation by efficiently allocating resources to under-supplied or underdeveloped sectors. Where the market does not do so efficiently, there is then a 'market failure' and, voila, a credible space opens for state intervention as a derivative of an otherwise isolated market failure (Bator 1958; Stiglitz 1994).[1] The hardcore assumption of markets and private firms first resolving economic problems is not seriously interrogated (Megginson 2005a). Consequently, a narrow and particular economic rationality tends to be conceptually grafted onto public banks that, despite the complexity of the public sphere's presence in social reproduction, remains subordinate to historically specific market imperatives. More funda-mentally, the 'market failure' concept itself reduces and sterilises multiple forms of societal inequalities, unequal power relations, and class exploitation to an after-the-fact failure of an otherwise idealised market mechanism. For those international financial institutions employing the market failure narrative to explain public interven-tions in financial markets, more often than not complex institutional histories and often unequal social relations are obscured (cf. World Bank 2012a, 46–47; IMF 2020, 51–52).

To question the conceptual accuracy of market failure is not to deny that public banks function and intervene in markets, and repeat-edly so especially at times of crisis and instability. It is rather to raise

---

[1] Mazzucato and Penna argue that market failure theory 'provides only a *partial and limited* justification for what NDBs (national development banks) do ... and it does not explain historical and contemporary developments' (2018, 257; emphasis in original). Mazzucato (2018) extends this argument in terms of public value creation. These works move beyond mainstream 'market failure' narratives in terms of mission-oriented and market-making frameworks.

the point that it is not *all* they do, nor not essentially *why* public banks exist, nor simply that they persist at the expense of private firms. I know of no research evidencing that public banks were only ever created to tackle a market failure. This is because market failure is a theoretical presupposition. By contrast, each of the six public banks discussed in subsequent chapters demonstrate multiple political and economic logics behind their historical foundation. More importantly, even when and where public banks intervene, it is never really in response to an abstract market failure but to concrete challenges and socially contested ambitions that require financing, expertise, and coordination. Such financing, expertise, and coordination may or may not be forthcoming from private banks and investors, governments, and even other public banks. But this is part of the wider political and economic context giving rise to time- and place-bound institutions. It is an exercise in extreme idealism to assert that markets and private firms alone intend to and can do all that public banks do. The point is that reducing the functions of public banks to market failure theory is ideological at base. It is also unnecessary, as it is easy enough to simply narrate what public banks do in practice. It is also misrepresentative insofar as what market failure captures is incomplete and inaccurate in any given case. Finally, it is misleading, as public banks can function in parallel to but also in direct competition with private banks, exercising firm-level competitive advantages over them quite independently of any presupposed market failure (Marois 2012; von Mettenheim and Butzbach 2017).

A brief look at the history of public banks substantiates the need to resist grafting market failure theory onto the whole of public banking. Indeed, public bank and bank-like institutions go back much further than many might imagine, long predating generalised markets, individual exchange relations, and monetary relations, not to mention capitalism itself (Hudson 2018; McNally 2020). The earliest forms of debt and credit institutions (the early bank-like institutions) appeared first in the ancient societies of Babylonia and Sumeria circa 2400 BCE (Graeber 2011, 64–65). Temples formed a centre of activity for trade and commerce, and local officials and private individuals developed practices of extending loans to facilitate this and for household spending. For better or worse, debt and credit institutions weaved themselves into social reproduction. When over-indebtedness threatened social instability or natural disasters under-mined peoples' capacity to repay, rulers would declare debt amnesties (Hudson 2018, 29–34).

The public and private credit institutions we know today to be banks, however, have their institutional lineages in the late Middle Ages. It was at this time that the infamous Medici family of Florence held financial power that extended across Europe. It is less well known that this is also the period when local state authorities first formed public municipal banks to address local political and eco-nomic problems. The first known public bank was the Taula de la Ciutat of Barcelona, created in 1401. The city was facing a crisis of private banking as over-indebtedness was leading to institutional collapses (Roberds and Velde 2014, 29). Authorities reasoned that a public bank could provide a reliable and stable banking option within the city while also drawing in deposits that could be used to finance the city's short-term debts more cheaply than by relying on private financiers. The Taula de la Ciutat proved to be remarkably stable, prevailing for some 450 years (Spufford 2014, 245–46). It was not alone. The second known public bank was founded in Genoa in 1408 for very similar reasons, only shutting its doors in 1815 after four centuries of operations (Felloni 2005).

Public banking persisted, expanded, and evolved. Municipal public banks appeared later in Venice and Naples and then in northern Europe. Public banks in Amsterdam (1609) and Hamburg (1619) began to innovate, developing new methods of dealing with the unreliability of coin money by substituting it with book-entry money, backed by precious metals (Roberds and Velde 2014, 83). By the late seventeenth century, national 'central banks' emerged – first with Sweden's public Riksbank (1668) followed soon after by the, at first, private Bank of

England (1694). These historical banking precedents began to have an effect on governing authorities' ideas of the possible. As Roberds and Velde write, 'From the fifteenth to the nineteenth century, the idea of a public bank had developed from that of a narrowly specialised facility in a commercial city, to that of an essential component of a nation's financial architecture' (2014, 84). Public banks were acquiring increasingly diverse functions and evolving as dynamic institutions. They were also bathed in prevailing power relations and exploitation. As David McNally narrates in depth, the Bank of England was founded to enable British imperial ambitions by financing war-making and to help underwrite British prosperity through the Atlantic slave trade, with one prosperous London slave merchant, Humphrey Morice, serving as a director then as governor of the Bank of England in its formative years (between 1716 and 1728) (McNally 2020, 155).

It is also during the historical period that other rationales for establishing public banks emerged, notably to service one's community. In the eighteenth-century American colonies, town hall meetings voiced popular demands (farmers and tradespersons) for establishing public land banks in opposition to elite merchant and propertied class demands for private ones (Thayer 1953, 148). Such was the case of British Quakers in the American colony of Pennsylvania, when the local government founded a public Land Bank in 1726 in response to the demands of farmers for more affordable and accessible credit (Rappaport 1996; Kulikoff 2000). Any returns to the Land Bank were channelled back into the community's public revenue. As much as the Land Bank responded to the 'failures' of mostly non-existent markets and private financiers, its rationale entailed class solidarity and political resistance to British imperial ambitions in the colony (though the Pennsylvania Land Bank eventually succumbed to pressure from British bankers to dominate finance in the colonies). Here again there are real contradictions. Insofar as early American colonists' and farmer interests combined to form a local public land bank in their interests, in *this* context it also entailed the often brutal dispossession and slaughter of American indigenous peoples to make way for European farmers: 'To ground money in land banks, as did South Carolina, Pennsylvania, New York, and other states, was to root it in soil drenched with the blood of indigenous peoples' (McNally 2020, 178). By contrast, during this same period in Europe, a more collective, less imperial, local political movement for small savings banks emerged in the late eighteenth century in Germany (the Sparkasse banks), which then spread to Great Britain by the early nineteenth century, thriving into the twentieth century (Butzbach 2012, 37). The social logic behind these savings banks was to enable ordinary, often very poor, workers to safely save modest amounts, earn a bit of interest, and take out all or some of these savings when needed.

The transition from more mercantilist to more capitalist industrial relations globally gave rise to new and more powerful expansionary economic and political pressures in the late nineteenth and early twentieth centuries (Beaud 2001). State formation, public service provisioning and infrastructure, and national industrialisation required great amounts of capital for large-scale, long-term investments. Bigger and more development-oriented national public banks offered an effective and direct means of mobilising and channelling finance in the capitalist core and periphery alike (von Mettenheim 2010). Then, as today, how public banks functioned and for whom was contested and contradictory within class-divided society. As much as public banks enabled small trades to flourish, farmers to farm, and municipalities to provide public services, so too did public banks (usually undemocratically) fund large-scale industrial conglomerates, thus helping politically well-connected families to accumulate enormous economic power and wealth in ways that entrenched capitalism's class-divided inequality (cf. Marois 2012).

In this period new public banks began to be erected worldwide, many of which prevail today. In 1816, the French Caisse des Dépôts et Consignations was created to deal with France's accumulated wartime and imperial debts.[2] In 1911, the Australian Labour Party founded the Commonwealth Bank as a savings and general commercial bank, which would later assume national central bank-like functions. Today's public savings bank, Sberbank, is linked back to the Russian monarchy under Tsar Nicholas I, who sanctioned the first openings of 'Savings Offices' in 1841. Following the 1917 October Revolution, these savings institutions were converted into the State Labour Savings Banks under the Soviet system and then in 1991 into Sberbank. Around the same period, the Ottoman Empire planted the seeds of a contemporary public universal banking giant in Turkey, Ziraat Bank. First created in 1863 as an agricultural fund to assist struggling farmers, it transformed into a farmer-oriented banking institution with an anti-imperialist (albeit deeply nationalist) ethos. As the nascent Turkish state struggled to take form after 1923, Ziraat Bank was tasked with bolstering domestic financial autonomy by curtailing dependency on European imperial financial powers.

In North America during the Great Depression years, provincial authorities in Alberta, Canada, established the Alberta Treasury Branch (ATB) in 1938 as an alternative source of credit for the mainly agricultural society. But it also came to hold cultural and class-related meanings. In the words of Doug Ross, a customer since 1949:[3]

> I was born a farm kid, and we had a lot of respect for what the leaders of the time were doing. We respected the function of the Treasury Branch, which was to benefit the farmers and small business. That's the reason I went to Treasury Branches. I felt some sort of bonding with them.

---

[2] The history of public banks is often missing, relatively incomplete, and sometimes inaccurate in the current literature. For example, Aghion states that the oldest government-backed financial institution was the Dutch Société Generale pour Favoriser l'Industrie Nationale, founded 1822 (1999, 85). The French Caisse des Dépôts preceded it, not to mention multiple other municipal banks. Mazzucato and Penna state that national development banks 'have their historical roots in the monetary agreements of Bretton Woods (1944)', which led to the creation of banks like Germany's KfW (2018, 259). Again, there are many more and much earlier cases of public banks.

[3] ATB Website www.atb.com/about/Pages/our-history.aspx. Accessed 4 June 2018.

The ATB followed on from similar such cases south of the border, wherein farming communities from Oregon to North Dakota created state banks to overcome natural disasters, like drought, and class-based oppression, like private bankers exploiting local farmers (for example, the Bank of North Dakota, Chapter 5). Nationally, the US Reconstruction Finance Corporation (RFC), founded in 1932, changed from initially providing banking sector liquidity to a direct financier of New Deal programmes through local banks and credit unions and to farmers, businesses, cooperatives, school districts, and so on (Olson 1988, 43–44; Nash 1959). By contrast, in the early twentieth century European fascist governments took over cooperative and savings banks as a mean of supporting their oppressive political movements (von Mettenheim and Butzbach 2014, 13).

Public banks, then and now, are what historically situated individual and collective agents make them to be – often resulting in contested and contradictory institutions hardly reducible to monochrome market failure explanations. This is especially so for public banks made to be countervailing political forces. In such instances, public banks were conceived of and created in response to the apparent 'market successes' of powerful, private, and foreign banks in exploiting a community. European imperialism and colonialism, alongside monarchic rule, embodied such structural forms of financial domination over states, societies, and classes that undermined domestic autonomy and human dignity in subjugated societies.[4] In certain cases of subordinated societies, it was understood that establishing some form of public control and ownership over the banks in order to mobilise domestic savings was an important factor of promoting national independence, supporting national revolutionary movements, establishing a balance of financial power, and for human liberation within one's borders (cf. Hilferding 2006[1910]; von Mettenheim 2012, 34).

---

[4] For a broader historical account of the connections between war, slavery, finance, and empire, see McNally (2020).

The post–World War II era of reconstruction, the consolidation of capitalism, drive towards industrial development, and decolonisation struggles each in different ways generated a surge in public banks worldwide. New public banks of the time included the Socialist Federal Republic of Yugoslavia's National Bank in 1946, Germany's founding of the KfW in 1948 (Chapter 6), and the post–Revolutionary People's Republic of China establishment of the People's Bank of China in 1948. At this time the small Central American country of Costa Rica nationalised its banks in 1948 as a step towards the 'democratization of credit' and national development (Marois 2005). Some years later the Democratic Republic of Vietnam's established its State Bank in 1951. Following the 1959 Revolution, Cuba nationalised the private banks within its borders in 1961. In Korea, after the 1961 coup, the military regime also nationalised the private banks. By contrast, in India the government of Indira Gandhi nationalised fourteen large private banks to facilitate a national, socialist-oriented developmental policy in 1969, after having already established several new national public banks (see Chapter 5). Algeria, Libya, Tanzania, and Egypt undertook bank nationalisations during the 1960s as part of their national liberation struggles. By the mid-twentieth century public banking had become significant, even dominant, within national economies. Estimates of the advanced capitalisms in the 1970s suggest that public banks controlled 40 per cent of the largest banks' assets while in the developing capitalisms 65 per cent were public (Levy Yeyati et al. 2007, 209–13). There were of course great differences among countries. In Latin America, for example, public ownership of the largest banks in Costa Rica reached 100 per cent; in Chile, Ecuador, and Peru around 90 per cent; Uruguay 42 per cent; and in Trinidad and Tobago less than 5 per cent.

Through public banks governments were able to coordinate and direct monetary resources across national spaces and into public and private sectors including housing, infrastructure, state-owned enterprises, farming, industrialisation, trades, municipalities, and so on. Public bank networks also ensured domestic payment and savings facilities. In many cases, the two were combined in universal banks or through collaborations between public commercial, universal, postal, and development banks. In this way, public banks financed capitalist industrialisation and development, as well as mediated class-divided social reproduction (Gerschenkron 1962; Bennett and Sharpe 1980; Marois and Güngen 2016). Nowhere did public banks exist without successes and setbacks or outside the pull of public and private interests within class-divided society. The demands of transitioning to capitalism and world market integration in the late nineteenth and early twentieth centuries gave rise to both unprecedented domestic financing requirements that could simply not be met by essentially non-existent private capital markets (in most cases) and to powerful national independence struggles that demanded greater domestic control over the financing of development. These economic and political motivations fostered the development and acquisition of a variety of institutional functions within public banks.

3.2   A HISTORY OF INSTITUTIONAL FUNCTIONS

Developmental processes and social reproduction, be they organised around capitalist, socialist, sustainable, or other rationales, require institutionalised means of pooling available money resources, magnifying them in quantity, and mobilizing them for costly and long-term investments (Itoh and Lapavitsas 1999; see Chapter 1). The function of transforming, magnifying, and converting short-term financial liabilities into long-term assets is a defining characteristic of the financial intermediation and money creation that banks do, in both temporal and geographical terms (Butzbach and von Mettenheim 2015). 'Fractional reserve banking' is key. The fractional reserve system enables banks to multiply the amount of loans made well above the actual cash reserves available for immediate withdrawal from a bank at any given time. A banking institution, that is, need only hold onto a 'fraction' of the money it lends out. The practice of fractional reserve banking emerged in history along with the rise of Europe's modern banking institutions during the middle ages. It is a politically authored and sustained economic practice that enables the speeding up of economic investment and expansion by increasing available capital resources. It is also a practice that has magnified the political and economic power of those classes and societies that have owned and controlled banking and financial institutions.

Modern human society has created different institutional types of public and private banks with different, sometimes overlapping, functions revolving around fractional reserves systems. I earlier elaborated on the various institutional types of public banks and why this book focuses on the three most common types, namely public commercial/retail banks (first tier), development or investment banks (second tier), and universal banks (combining commercial and development/investment functions) at the sub-national and national scale (see Chapter 1). I have also specified what it is that qualifies a bank as a public bank, namely that it is located within the public sphere; performs financial intermediation and banking functions but with no ultimate purpose or policy orientation; can function in public and private interests; and persists as a credible, contested, and evolving institution (see Introduction).

Commercial, development, and universal public banks will often service different combinations of target groups (or clients), including corporations, households, governments, micro-, small- and medium-sized enterprises (MSMEs), local and national financial institutions, non-financial corporations, public and state agencies, farmers, and so on. The motivations of target groups to borrow will range from a personal need for basic food supplies, to a family's desire for a home, to a local firm's need to expand operations, to a business' strategy to invest in new technologies, to a bank wanting to access additional loanable funds, to a community's need to upgrade water or transportation infrastructure, and to a government's need to cover fiscal shortfalls, wage war, overcome economic crisis, or confront a pandemic. Any one of these target groups may also borrow simply to service already-existing debts or to shift debts between institutions (displacing current debt obligations in time and/or place). Anyone of them might also borrow on speculation, that is, to use the money to make more money through various 'casino-like' ventures (though this would be less likely, but not impossible, among public sector borrowers).

This is all made possible through a variety of financial contracts, which become an *asset* for the one lending (from which a future benefit should be derived) and a *liability* for the one borrowing (a future obligation to pay). These contracts form a legal claim to future money flows. Banks typically loan money for 'interest' (I do not here address sharia-compliant finance), which is in effect the cost of borrowing money (extra fees are also often charged). At base, both the interest and principal need be repaid to complete the contract in full and without default. This process involves greater and lesser levels of risk that the loan may not be paid back, affecting its financial return profile. If a bank extends too many risky 'non-performing loans', there is a chance the bank will go bust – unless it is bailed out by other banks or by a public authority. Private banks are typically profit driven while public banks are typically mandate driven, though there are private banks that are not-for-profit and profit-maximising public banks. It depends on how those who control a bank make it, rather than on any universal principle, per se, derived from a public or private ownership form.

Most of what public commercial, development, and universal banks do and the financial resources they command have been mostly built up and acquired over the last century or so. While mainstream economists would prefer these be merely derivatives of market failure, we know that there are more diverse economic and political forces at play. In general, therefore, we can refer to three broad public banking historical legacies: an enduring economic legacy of mobilising and magnifying money capital; an enduring political legacy as countervailing forces against foreign domination, class inequalities, and private interest supremacy; and an enduring knowledge legacy as repositories of financial expertise and know-how within the public sphere (a function bridging the economic and political illustrated in the case study chapters). No doubt, as our case studies attest to, public banks also have enduring economic and political legacies that reinforce class-divided inequality and economic processes that can undermine the public interest.

Across these legacies, public banks have acquired multiple functions that provide, sometimes transient, sometimes enduring, financial solutions to the challenges of economic development and social reproduction. It is for these credible yet class-divided legacies and functions that public banks persist within capitalism. It is for what public banks do that they garner collective support from contending public and private interests within class-divided society.

Table 3.1 provides an indicative list of functions acquired and performed by public commercial, development, and universal banks. There is an interconnectedness. In seeking to mobilise scarce financial resources to industrialise economies, public banks had to develop savings, loans, chequing, and payment services. This linked public banks to state formation processes and spatial strategies of national territorial and monetary integration. The geographically targeted provisioning of small town and rural financial services is similarly tied to mobilising and magnifying capital nationally, but it too involves building up in-house 'finance for development' expertise. In some cases, public banks (as well as savings and cooperative) were founded in order to counteract usury and the exploitation of peasants and a society's nascent working class.

New political and economic pressures associated with world market integration intensified pressures to connect national and regional development to varied strategies of import substitution and export-oriented industrialisation. In theory, bank intermediation should channel money from capital rich to capital poor regions, facilitating combined development. In practice, money begets money, and already capital rich areas have tended to absorb more and more capital

Table 3.1. *The acquired functions of public banks*

General categories of functions	Instances of particular functions	Performed by ... public banks
Household retail and commercial services	Standard loans; lines of credit and credit cards; payments and chequing; deposits and savings; mortgages; retirement planning; investment services; insurance; forex; etc.	Retail/ Commercial Universal
Corporate retail and commercial services	Standard loans; lines of credit and credit cards; payments and chequing; deposits and savings; mortgages; investment services; insurance; forex; employer services; asset management; etc.	Retail/ Commercial Universal
Development finance and investment services	Long- and short-term development loans; infrastructure (energy; transport; water and sanitation; health; education; etc.); investment services and advising; bond issuances; technical expertise; import–export finance and guarantees; public–public partnerships; public–private partnerships; in-house research and development	Development Universal
Concessional lending and service provisioning	Subsidised interest rates; preferential terms and conditions; reduced fees; subsidised or free technical advice	Retail/ Commercial Development Universal

Table 3.1. (*cont.*)

General categories of functions	Instances of particular functions	Performed by ... public banks
Venture capital and equity financing	Taking a direct ownership stake in a project, start-up company, or small business	Development Universal
Mandate-driven and emergency lending	Officially targeted lending and support to mandated areas (social sectors; regional; economic; environmental; etc.); crisis interventions (financial crises; natural and human-made environmental disasters; pandemics); economic stabilisation; counter-cyclical lending	Retail/ Commercial Development Universal
Public sector collaborations and support services	Ownership, financial risks, and expertise are shared among public sector entities; cross-funding of public sector banks; deposit-taking and credit services for public employees and services	Retail/ Commercial Development Universal
Micro-, small-, and medium-sized enterprise (MSMEs) support	Provide credit and payments services; preferential loan facilities; support, advice and expertise	Retail/ Commercial Development Universal
Knowledge services	Provide technical advice and expertise to enterprises (MSMEs to large corporations) and government authorities (municipal to national); national, regional, and local developmental planning	Retail/ Commercial Development Universal

Table 3.1. (cont.)

General categories of functions	Instances of particular functions	Performed by ... public banks
	support; project preparation services; sectoral expertise; performance standard-setting and monitoring	
Financial integration and access	National payments systems; small community and rural service provisioning; government assistance program administrators; social integration and protection of vulnerable groups support and services	Retail/ Commercial Universal
Aid and development (domestic and international)	Administer directed loan and grant support programmes for governments and official donors; provide knowledge services; offer concessional lending and facilitate transfers	Development Universal

Source: Compiled by author

resources, especially when left to the strategies of private banks alone (Myrdal 1963; Bennett and Sharpe 1980). More has money poured into cities, depriving the countryside of employment opportunities and encouraging migration to the cities. Public policy and public banks have helped to offset this tendency, if not eliminate it, by moving money from core to peripheral regions as an expression of public policy and financial autonomy.

National developmental strategies also faced investment barriers. Public banks became known as home-grown solutions for the provisioning of long-term and often subsidised credits. The most obvious examples are in public infrastructure and technological imports, but historically this has also included industrialisation projects around resource extraction, inputs into manufacturing (steel, paper, and so on), and large-scale energy projects. The long-term effects of building up public banks as financial institutions and of extending their range of functions combine to offer governing authorities an 'in-house' repository of public financial and developmental expertise from which the government and public sector can benefit. Public banks can amass significant institutional and inter-generational memory at the international, national, and local levels, quite literally becoming 'knowledge' banks, which can be shared collaboratively within the public sphere. Governing authorities benefit by having a ready pool of public bank employees versed in and practicing financial, monetary, and development economics. Public bank employees will have knowledge of their local conditions, too, which is a benefit to the community and to planning authorities.

The role of emergency economic stabilisation and counter-cyclical lending are forms of (not necessarily progressive) wealth redistribution undertaken by public banks. At times of instability and crisis, public banks can function counter-cyclically, that is, lend into the crisis. Private banks tend to function pro-cyclically, constraining thus worsening crisis. In the absence of democratic deliberation and social equity governance frameworks, however, this will not necessarily occur in the public interest. Public banks can rescue private banks or bail out corporations, socialising the costs of the crisis in class-divided ways. Most likely the function will be realised in a complicated mix of both (sustaining a private industry, hence employment, hence incoming personal tax receipts) but not without contradictions. Finally, at times of crisis public banks can function as safe havens for people's savings, backed by sovereign guarantees to reduce the risk of personal savings losses. The accumulated legacies of public banks and the functions they have acquired across time and in different places are extensive. They are subject to change as capitalism and the relative power of public and private interests evolves.

Chapter 7 elaborates on a proposal of how a democratised green and just public bank might function.

3.3 THE TRANSITION TO NEOLIBERALISM

In the finance and development literature, neoliberal 'casino capitalism' is understood as a substantive break with post-war state-led strategies of capitalist development (Strange 1994). Development was increasingly understood to be achieved via market exposure, and making money from money in finance increasingly displaced investing to facilitate industrial production (Mazzucato 2018, 135–36). This post-1980s neoliberal shift entailed a broad move towards the so-called Washington consensus assortment of neoclassical structural adjustment policies (cf. Williamson 1990). Yet neoliberalism is more than just a set of economic policies (Pradella and Marois 2015). It is also a class-based and global process led by individual and collective agents that has restructured state and society such that social, political, economic, and ecological reproductive processes are more directly and intensely subordinated to capital accumulation imperatives and market rationalities (Harvey 2005; Fine and Saad-Filho 2017; Carroll et al. 2019). To usher change in, neoliberal advocates attacked and often defeated the collective capacity of organised labour, the poor, the peasantry, and popular classes to resist neoliberal transformation. This involved policies of liberalisation, deregulation, and privatisation. More fundamentally, though, these policies are expressions of deeper social reconfigurations of state, capital, and labour relations in favour of capital accumulation concentrated in the hands of those who own and control capital.

Alongside neoliberal transformation, finance capital has come to exert an enormous impact on overall economic activity, corporate strategies, personal decisions, and government planning and policy-making in ways that intensify financial pressures on societal reproduction (Ghosh 2005; Orhangazi 2008a; Fine 2010; Garcia-Arias 2015; Konings 2018). Therein, the ways in which finance capital interacts with society is class-divided and socially unequal in complex ways (Lapavitsas 2009; Marois 2012; Chesnais 2016; Hanieh 2018). As critical geographer David Harvey explains, class 'is a role, not a label that attaches to persons. We play multiple roles all the time.... The role of the capitalist is to use money to command the labor or the assets of others and to use that command to make profit, to accumulate capital and thereby augment personal command over wealth and power' (2010, 232). Capitalists leverage their accumulated wealth and societal power to ensure that their self-interests are preserved. For example, corporate capital actively works to shape global green transitions so that they are growth and consumption oriented 'with a minor tweak' (Ervine 2018, 121). The vast majority of wage-labouring people, by contrast, consume what they earn in order to survive and reproduce themselves by purchasing food, clothing, shelter, and so on, often having to rely on credit to do so. The rollback of the state and public provisioning alongside the commodification of practically everything under neoliberalism has forced workers, and particularly women, to use interest-bearing finance (consumer credit and micro-finance) to secure their most basic human needs (Ghosh 2013; Soederberg 2013a, 2013b; Roberts 2015; Bateman et al. 2019). Individuals, families, and workers with savings, debts, and shareholding (for example, pensions) are now more directly integrated into global finance but *without* having any new rights or control mechanisms over the financial institutions in control of their savings (de Brunhoff 2003; Soederberg 2014). At the same time neoliberal depoliticisation strategies have insulated the state financial apparatus, regulatory institutions, and related processes from democratic input and influence. As a whole, these neoliberal and finance-led changes have facilitated massive financial expansionism, class-divided concentrations of wealth, recurrent financial crises, and even de-development as financial resources flow towards speculative rather than productive investment (Duménil and Lévy 2013; Mazzucato 2018). As more than just a set of rightly or wrongly engineered economic policies, neoliberal financial transformation has enable capital to retain a much greater proportion of the social surplus, resulting in skyrocketing inequality between classes, within societies, and among countries globally – all of which has been to the detriment of workers, the poor, women, and marginalised (Kapsos and Bourmpoula 2013; Goda et al. 2016; Lockwood 2020).

The neoliberal ideological revolution initially brought the developmental credibility of public services and banking to a grinding halt (Bayliss and Fine 2008). Neoclassical economists and neoliberal advocates worked to expose cases of poorly run institutions and evidence of abuse by state elites and domestic capitalists (Caprio et al. 2004; Haber 2005). While unrepresentative of all, or even most, public banks, problematic public banks no doubt added narrative weight to the neoliberal assault. The World Bank has acknowledged the thin evidentiary basis, noting that for the first two decades of neoliberal privatisation efforts the 'primary evidence' against public banking in development finance was largely 'anecdotal' (World Bank 2001, 127). The evidence for and against public banks in economic development, however, continues to be contrasting and inconclusive (Chapter 2). Proof was mostly beside the point for advocates of neoliberalism, however, especially for hardcore public choice advocates and 'government failure' proponents (Tullock et al. 2002; see MacLean 2017). It was more about the promised benefits (freedom, wealth, rising tides) and the ideological commitment to jettisoning government influence over private corporations (cf. Mazzucato 2018, 249–51). For their part, private and foreign bankers had long grasped the opportunities generated by the 1980s debt crises to profit off the privatisation of public enterprises, including banks (Cypher 1989; Weizsäcker et al. 2005). All of this was ideologically backed by northern development agencies like the USAID, the IMF, and the World Bank. In scholarly circles well into the 2000s, relatively little was heard or written about public banks and development except by advocates of privatisation, who presaged no real future for public banks (Maxfield 1992; Caprio et al. 2004; Andrews 2005; cf. Aghion 1999). In mainstream circles, the future of banking and development was decidedly private – and advocates were set on making it so (World Bank 2001; Clarke et al. 2005; Megginson 2005b; Rodríguez and Santiso 2007).

An underappreciated but important aspect of neoliberal transformation is how governing elites have restructured the state apparatus to better manage recurrent financial crises to the benefit of financial capital and private investors (Panitch and Gindin 2012; Yalman et al. 2019; Karwowski and Centurion-Vicencio 2018). During the financially turbulent 1990s, state and government elites developed institutional expertise and material capacity to absorb financial risks at times of crisis in order to stabilise otherwise unstable neoliberal transformations. This process involved the socialisation of financial risks (Marois 2011, 2014; Ho and Marois 2019) or, alternatively, the socialisation of crisis (Whitener 2019) by authorities through the state apparatus. Either way, workers and the poor are forced to pay for the costs of recurrent financial crises, directly through increased taxation and indirectly through austerity, to the benefit of financial capital and neoliberal continuity, exacerbating inequalities in class-divided society. This has occurred in countries north and south since the 1980s, including Turkey, Mexico, across East Asia, New Zealand, Ireland, Russia, Brazil, the UK, the United States, and so on (see Marois 2012; Lapavitsas 2013; Clark 2016; McNally 2015). I have argued elsewhere in the case of Mexico's 1982, 1994–95, and 2008–09 financial crises that society does not get financialisation without the class-divided socialisation of financial risks by state authorities (Marois 2014, 324–25):

> the recurrent socialization of financial risks ... cannot occur
> without the institutionalized subordination of workers and popular
> classes to financial imperatives. This unequal power relation exists
> because financial capital has won the political battle around
> establishing policy matrixes that enable state authorities to push
> the costs of financial risks gone bad onto society – be it in the form
> of bank nationalization, recapitalization, official guarantees, or
> foreign reserve accumulation – via state fictitious capital, working
> class taxation, and budget allocations.

These same class-divided processes followed the 2008–09 global financial crisis. Then Bank of England Governor Mervyn King recognised the social iniquity of the bailouts, acknowledging that the price of 'financial crisis is being borne by people who absolutely did not cause it'.[5] Insofar as the state is integral to financialisation, so too has the socialisation of private financial risks emerged as the one thing that financialised capitalism cannot do without.

The state-led socialisation of private financial risks, moreover, provides further insight into why public banks remain credible for private interests under neoliberalism. Public banks have proven functionally capable of helping to stabilise recurrent financial crises (definancialisation) and of absorbing the private risks of green infrastructure investments (decarbonisation) in ways that can help to preserve global capitalism and retain its class-divided power structures. This is the basis for the convergence of economists around a pro-market additionality framework: public banks can disproportionately serve private interests and capital accumulation by socialising risks to enhance investors' rewards. But this does not occur outside of class-divided society and independently from being held up against more common, public interest goals (either in practice or in discourse). To the extent public banks can be and are held to account (democratisation), this has never been much of a concern in the mainstream literature (other than to remove and depoliticise any such governance structures). There is no escaping, however, that the historical functions performed by public banks in the public and private interest are a matter of contestation in ideological, discursive, and material terms and that neoliberal transition has shifted the terrain of that struggle towards the interests of financial accumulation. This is neither natural nor inevitable, but subject to change.

---

[5] Philip Inman, 'Bank of England Governor Blames Spending Cuts on Bank Bailouts', *The Guardian*, 1 March 2011. Available at www.theguardian.com/business/2011/mar/01/mervyn-king-blames-banks-cuts. Accessed 18 August 2019.

Public banks have a long history of credible and diverse functions well in excess of market failure narratives. A genuinely historical and dynamic approach points instead towards a non-essentialist worldview that leaves open the potential to experiment with and mobilise public banks in a multitude of ways. Nothing in the past or in the foreseeable future will guarantee that public banks function in the public interest, but neither does anything past or present guarantee they cannot. Historical structural context matters, however. In contemporary neoliberal reality, public banks function before a series of contradictions. Do they mobilise public resources to support the well-organised, dominant, and collective interests of private finance, who as a class are in search of expanded power, profit, and market control in ways that can in turn threaten the future of public banks and a public *ethos*? In other words, should public banks be 'institutionally responsible *for* and politically subordinate *to* the fate of financial capital', publicly socialising the losses while privatising the gains (which is the preferred strategy of the World Bank) (cf. Marois 2014, 325)? Or should public banks break with structurally oppressive neoliberal financialisation by supporting the collective interests of workers, women, popular classes, and the marginalised – that is, by supporting the public interest? The answers can only be realised in context. As dynamic entities, the legacies of public banks cannot avoid the pull of public and private interests. As much as public banks help to sustain global finance capitalism and, by extension, class-divided private interests, case study research also demonstrates that public banks can be made to function in the public interest via decarbonisation, definancialisation, and democratisation, not to mention being made to respond to emergencies like the Covid-19 pandemic. The future legacies of public banks remain to be forged. But for whom?

4   Decarbonisation

So far I have developed three of the book's premises – that public banks persist with more capacity than commonly realised; that a dynamic view of public banks is best able to explain their contested resurgence; and that public banks have a more diverse historical legacy of functions than allowed for within market failure paradigms. We now turn to the fourth premise, which is based on case studies of public banks functioning in the public interest, if not free of the pull of private interests.

In this chapter on 'decarbonisation', I argue that the ways in which the China Development Bank and the Nordic Investment Bank function to tackle the crisis of climate finance bolsters their credibility and persistence within class-divided society. These public banks are scaling up financial capacity, directing it towards decarbonisation and environmental sustainability, and developing accountable floors for green funding decisions in ways that can inform needed debate on what pro-public green and just public banks should be like. However, neither the China Development Bank nor the Nordic Investment Bank are without contradictions or free of the need to be *made* better. Public interest demands for a sustainable future have constituted a motivating force for their greening. Yet the trajectory of global climate finance policy is disproportionately influenced by the shadow of contemporary capitalism, that is, by capitalist accumulation and growth imperatives that favour market expansion, private interests, and investor priorities. The shadow of carbonising capitalism can and does undermine the decarbonisation activities of these two banks, yet they can be made to do better.

Three premises substantiate this argument. First, the World Bank and mainstream economists disproportionately frame the problem of public banks financing decarbonisation according to a logic of pro-market additionality. Second, the China Development Bank and the Nordic Investment Bank evidence that public banks have acquired the financial capacity and expertise to fund decarbonisation and climate change mitigation in public interest ways. Third, the 'greening' of these two public banks is contradictory. Despite committing substantial resources to combatting climate change, the China Development Bank and the Nordic Investment Bank also fuel it by disproportionately funding otherwise carbonising economic activities, exposing the green and growth contradictions of global financialised capitalism.

4.1 THE PROBLEM OF PUBLIC BANKS FINANCING DECARBONISATION

At the highest levels of international policymaking, the problem of public banks financing decarbonisation is increasingly being framed around an economic principle of 'pro-market additionality'. The gist of this melange of orthodox and heterodox thinking is that the accumulation interests of private finance suffer no harm – for it is they who are still best able to respond to the crisis of climate finance.[1] In this, pro-market additionality is premised on mobilising the mass of capital under private control by using public resources to socialise private investment risks to maximise private returns. This ideological principle cum policy strategy of financing decarbonisation is most

---

[1] The problem of public banks financing decarbonisation, of course, sits within a broader debate on the financing of decarbonisation (Newell and Paterson 2010). A significant element of this debate has focused on neoliberal idealism that if exposed to the market, then *carbon* markets will resolve the environmental problem on its own. The evidence is the opposite, as the global political economy of carbon has neither contained carbonising growth nor offered any substantive alternative pathway away from the incessant productivist and profit-maximising system of capitalist exploitation of the environment and workers driving carbonisation of the environment and social inequality. The literature on this is extensive and beyond the limits of this chapter, but for a useful start of the wider contours of financing green transformation, see the following: Lohmann 2006; Newell 2011; Bracking 2012; Eccles 2013; Sullivan 2013; Ervine 2013, 2018; Michaelowa et al. 2019.

evident in the World Bank's 'Maximizing Finance for Development' strategy and its related 'Billions to Trillions' agenda (IMF/World Bank 2015; cf. Badré 2018). The World Bank strategy/agenda demands the subordination of public banks to some variation of growth- or accumulation-oriented green investing without (and this is key) public banks ever seeking to compete with, out-compete, or displace private markets, banks, or investors and their profit motives. The ideology of pro-market additionality, by design, excludes any credible potential for public banks to act on decarbonisation autonomously, in the public interest, or in ways that bolster future public capacity and public sphere collaboration.

For this pro-market additionality narrative to be compelling, two assumptions need accepting: (1) that public banks cannot fulfil the demand for climate finance independently, so private investors must be courted and (2) that public banks exist a priori to support the private sector and capital growth. The first is yet evidenced in the decarbonisation literature and the second is an ideological presupposition. Yet the two together over-determine the narrative and material limits of what public banks can do to finance decarbonisation. To inquire how public banks might finance decarbonisation independently or in ways contrary to a principle of pro-market additionality is rendered an illegitimate and practically absurd proposition. The problem of financing decarbonisation is as such impoverished.

But it is no less pressing. The financing of decarbonisation is an urgent and desirable societal process necessary for the reduction of global carbon emissions (UNCTAD 2019). As a societal process, financing decarbonisation entails intersecting and contentious environmental, political, economic, gendered, and racialised dimensions (see Newsham and Bhagwat 2016; Magdoff and Williams 2017; Ervine 2018; Nightingale et al. 2020). It therefore entails important technical elements, including specific expertise, and contested elements, insofar as competing technologies, strategies, and relationships of power, privilege, and social reproduction come to bear on decarbonisation and its financing in practice. To be certain, decarbonisation cannot be isolated from overlapping climate change mitigation and adaptation strategies. Yet decarbonisation, in particular, has reached a global consensus around the immediacy of reducing human activities that produce greenhouse gas (GHG) emissions. This means financing the replacement of high carbon with low carbon infrastructure, as infrastructure accounts for over 60 per cent of all GHG emissions (Bhattacharya et al. 2016; IPCC 2018). Without changing the infrastructure of social reproduction, now and into the future, there is no hope of stemming and reversing carbon-generated climate change – a now extinction-level threat to humanity. This is the underlying challenge and the foundation of the crisis of climate finance.

The transition to a low-carbon future will be costly and so the problem of financing decarbonisation is real. The exact amount of financing required varies. However, estimates given in the benchmark 2016 report, *Delivering on Sustainable Infrastructure for Better Development and Better Climate*, provide the touchstone for most discussions (Bhattacharya et al. 2016; cf. UNEP 2015). Accordingly, between 2015 and 2030 global society will need to spend about $90 trillion to meet global climate mitigation ambitions by holding global temperatures below a 2°C rise. The $90 trillion is an amount that exceeds the total combined costs of all current infrastructure stock, hence truly historic in scale. The $90 trillion estimate also accounts for aging infrastructure in the advanced capitalisms and new requirements for the developing and emerging capitalisms. In short, total global public and private low-carbon investments will need to nearly double, from about $3.4 trillion annually to over $6 trillion (Bhattacharya et al. 2016, 26).

Where will these trillions of dollars in climate finance come from? For the World Bank, it is pro-market additionality and using public funds to leverage private capital. The United Nations Environmental Programme (UNEP) further suggests *greening* the financial system by internalising sustainable development into decision-making by financial regulators and central banks (UNEP

2015, xiv; cf. Volz et al. 2015). It is no small task, and observers increasingly recognise the real limits to existing market-based, profit-oriented strategies. As United Nations (UN) Secretary-General Guterres acknowledges, 'It is clear that the world will not achieve the Sustainable Development Goals without a fundamental shift in the international financial system' (UN IATF 2019, iii). This will demand changes at the national level. President of the German Central Bank (Bundesbank), Jens Weidmann, writes that a 'financial system that facilitates this [green] transition is indispensable'.[2] The governors of the Bank of England and France, Mark Carney and François Villeroy de Galhau, also argue that the 'financial sector must be at the heart of tackling climate change'.[3] Consensus is for the need for change, beginning at home and from within the financial system (cf. Durrani et al. 2020). But how and in whose interests?

Behind these somewhat recent calls to 'green' the financial system lies an often implicit (sometimes explicit) recognition that financial markets alone have failed to resolve the problem of financing decarbonisation, and this failure has something to do with the risk-return preferences of private banks and investors (Mazzucato 2015; Spratt 2015; UNCTAD 2019). Decades of neoliberalism, financialisation, and the intensification of capitalism's profit-maximising logic in society have not fostered a global financial system willing to confront the decarbonisation challenge in anything but private interests and the desire to amass ever-growing masses of money. As a *Financial Times* special report highlights, private financial investors show little interest in riskier longer-term and/or lower-return green infrastructure or technology investments.[4] The European

---

[2] Speech at the OMFIF Global Public Investor Symposium on 'Green Bond Issuance and Other Forms of Low-Carbon Finance', 13 July 2017. Available at www .bundesbank.de/en. Accessed 18 March 2020.

[3] 'The Financial Sector Must Be at the Heart of Tackling Climate Change', *The Guardian*, 17 April 2019. Available at www.theguardian.com/commentisfree/2019/apr/17/the-financial-sector-must-be-at-the-heart-of-tackling-climate-change. Accessed 18 March 2020.

[4] *Financial Times* (2016) 'Modern Energy', Special Report, 26 July 2016.

Commission's European Political Strategy Centre (EPSC) puts it bluntly: the 'financial system has been structured around short-term frameworks and horizons ... where the primary concern is typically making a fast profit' (2017, 11). The UN Conference on Trade and Development, too, realises that 'private (and especially foreign) banks are known for avoiding such lending as they pick profitable cherries elsewhere' (UNCTAD 2019, XII). For many, this comes as no surprise given the expansive literature on the financial pressures and problems of maximising shareholder value and corporate governance strategies under neoliberal capitalism (Soederberg 2010; Lazonick and Shin 2020). In financialised capitalism private finance is uninterested in bearing the risks of climate finance without a public guarantee of the rewards.

So the problem of financing decarbonisation remains, albeit in an intensely financialised context where private finance has restructured global financial markets in its interests, vastly increased its mass of wealth, deepened its structural power within the financial apparatuses of states, and solidified its pro-market logic within the international financial institutions (Marois 2012; Panitch and Gindin 2012; Soederberg 2014; Babb and Kentikelenis 2018; Hanieh 2018). The result is a materially and discursively powerful neoliberal logic and financialised structure favouring finance capital. When applied to public banks, common sense dictates that they should align themselves with private investment strategies and priorities (see IMF/ World Bank 2015; OECD 2017b). The UN Inter-Agency Task Force (IATF) on Financing for Development agrees: the future of decarbonisation needs the de-risking of private investments by public finance, including public banks (UN IATF 2019). Following the logic of pro-market additionality, the UN IATF accepts the socialisation of risks and the privatisation of returns.

The vitality of the pro-market additionality narrative further relies on the perceived incapacity of public banks to confront the crisis of climate finance independently of private interests. On the one hand, the 2015 UN *Addis Ababa Financing for Development*

Report (the Addis Ababa Action Agenda, AAAA) lifts up the potential of public banks, stating, 'We note the role that well-functioning national and regional development banks can play in financing sustainable development' (AAAA 2015, 13–14). Yet, on the other hand, subsequent UN reporting flushes away this potential by misrepresenting and under-representing public banking assets at a mere $5 trillion in combined assets, or about one-tenth of the actual capacity (UN IATF 2019, 143). Mainstream economists reinforce the incapacity message, writing that '[o]bviously, the considerable demand for infrastructure investment cannot be satisfied by the public sector alone. Private capitals should be encouraged to flow into the infrastructure sectors to narrow the prevailing gap' (Wang 2016, 1). As already shown in Chapter 1, however, there are over 900 public banks worldwide with nearly $49 trillion in assets.

The incapacity message further obscures how public banks already punch well above their relative weight in climate finance. Private banks hold over four times the financial assets of public banks and have far greater institutional numbers. Yet combined private finance barely out-fund public finance. Climate Policy Initiative (CPI) research shows that of an estimated $454 billion in climate finance in 2016, private investors contributed $230 billion whereas the public sector contributed $224 billion, nearly a fifty-fifty split (Table 4.1). In 2017–18, private investments jumped significantly (and unusually), but public sources still accounted for 44 per cent of the total climate finance commitments, maintaining a steady increase since 2012 (CPI 2019, 5).

Table 4.1. *Estimated global climate finance, 2012–18, USD billions*

	2012	2013	2014	2015	2016	2017/18*
Private	224	199	241	267	230	326
Public	136	143	147	205	224	253
Total	359	342	388	472	455	579

Sources: CPI (2017, 1; 2018, 2; 2019, 3)

The CPI public sources of climate finance include foreign donor governments and their agencies, multilateral climate funds, and above all public development finance institutions (DFIs), which account for nearly 90 per cent of public climate investments (CPI 2017, 4). It should be noted that actual public bank contributions are likely far higher as CPI data exclude public commercial/retail and universal banks, which hold trillions more in banking assets. Add to this that the CPI cannot account for actual government-spent climate finance, such as 'public budgets dedicated to domestic climate action, in particular domestic public procurement or infrastructure investment and government shares in state-owned enterprises investments' (CPI 2017, 9), and public climate finance is undoubtedly more significant. The CPI private sources include corporations, project developers, commercial banks, institutional investors, and households (CPI 2017, 6). Therein, project developers are the largest climate financiers, accounting for about half of 2016 investments of $230 billion. Corporations, households, and commercial banks invested around $30 to $35 billion each (why CPI includes private commercial banks but not public ones is unclear). Private equity, venture capital, infrastructure funds, and institutional investors only added about $3 billion combined (CPI 2017, 6).

One of the most preferred destinations for private investors is renewable energy due to its favourable risk-return profile. Empirical work by Mazzucato and Semieniuk (2018) shows that private investments in renewable energy technologies account for about 70 per cent and public about 30 per cent of total investments since 2008 (nearly 90 per cent of these investments are in onshore/offshore wind, solar and photovoltaics, and biomass and waste energies).[5] Public investments, however, grew by 230 per cent from 2006 to 2014 whereas private investments fell by 12 per cent, leading the authors to

---

[5] It needs stressing that the destinations of financing for renewable energies and green technologies need to be subject to intense scrutiny, in both the global north and south, to guard against greenwashing or the calling of carbonising investments as decarbonising ones (see Adkin 2019).

conclude that 'public sources of finance have been playing a pivotal role in stabilizing the investment volume' in renewable energy (Mazzucato and Semieniuk 2018, 14). This is the case in even the most preferred climate finance destination for private finance.

Elsewhere public finance is dominant. For example, about 90 per cent of the world's water services are publicly owned and operated, with about equal amounts of financing being of public origin (UN Water 2015; UN IATF 2019). In the United States, public investment accounts for about 90 per cent of water and sewage and transport infrastructure investments (UN IATF 2017, 12; cf. Hanna 2018a). In developing countries, the UN estimates that the public sector covers about three-quarters of combined infrastructure investments. Outside of the profitable renewable energy sectors and, to a lesser extent, transport sectors, private climate finance investment is almost invisible, especially in crucial areas like adaptation, land use, energy efficiency, and so on (CPI 2019, 10). Private investors have structural risk-return profiles that demand maximised returns above all else.

This stark reality has led civil society and research institutes to call for greater *pro-public* public financing of a global green and just transition, calls that have drawn inspiration from the popular 'Green New Deal' framework popularised by US Congressional representative Alexandria Ocasio-Cortez (Romero 2017; Mazzucato and McPherson 2018; Marois and Güngen 2019b; Steinfort and Kishimoto 2019). A clearer understanding of the ways, for better and worse, that existing public banks finance decarbonisation and climate change mitigation strategies is urgent.

4.2 THE WAYS OF PUBLIC BANKS FINANCING DECARBONISATION: THE CHINA DEVELOPMENT BANK AND NORDIC INVESTMENT BANK

Public banks are well-positioned to respond to the problem of financing decarbonisation as they already play a much larger role in infrastructure finance than is commonly known and they can be made to scale up climate financing rapidly (ADFIAP 2009; Barrowclough and Gottschalk 2018; Peetz 2019; UNCTAD 2019; Ray et al. 2020). Yet decarbonisation does not, indeed cannot, *naturally* emerge as a priority of public banks. There is essentially nothing in public bank ownership that destines these financial institutions to confront climate change. There are public banks that disproportionately fuel climate change, including, for example, the big public banks in the United Arab Emirates and Saudi Arabia that depend on hydrocarbon revenues channelled through the state (see Hanieh 2018; BankTrack 2019). And there are others that have or are developing explicit climate finance and environmental programmes (including the US-based Bank of North Dakota, India's NABARD, Costa Rica's Banco Popular, and Germany's KfW discussed elsewhere in the book). In most cases public banks do both, traversing the contradictory reality of a highly carbonising form of global capitalism and increasingly pressing green imperatives to protect the future of humanity. Whatever public banks do, or do not do, social forces are the linchpin.

As with definancialisation and democratisation in later chapters, so too here with decarbonisation. The China Development Bank and the Nordic Investment Bank are not presented as idealised examples of public banks financing decarbonisation. As dynamic historically and socially constituted entities, these two banks are necessarily imperfect and evolving, as are our assessments of them. Rather, the China Development Bank and the Nordic Investment Bank illustrate the existing possibilities for mobilising public banking capacity and expertise towards confronting one of society's greatest threats, global warming, by directly financing decarbonisation. Yet the two public banks also expose undeniable pitfalls by virtue of functioning within the shadow global financialised capitalism.

4.2.1   The China Development Bank

The extraordinary case of the China Development Bank (CDB) forces scholars, activists, and policymakers to re-evaluate the 'realm of the possible' for mobilising public banks to confront climate change, and

Table 4.2. *The China Development Bank and Nordic Investment Bank at a glance*

	CDB	NIB
Board of governors	13 members: 3 directors, including the chair; 4 government agency directors (National Development and Reform Commission; Ministry of Finance; Ministry of Commerce; People's Bank of China); 6 equity directors (unspecified).	8 members: comprising the finance ministers of the eight member countries.
Mission	To support national development and deliver a better life for the people.	To finance projects that improve productivity and benefit the environment of the Nordic and Baltic countries.
Mandate vis-à-vis decarbonisation	To implement 'green financing, promote green lending, design and offer innovative green financial products, and support our top priorities in the environmental protection cause, including energy saving and emission reduction, prevention and remediation of pollutions, clean energies, and ecological restoration'.	To promote the 'sustainable growth of its member countries by providing long-term complementary financing, based on sound banking principles, to projects that strengthen competitiveness and enhance the environment'.
Type of bank (year established)	National Development (1994)	Regional Multilateral Development (1975)

Table 4.2. (*cont.*)

	CDB	NIB
Ownership	4 state entities (Orbis names its owner as the People's Republic of China)[6]	8 government shareholders
Total assets	$2.4 trillion (2018)	$36.7 billion (2019)
Return on assets (annual average)	0.88% (2013–18)	0.75% (2012–19)
Net profit after tax (annual average)	$15.81 billion (2013–18)	$243 million (2012–19)
No. of employees	9,507	229
No. of branches	40	1
Credit rating	A1 (Moody's); A+ (S&P)	Aaa (Moody's); AAA (S&P)

Sources: Annual Reports of CDB and NIB; Orbis Bank Focus (Data update 633 – 31/01/2018 and 29/01/2018; 09/03/2020)

to seriously heed the pitfalls. There is no other public bank in the world with as much green financial capacity as the CDB that is so equally contradictory. The CDB's relative institutional youth yet unmatched scale of operations exemplify how a public bank can scale up capacity and build expertise given the political will to do so (see Xu 2018; Chen 2019). The CDB also exemplifies how public banks can be subject to global capitalist growth and expansionary imperatives,

---

[6] Four state entities own the CDB, including the Ministry of Finance (36.54 per cent); Central Huijin Investment (34.68 per cent); Buttonwood Investment Holding Co. (27.19 per cent); and National Council for Social Security Fund (1.59 per cent) (see CDB website www.cdb.com.cn/English/gykh_512/khjj/. Accessed 3 March 2020). According to Wang, in 2015 an investment vehicle of the People's Bank of China injected $38 billion to support CDB activity in the 'One Belt and One Road' initiative, giving it a 27.19 per cent stake in the CDB via Buttonwood.

which are in this case connected to China's aim of greater integration into global financial and commodity markets. The institutional credibility of the CDB is bolstered both by its green and its economic expansionary credentials.

4.2.1.1 History and Current Structure of the CDB

The CDB emerged and reproduces itself within the specificity of China's transition to capitalism, the characteristics of which remain open to debate (Karmel 1994; Ho 2017). That said, China presents us with a type of variegated and state-permeated capitalism that is deeply integrated into the world market (Ten Brink 2013). Heterodox development scholars tend to praise China's state-led strategy of pursuing rapid growth and productive capacity (Lo and Zhang 2011). Others have been more critical of China's increasingly marketised approach that offers few, if any, alternatives to growth-, competition-, and carbon-intensive capitalist development that is also low-wage and labour-unfriendly (Hart-Landsberg and Burkett 2005; Pringle 2011, 2015; Malm 2015).

China's large and sophisticated banking and credit system has been at the core of its transition to capitalism and world market integration, helping to smooth its otherwise unstable if remarkable economic transition over the last three decades (Chui and Lewis 2006; Ju and Lo 2012; Wang 2016; Xu 2018; Ho and Marois 2019). Since the 1990s state authorities have undertaken financial liberalisation measures and created an active market-based financial system. Yet the domestic financial structure remains largely bank-based, publicly owned, funded by domestic deposits, and geared towards financing industrialisation, medium- and large-scale business, and other Chinese state-owned enterprises according to official state policy directives (Yeung 2009; Turner et al. 2012; Chen 2019). Presently, China's largest banks are public and among the largest in the world, public or private, controlling over $20 trillion in assets (Chapter 1).

As a financial institution in Chinese society, the CDB has evolved in line with the exigencies of the country's neoliberal transition. Established in 1994, the CDB was part of the government's strategy to create three new policy-oriented specialised development banks (the other two being the Agricultural Development Bank of China and the Export–Import Bank of China, also founded in 1994). During the 1990s the Chinese economy and state apparatus was under economic stress as state-owned enterprises (SOEs) were suffering from declining performance due to mounting competitive pressures. This put pressure on the country's public commercial banks, which were impacted by snowballing non-performing loans (NPLs) (Chiu and Lewis 2006, 186–87). State authorities envisioned the new CDB absorbing these financial risks gone bad, which in turn would enable the public commercial banks to reform and become more marketised (Chen 2019). The new CDB at the same time absorbed significant amounts of local authorities' non-performing loans (Xu 2018). Consequently, the CDB faced an immediately uncertain future, suffocating on toxic debts.

There were other political economic forces in play. Reforms after 1998 pushed the CDB towards a more growth-oriented and expansionary future. Xu reports that in 1994 the CDB had only $11 billion in assets (2018, 47). By 2019, its assets exceed $2.3 trillion (Table 4.3). In doing so, the CDB has been tied to China's global developmental ambitions. By bolstering state financial capacity via the three new policy banks, the CDB included, Chinese authorities could manage economy-wide reforms but without shedding state

Table 4.3. *CDB operational data, 2013–18*

	2013	2014	2015	2016	2017	2018
Total assets (billion USD)	1,342	1,686	1,944	2,063	2,451	2,361
Net profit after tax (billion USD)	13.10	16.05	16.09	15.79	17.45	16.35
ROAE	15.09	15.72	11.94	9.83	9.46	8.82
ROAA	1.02	1.06	0.91	0.81	0.75	0.70

Source: Orbis Bank Focus (Data update 633 – 31/01/2018 and Data update 1680 – 09/03/2020)

financial power to the private sector (Hart-Landsberg and Burkett 2005, 64). As and when the expanding public banking sector experienced turbulence, state authorities further managed and displaced financial crises by building parallel financial structures including, for example, new state-owned asset management companies (Ho and Marois 2019). As a top-down strategic policy objective of financial transformation for national development and growth, China has achieved its aim, and spectacularly so.

While becoming increasingly marketised and profit oriented, so in some ways more distant from direct political control, there remain political and economic ways by which state authorities shape and control public banks and credit allocation (Chen 2019). Governance over the CDB flows from the Central Committee of the Chinese Communist Party and the State Council to shape broad mandate decisions within the institution (in ways in line with other public banks, like the KfW, the NIB, the State Bank of India, the North American Development Bank, and so on, if more directly so) (CDB 2017, 20). High-level reforms in 2016, however, dispersed decision-making power within the CDB more broadly across the Chinese state apparatus by expanding the board of directors (responsible for strategic planning and overall business development policies) to include officials from the National Development and Reform Commission, Ministry of Finance, Ministry of Commerce, and People's Bank of China (PBOC) (CDB 2019, 12). The exact motivation is unstated, but it may be a strategic move to smooth out recurrent internal political power struggles within the state financial apparatus for control over China's powerful public financial institutions, their resources, and the redistribution of losses at times of crisis (cf. Shih 2004; Walter and Howie 2012; Ho and Marois 2019). While governance reforms have not extended to including civil society participation, it is also the case that, as a financial intermediary, the CDB works and negotiates with local, regional, national, and foreign governments to identify priorities and execute project (Gallagher et al. 2012; Sanderson and Forsythe 2013). It is an institution in and of Chinese society such that its financial power is mediated, if unequally so, by the social forces involved and the local and global spheres in which it functions and reproduces itself.

Therein the CDB's mandate is to enhance China's 'national power' and to improve 'people's livelihood' (CDB 2015, 17). While marketisation has penetrated the bank's operational logic since China's 2001 accession to the World Trade Organisation, there is no institutional ambiguity as to its government-led expansionary orientation (or willingness to respond to government demands, as per its Covid-19 response; see the Epilogue). The CDB's operating ethos states (2015, 17):

> By integrating the advantages of the government in organization and coordination with the market-oriented financing skills, we have given full scope to our advantages of medium- and long-term investment and financing, going a long way to accelerate the process of China's industrialization, urbanization and internationalisation and the economic and social development.

Within twenty-five years of its founding, the CDB has amassed unprecedented financial power, holding assets of over $2.3 trillion and generating over $16 billion in annual income (Table 4.3). It does so while lending long term, that is, by providing between 40 to 50 per cent of its loans for terms over five years (Orbis 2018, 2020). State authorities have enabled this by directing domestic financial resources into CDB coffers from the other public commercial banks and the Postal Savings Bank of China (established in 2007) – as done in France, Japan, India, and so on (see Chen 2019). The CDB converts these short-term savings into long-term liabilities, magnifying existing financial resources. Sovereign backing for the CDB enables it to also raise cheap, long-term capital by issuing its own CDB bonds in financial markets (mostly domestic) and to a wide range of institutional and commercial investors (Wang 2016, 10; Xu 2018). The CDB concentrates on channelling its financial resources into large-scale investments and economically significant infrastructure projects across the energy, rail, public transport, aviation, telecommunications, oil and gas, petroleum refining, solar-, thermal-, and hydropower, mining, machinery, construction and real estate, electronics and motor industry, as well as other sectors (Wang 2016, 13–14; Macfarlane and Mazzucato 2018, 28). Less known or appreciated, the CDB also lends towards a social mission by offering educational loans and poverty alleviation programmes (Xu 2018, 48). More recently, however, its green lending portfolio has captured attention.

4.2.1.2 The CDB and Financing Decarbonisation

The crisis of climate finance has raised the profile of the CDB as one of the more aggressive, and largest, development banks active in this field (Barone and Spratt 2015; UNCTAD 2019). Institutionally, the CDB self-identifies as a public agent of sustainable climate finance and what China refers to as 'ecological civilization'. CDB Chair Hu Huaibang writes (CDB 2017, 50):

> We will stay committed to green development and drive ecological civilization. We will focus on supporting key ecological protection efforts, including the prevention and remediation of air, water and soil pollutions. We will support the state's efforts in building national reserve forest bases, promote the green, low-carbon and renewable solutions for economic development, including new energies and renewable energies, energy saving, environment protection, and modern agriculture, in order to improve the ecological robustness and sustainability.

The CDB's financing of decarbonisation has occurred within a series of domestic environmental policy changes. For example, the China Banking Regulatory Commission (CBRC) requires that all public and private financial institutions, including the CDB, report on a set of new green key performance indicators (KPIs) (CBRC 2014). China's green KPIs flow from four previous government documents: the *Comprehensive Energy Saving and Emission Reduction Scheme of the 12th Five-Year Plan* (State Council [2011] No. 26); the

Environmental Protection Planning of the 12th Five-Year Plan (State Council [2011] No. 42); the *Opinions of the State Council on Accelerating the Development of Energy Saving and Environmental Protection Industries* (State Council [2013] No. 30); and, significantly, the 2012 Green Credit Guidelines.

Yet the CDB was already functioning ahead of the green curve. It was the first Chinese public bank to sign up for the UN Global Compact, a voluntary initiative that commits institutions to pursuing sustainability principles and supporting UN goals, joining in 2006. This signalled the bank's opening step towards its current operating narrative of 'driving development through sustainability' (CDB 2017, 5). In 2009 the CDB established six core operational priorities, one of which involved raising awareness of climate change and climate issues (the other five priorities involved enhancing governance; supporting state strategies; fulfilling global commitments; delivering inclusive finance; and promoting social harmony) (CDB 2017, 12). The CDB's environmental mandate has since been fortified according to three green development guidelines, which include promoting (a) ecological civilisation; (b) the greening of clients' development; and (c) self-sustainable development (CDB 2017, 52).

The notion of building an ecological civilisation, written into the constitution of the Communist Party in 2012, is a centrepiece of China's response to the intertwined problems of accelerating growth and environmental destruction (see Wang et al. 2014; Pan 2016). Following on from this, China committed to reducing GHG emissions by 60–65 per cent below 2005 levels by 2030 in response to the 2015 Paris Agreement, with its state-owned enterprises and banks leading the initiative (Coady et al. 2019, 30). Empirical research suggests that China's top-down, high-level directives have been an important causal force driving China's move towards 'green growth practices' (Guo et al. 2018).

The CDB has subsequently dedicated massive financial resources to green lending. By the end of 2018, the CDB reports having

$1.9 trillion in outstanding green credits (CDB 2019, 47). This makes the CDB the single largest green lender not only in China but in the world, and its green portfolio is expanding. Empirical research shows that between 2004 and 2014 China increased renewable energy investments from 8 per cent to 46 per cent of total global investments (Mazzucato and Semieniuk 2018, 14). Disaggregating lending for 2014, the CDB lent out some $30 billion for wind and solar power projects, $33 billion for renewable energy power projects, and $65.5 billion for over 2,500 water conservation projects (Wang 2016, 16). Based on CDB estimates, sustainable infrastructure lending accounts for about one-third of CDB lending (Wang 2016, 21). As a result, the CDB reports significant GHGs reductions flowing from its green credits. Between 2014 and 2019, CDB green projects reduced carbon dioxide emissions in the range of 131 to 174 million tons annually (CDB 2014–19).

The CDB reports internationally on its green financing activities and is active within global forums concerned with sustainable finance. For example, the CDB participates in the UN Environment Programme and UN Global Compact, contributed to the 2030 UN SDG research meetings, and reports to the Global Reporting Initiative (GRI) (CDB 2017, 14). The CDB has also sought to green itself via its 'Green Office Solutions' (CDB 2017, 57). Most likely taken in response to GRI reporting requirements, the CDB tries to minimise its operations' energy consumption and to limit negative environmental impacts (admittedly, however, actions have been largely restricted to promoting video conferencing and reducing paper usage). For its efforts, the CDB has been internationally recognised. In 2016 the United Nations Global Compact Network China named the CDB as one of less than forty Lead Enterprises in Achieving Sustainable Development Goals (meaning the CDB actively engages with the UN Global Compact and submits annual advanced communications on progress).

In reporting, lending, and even transparency terms, the CDB has moved well beyond what most public banks have done to date on climate finance. In doing so, it has substantively positioned itself to tackle the crisis of climate finance. China authorities have made it so. Still, as one early report notes, China 'has made significant progress in incorporating social and environmentally responsible guidelines into its official guidelines, but further progress can be made' (Gallagher et al. 2012, 26). Others agree: 'although the CDB's environmental policy has been greatly improved, the bank has not yet adopted international standards such as the Equator Principles' (Barone and Spratt 2015, 36). The contradictions of the CDB's green lending and growth ambitions are picked up on again later.

4.2.2   The Nordic Investment Bank

The Nordic Investment Bank (NIB) is also a public development bank, if multilateral, with an institutionally distinct history and context.[7] It too illustrates that a public bank can evolve to target the financing of decarbonisation and climate change mitigation projects in the public interest, if never independently of capitalism's growth imperatives. It has done so, notably, while establishing an accountable and transparent floor for green lending. This has bolstered its credibility within the Nordic region.

4.2.2.1   History and Current Structure of the NIB

The NIB is not owned and controlled by a single government. It is a wholly 'state'-owned multilateral bank founded in 1975 by the five Nordic countries of Denmark, Finland, Iceland, Norway, and Sweden. The NIB expanded its membership by three in 2005 to include the Baltic countries of Estonia, Latvia, and Lithuania. With assets of just under $37 billion, the NIB is of a much smaller scale than the CDB (Table 4.4). There are, however, other compelling reasons to look at this public bank.

---

[7] For a comprehensive study of regional multilateral development banks, see Clifton et al. 2021a.

Table 4.4. *NIB operational data, 2012–19*

	2012	2013	2014	2015	2016	2017	2018	2019
Total assets (billion USD)	34.2	32.4	30.2	29.7	31.8	35.9	36.3	36.7
Net profit after tax (million USD)	276	300	255	235	223	253	198	204
ROAE	8.17	7.90	7.23	7.03	6.60	6.27	4.92	4.98
ROAA	0.84	0.88	0.87	0.83	0.74	0.70	0.56	0.57

Source: Orbis Bank Focus (Data update – 29/01/2018; 09/03/2020)

The history of creating a Nordic regional bank goes back to the 1950s and unrealised plans to form a Nordic customs union (cf. Montgomery 1960). Yet the turning point for the NIB did not arrive until the 1970s petrol shock and as the Nordic countries faced a deteriorating balance of payments crisis (Sipilä 2016; cf. Jonung 2008, 67–68). According to Bengt Dennis, a former Swedish under-secretary of state who helped to found and then sit on the NIB's first board of governors, it was at this conjuncture that sufficient political will and cooperation gelled around establishing the new public bank (NIB 2017, 37–40). In the face of crisis, state authorities recognised the benefits of having a regional bank capable of accessing cheaper global capital and channelling it locally (that is, able to 'fix' mobile capital). Relatedly, the initial ethos of the NIB was about directing long-term finance towards projects that generated economic growth, realised productivity gains, and combatted unemployment (Skidelsky et al. 2011, 13; Cogen 2015, 77).

Societal and cultural factors also shaped the NIB. Dennis writes that whereas Sweden resisted, Denmark, Finland, Iceland, and Norway insisted that the NIB integrate socio-economic factors into financial decision-making (NIB 2017, 37–40). At the same time, governance parity among the otherwise unequal member countries (in wealth and demographic size) became an institutional pre-condition for the broad-based political and societal support that arose behind the new NIB. This is not to suggest that the NIB was uncontested. On the political right and among some business associations, there was opposition to the idea of any new public bank on ideological grounds. On the political left, some argued against the NIB placing profitability before socio-economic factors. Geopolitical forces also played a part in defining the NIB as an institution. The five founding members decided to place the headquarters in Helsinki as a political strategy of drawing Finland away from Soviet influence by hosting its first important trans-Nordic institution. Geopolitics would again play a redefining role fifteen years later. With the collapse of the Soviet Union in 1989, a space opened for greater Nordic–Baltic cooperation through the NIB, culminating in Estonia, Latvia, and Lithuania becoming NIB members in 2005 (Confidential Interview, SEO, February 2020).[8] Notably, the NIB's first act in response to the Covid-19 pandemic in early 2020 was to channel €1.6 billion in supportive credits to its three newest members (see Epilogue).

With its founding in the 1970s, the NIB's initial capital foundation was public in origin, and it remains so. Authorised capital (paid in and callable) now totals €6.14 billion, of which member states subscribe to in proportion of their gross national income (GNI) (NIB 2017, 60). The NIB can lend up to 250 per cent (that is, a multiple of 2.5 times) of its combined authorised capital and accumulated reserves, magnifying them in order to direct them regionally. Like most public banks, the NIB benefits from a sovereign guarantee, which enables it to access global financial markets cheaply based on its AAA credit rating (Table 4.2; cf. Macfarlane and Mazzucato 2018, 50). According to Standard and Poor's, 'Since its establishment, NIB has enjoyed the unwavering support of member governments, which provide high-quality callable capital' (2017, 5). In ways similar to the CDB's 'green

---

[8] On 27 February 2020 I conducted a confidential interview with a senior environmental officer (SEO) at the Nordic Investment Bank Headquarters in Helsinki, Finland.

growth' approach, the NIB's current mission is 'to finance projects that improve productivity and benefit the environment of the Nordic and Baltic countries' (Table 4.2). It likewise aims for growth that is 'green' (Confidential Interview, HLM, February 2020).[9] Like the CDB, long-term lending of over five years forms a substantive part of this, typically accounting for between 35 per cent and 50 per cent of lending (Orbis 2018, 2020).

NIB-financed projects tend mostly towards supporting productivity growth and improvements in infrastructure. In 2016, for example, new loans totalled €3.4 billion, of which energy and environment accounted for 34 per cent; infrastructure, transport, and telecoms 23 per cent; industries and services 25 per cent; and financial institutions and SME lending 18 per cent (NIB 2017, 6–7). In 2019 new loans totalled €2.7 billion, of which water and waste management accounted for 18 per cent; research and development investments 17 per cent; financial intermediation 12 per cent; electricity networks 11 per cent; buildings 10 per cent; health 8 per cent; followed by business expansion, transportation, education, energy generation, telecommunications, and mergers and acquisitions at between 1 and 7 per cent of lending.[10] Lending to the public sector constitutes an important but not dominant portion of NIB activities, averaging around 30–40 per cent overall, although some years can stretch to over 50 per cent of lending because of infrastructure demands (NIB 2017–19). Due to pandemic-related lending in 2020, the proportion of public lending should significantly increase. Credits to the public sector tend to fortify the bank's risk profile because they are rated as low risk (the same applies in China).

To reproduce itself institutionally, however, the NIB competes in financial markets and with other public and private banks, adjusting its terms and rates accordingly to make its offerings more

[9] On 27 February 2020 I conducted a confidential interview with a high-level manager (HLM) at the Nordic Investment Bank Headquarters in Helsinki, Finland.
[10] See NIB website www.nib.int/who_we_are/our_year_in_brief. Accessed 10 March 2020.

attractive to clients. In other words, the NIB does not just provide 'additionality' finance. Yet the bank is not mandated to maximise returns. Rather, the NIB funds projects with a clear purpose, with the 'purpose' being judged according to the bank's mandate of productivity and/or environmental gains (Confidential Interview, SEO, February 2020). According to NIB staff, this 'mandate check' distinguishes the NIB from private commercial banks because staff must follow a credible process of compliance with transparent guidelines from both within the NIB and externally in accordance with national legislation and permit-granting public agencies (Confidential Interview, SEO, February 2020; cf. NIB 2012). This mandate compliance constitutes the 'floor' for NIB lending operations. Moreover, to reduce the bank's risk profile, the NIB board stipulates that the bank should not fund more than 50 per cent of any single project, be it public or private sector (2018b, 55).

As an institution the NIB is financially stable and generates regular, if modest, returns for its government shareholders. From 2012 to 2019, NIB's return of assets (ROA) averaged 0.75 with an average annual income of $243 million (NIB 2017, 57). In the last three years the NIB has paid out annual dividends of $66 million in 2017, $46 million in 2018, and $51 million in 2019 to its member governments (Orbis 10/03/2020). Here we see some of the variety among public banks. In contrast to the NIB, the German development bank KfW ROA is much lower (less than 0.40 per cent) and it recycles its returns back into lending. Turkey's universal bank, Ziraat Bank, is legally mandated to maximise returns and pays out significant annual returns to its government owner. The universal Banco Popular of Costa Rica maximises returns and uses a portion of them to support not-for-profit activities. The commercial Bank of North Dakota pays out annual dividends to the state, like the NIB. According to Finnish Prime Minister Juha Sipilä (2016), the NIB's member governments welcome the dividends but view the bank primarily as an institutional tool for regional policy and cooperation. Therein, financing decarbonisation has emerged as an increasingly prominent regional political and economic orientation over the last decade.

4.2.2.2   The NIB and Financing Decarbonisation

Nordic societies, while differing in their own ways, have tended to demand more socially responsible practices from those financial actors and institutions operating within their borders (Bengtsson 2008a, 2008b; Scholtens and Sievänen 2013). The 1980s and early 1990s were a turning point, inspired by the impact of the UN Brundtland Commission (1983–87) – headed by the former prime minister of Norway, Gro Harlem Brundtland (Bengtsson 2008a, 973) – on raising environmental awareness. Nordic trade unions, civil society, and NGOs have since taken a more activist stance towards finance paying heed to societal and environmental factors, especially within the region's pension and sovereign wealth funds (Clement 2004; Bengtsson 2008a; Reiche 2008). The 2008–09 global financial crisis further underscored the need to insist upon greater democratic financial oversight and social responsibility (Scholtens and Sievänen 2013). So when the 2015 Paris Agreement fully exposed the crisis of climate finance, this crystallised movement towards demanding more sustainable finance at the highest levels of Nordic governments. According to Finland's Minister of Finance Petteri Orpo, 'Nordic countries have collectively recognized that climate action should be our primary goal.'[11]

In consequence, the mandate of the NIB has been *made* to evolve towards environmental sustainability. Like the CDB, the NIB was not founded on a 'green' mandate, but it was an early mover (Confidential Interview, HLM, February 2020). Indeed, material environmental necessity was a key driver, specifically the dire situation of pollution in the Baltic Sea – one of the dirtiest seas in the world (Confidential Interview, SEO, February 2020;

---

[11] 'Finance Ministry Coalition for Climate Action to Meet in Helsinki', NIB News, 20 February 2019. Available at www.nib.int. Accessed 11 March 2020.

cf. SIWI 2018). The Nordic countries came together to mobilise the NIB. The bank responded by financing regionally significant water, wastewater, and sanitation projects. In the process, the NIB signed up to the Helsinki Commission (HELCOM), otherwise referred to as the Baltic Marine Environment Protection Commission, which sets the standard for Baltic Sea discharges. Subsequent public bank–public water collaborations have taken root between the NIB and Baltic-region public and municipal water providers, including, but not limited to, Stockholm in Sweden, Grodno and Brest in Belarus, and St. Petersburg in Russia. The regional Northern Dimension Environmental Partnership (NDEP) framework, which the NIB joined in 2001, further facilitates ongoing environmental and climate political cooperation. It was thus in response to both societal and environmental necessity that the NIB began working on the Baltic seas. Now 'clean seas' and water are constitutive of how the NIB functions.[12]

There is, regrettably, relatively little historical data on the NIB's early environmental lending. One Artic Council Report states that between 1988 and 2002 the NIB dispersed €2 billion in loans for 200 different environmental projects, with average credit offerings ranging between €100 to €200 million per year (Randefelt 2002). In 1997 the NIB established a new dedicated environmental loan facility. In the early 2000s the NIB deepened and then formalised its environmental mandate, as endorsed by its eight public owners, to support projects that improve resource efficiency; the development of a competitive low carbon economy; protection of the environment and its ecosystem; and the development of clean technology (NIB 2012; Sipilä 2016). According to NIB staff, its mandated environmental lending qualitatively distinguishes the NIB from the private investment banks (Confidential Interview, SEO, February 2020; cf. Lessambo 2015, 148).

---

[12] See 'Cleans Seas in the Nordic-Baltic Region', NIB News, 24 January 2019. Available at www.nib.int/who_we_are/news_and_media/news_press_releases/3178/clean_seas_in_the_nordic-baltic_region.

This points to how public banks can be made to internalise the political and economic priorities of social forces and society.

The NIB has, moreover, institutionalised procedures to enforce and monitor environmental lending, applying a sustainability lens to all projects. Internally staff work according to the NIB 'Sustainability Policy and Guidelines' (SPG), in force since 2012 (NIB 2012). Prior to financing a project, the SPG guides NIB staff in identifying and addressing potential problems (Confidential Interview, HLM, February 2020). For example, the SPG has a list of exclusions that the NIB must not finance, including projects deemed illegal under national law or international conventions, such as activities involving certain PCBs and asbestos, illegal animal trade, threats to biodiversity or cultural heritage, and so on; weapons production; ethically controversial projects (like gambling and tobacco); production of radioactive, non-medical materials; and certain high-carbon power plants. These provide a firm socially determined 'floor' for NIB's lending decisions.

By having a firm internal standard, NIB staff can use its sustainability criteria, the SPG, to engage with and push its clients to go greener than they might have otherwise (Confidential Interview, HLM, February 2020). Staff do so by pulling on various levers. For example, the NIB can leverage its accumulated expertise and knowledge to make clients aware of viable green alternatives. The NIB can also play with the financial conditions, such as offering longer terms, repayment grace periods, and even better pricing (albeit to a lesser extent as the NIB functions on market terms). Clients may perceive benefits in having their funded projects certified NIB 'green' (the German KfW also has an energy-efficiency certification standard). On the one hand, NIB certification enables clients to participate in NIB Green Bond issuances. On the other hand, NIB certification imparts a positive environmental narrative upon a client's project. Furthermore, the NIB's sustainability standards enable the bank to influence other financial institutions by setting conditions for the on-lending of its funds (that is, it can exercise green loan conditionality through its retail bank customers) (cf. Skidelsky et al. 2011, 15). In

2019, for example, the NIB provided €35 million over seven years to Bonum Bank, a coop bank owned by the POP Bank Alliance Coop (an alliance of twenty-six cooperative banks in Finland). The NIB loan is conditional on Bonum Bank credits conforming to the NIB's 2012 Sustainability Policy and Guidelines. By having a firm and transparent 'green' floor, the NIB can outwardly project the reach of its environmental mandate through its loan programmes in ways that leverage public lending for public good sustainability ends.

Externally, the NIB subscribes to certain environmental anchors as a means of transparency and accountability (NIB 2017, 30). In addition to its Northern Dimension Environmental Partnership and HELCOM membership, the NIB has signed the Declaration on the European Principles for the Environment. Like the CDB, the NIB reports annually to the Global Reporting Initiative (GRI) on sustainability indicators. It is part of the Multilateral Financial Institutions' Environmental Working Group and since 2014 the Green Bond Principles group. Following the 2015 Paris meeting, the NIB joined the European Association of Long-Term Investors' declaration for COP21, committing to financing decarbonisation. In recognition, the European Commission made the NIB an observer to the High-Level Expert Group on sustainable finance in January 2017. In 2019 the NIB joined the Network for Greening the Financial System (comprising central banks and financial supervisors) as an observer institution. As a regional public bank, the NIB has situated itself within global sustainable finance networks.

In making its way towards financing decarbonisation and environmental sustainability, the NIB has begun to classify and measure the impact of its loans vis-à-vis its environmental mandate and policy guidelines. To be classified as 'environmental', a NIB loan must have significant direct or indirect environmental impacts, regardless of sector (NIB 2018b, 6). This gives the bank, its staff, and outsiders a transparent 'green' marker. Not all loans, however, are 'green' and lending levels vary considerably from year to year (Table 4.5). In 2014, for example, 46 per cent of NIB loans received a good or excellent

Table 4.5. *NIB financing decarbonisation*

	2014	2015	2016	2017	2018	2019
Loans with good or excellent environmental mandate rating	46%	36%	37%	27%	20%	42%
Total value of loans with good or excellent environmental mandate rating	€1.1 billion	€1.02 billion	€1.57 billion	€0.94 billion	n/a	€1.12 billion
Estimated reduction in CO2 emissions	260,000 tonnes	50,100 tonnes	280,000 tonnes	49,000 tonnes	817,600 tonnes	504,000 tonnes

Sources: NIB (2015–19, 2018b)

environmental rating but only 36 per cent the following year (making NIB green loans comparable to Germany's KfW levels, see Chapter 6). In 2017 and 2018, however, levels fell to below 30 per cent before jumping back up to 42 per cent in 2019. Environmental lending includes wastewater treatment, public transit, and renewable energy, among other allowable projects.

In 2011 the NIB opened a new phase in the financing of decarbonisation and climate change mitigation when it initiated the NIB Environmental Bond framework. According to the Climate Bond Initiative, from 2011 to 2017, the NIB issued €3 billion worth of green bonds, becoming the region's largest issuer of green bonds (although Nordic local governments are increasingly active) (CBI 2018, 6). NIB green bonds channelled funds into public transport (17 per cent of projects), green buildings (14 per cent), energy efficiency (7 per cent), waste management (5 per cent), wastewater treatment (23 per cent), and renewable energy (34 per cent) (NIB 2017, 30). By the end of 2019, total green bond issuance had jumped to €3.9 billion (NIB 2019, 56).

Green Bonds issued by the NIB and others are taking a notably public–public character. Two-thirds of new green bond issuances in 2017 were of public origin, which included the NIB, other public banks, as well as local and national governments and other government-backed entities (CBI 2018, 8). Public authorities benefit from what is a more stable form of lending. On average, Nordic-originated green bonds have longer-terms, from three to five years. Public bank–originated bonds can stretch even longer: the NIB and the KBN Kommunalbanken (a Norwegian public bank) have issued fifteen- and twenty-year bonds. For public authorities, especially local and municipal governments, long-term funding is vital for developing sustainable infrastructure (CBI 2018, 9; cf. Warner 2015; Kumari and Sharma 2017; Xu 2018). The type of green bonds being offered also suggests a form of definancialisation (see Chapter 5): they transform globally mobile finance capital into regionally situated, fixed, longer-term, and (often) public sector and public goods investments.[13]

Levels of green lending by the NIB are broadly in line with regional sustainability trends. According to the Nordic Council of Ministers, a regional political body, 37 per cent of energy consumption in 2014 came from renewables and 54 per cent from fossil-free sources; by 2030 the Nordic countries are projecting to reduce GHG emissions to at least 40 per cent of 1990 levels (NCM 2017, 7). The Nordic Council of Ministers identifies the NIB as a key financial institution behind the region's sustainable growth and climate mitigation ambitions. So too in more bottom-up views. A 2015 survey involving 123 interviews with NIB clients and stakeholders reports that the NIB is perceived as acting ethically and sustainably, supported by a high-level of institutional expertise and knowledge (NIB 2017, 50). The perceived institutional credibility of the NIB, from

---

[13] These bonds may also help to counter pressures on local authorities to invest in return-generating speculative instruments, as happened with the global financial crisis debacle that then saddled Nordic communities with significant losses from the US-based sub-prime 'mortgage-backed security' investment frenzy, resulting in lost financial resources and public sector austerity (Aalbers and Pollard 2016).

above and below, may be related to how it institutionalises contending societal priorities. NIB President and CEO Henrik Normann, writes:[14]

> When we now see a growth in sustainable finance I think it's quite important that we look at if there are victims in this process of green transition. Therefore we at NIB focus not only on the environment, but also on productivity. When those two factors work together we achieve sustainable growth. That way we create new jobs and prosperity also for our children.

The NIB has also been greening itself. While an operationally small organisation with fewer than 250 employees at its headquarters in Helsinki, the NIB forms part of the WWF's Green Office Network, which aims to reduce the ecological footprints of organisations in a cost-effective way. In doing so, the NIB was awarded the use of the Green Office logo in 2016 for a three-year period (an aspect of GRI reporting). Therein, the NIB supports a culture of workplace sustainability, including green cleaning services and recycling practices. The NIB has refurbished its building and moved its energy source to 100 per cent wind, certified by the European Energy Certificate System. While on its own quantitatively insignificant, this institutional commitment goes some way to demonstrating an organisational ethos around sustainability. Still, the NIB is not without contradictions. Much like the CDB, its carbonising 'competitiveness' portfolio continues to outpace its green 'decarbonisation' efforts.

4.3   CONTRADICTING GREEN AND GROWTH IMPERATIVES

Notwithstanding what the China Development Bank (CDB) and the Nordic Investment Bank (NIB) do to finance decarbonisation and environmental sustainability, carbonising growth functions continue

[14] '40 Years of Experience Have Proven Its Point: Sustainable Financing Actually Works' Nordic Co-operation', Available at www.norden.org/en/news/40-years-experience-have-proven-its-point-sustainable-financing-actually-works. Accessed 10 March 2020.

to outweigh decarbonising green ones. This is because despite being differentially mediated by collective demands for green transformation, these institutions must also reproduce themselves within class-divided societies that are integrated into global capitalism. This gives rise to contradicting green and growth imperatives vis-à-vis contending public and private interests.

In the case of China and the CDB, the country's 'green credit directive' and the CDB's external reporting should push credit decisions towards accounting for environmental, social, and economic risks, as well as local regulations, at home and abroad (Ray et al. 2015, 14). We see the CDB moving in the direction of environmental reporting and towards increasing its total mass of finance directed towards decarbonisation. Yet there are widespread concerns over the (im)balance of China's green versus growth imperatives. Weighing most heavily are China's interconnected global and domestic economic growth ambitions, which are unachievable without systematically carbonising the world's atmosphere (Wang et al. 2020). China's expansionary, consumptionist, and carbonising growth orientation was made clear by former Premier Wen Jiabao in China's twelfth five-year plan (2011–15) (2011, 19):

> Expanding domestic demand is a long-term strategic principle and basic standpoint of China's economic development, as well as a fundamental means and an internal requirement for promoting balanced economic development. [...] We will actively boost consumer demand. We will continue to increase government spending used to help expand consumption and increase subsidies to low-income urban residents and farmers.

The CDB situates its 'market-driven pursuit of sustainable development' in line with China's larger ambitions, acknowledging the special role it serves in fulfilling China's infrastructural needs vis-à-vis its growth strategies (CDB 2017, 5, 24, 30; cf. Xu 2018). Growth imperatives can thus override and obscure otherwise green initiatives. In transportation, for example, the CDB provided cumulative lending totalling ¥1.5 trillion by 2016 (about $237 billion in 2018 dollars) for railways (CDB 2017, 30), which can be viewed as a relatively greener and lower carbon form of transport. Yet rail investment was dwarfed by cumulative lending of ¥2.6 trillion (about $411 billion) to highways and by the CDB's support for ninety new airports (no lending figures given). In energy infrastructure the CDB has provided cumulative lending to nuclear power totalling ¥296 billion (about $47 billion), equalling 30 per cent of all domestic nuclear investment (CDB 2017, 31). Abroad, the Chinese development banks with the CDB in the lead, massively fund greenhouse gas emissions, particularly through coal-fired energy generation (Li and Gallagher 2019). A third of foreign investments is classified as sustainable infrastructure, despite CDB figures throwing together public transport, rail, solar, and hydro investments with nuclear, oil energy and pipelines, highways, and telecommunications investments (Wang 2016, 22). China also wears the dubious crown of king of fossil fuel subsidies. According to IMF estimates, China is, by far, the largest fossil fuel subsidiser at $1.4 trillion for 2015, followed by the United States ($649 billion), Russia ($551 billion), the EU ($289 billion), and India ($209 billion) (Coady et al. 2019, 23).

China's carbonising growth is enmeshed within the internationalisation of the Chinese state and capital, a strategy wherein state-owned enterprises and public banks have unambiguous economic expansionary and growth-inducing roles (Jones and Zeng 2019, 1422). The CDB is heavily involved. For example, the CDB partners with the country's oil (and carbon) giant, the China National Petroleum Corporation, to drive forward the Belt and Road Initiative (BRI).[15] Therein the CDB facilitates Chinese oil purchases, both extending loans and handling foreign payments. Related energy contracts are often conditional on buying Chinese infrastructure

---

[15] See China National Petroleum Corporation, 'A Number of Cooperation Agreements Signed between CNPC and Its Partners', 22 May 2017. Available at www.cnpc.com.cn/en/nr2017/201705/7e79d750e7524d60b786a913d9bac7a7.shtml. Accessed 23 July 2020.

equipment in support of domestic industry (Wang 2016, 8; cf. Barone and Spratt 2015). While the bank's contribution to the BRI is discursively tied to an interpretation of sustainable development premised on increased prosperity, materially, it pumps billions into ramping up industrial capacity, manufacturing, infrastructure connectivity, and energy and resource extraction to support the globalisation of Chinese capital along the BRI (CDB 2017, 39; 2018, 41; 2019, 1; cf. Summers 2016). There is little transparency or accountability behind these actions. Once the rose-coloured glasses of the CDB's enormous financial capacity and ability to direct finance are removed, then its green credentials turn rather murky brown.

The strategic blurring of green and growth-oriented lending by Chinese authorities has given rise to pervasive accusations of financial 'greenwashing' from across the green investor and civil society communities.[16] A Friends of the Earth United States (FoEUS) report acknowledges that China's Green Credit Guidelines are 'one of the most progressive and interesting examples of a sustainable finance policy in the world' both for their environmental ambitions and for requiring that Chinese banks comply with host country laws and international norms in foreign lending (FoEUS 2017, 6). The report concludes, however, that the operations of Chinese banks abroad do not yet reflect these progressive standards – a conclusion drawn by others too (Gokkon 2018; Shishlov et al. 2018). Tukic and Burgess (2016) find that the profit imperatives of Chinese companies abroad limit their investments in areas of higher social need but lower profitability. The FoEUS further points out that the Chinese banks are weak on 'ensuring that public consultations are conducted based on Free, Prior and Informed Consent' (2017, 6). Such weak regulatory transparency and compliance extend to China's flourishing green bond market, which within three years of opening in 2015 issued over

---

[16] See W. Shepard, 'Inside China's "Greenwashing" of the Belt and Road', *Forbes*, 29 February 2020. Available at www.forbes.com/sites/wadeshepard/2020/02/29/inside-chinas-greenwashing-of-the-belt-and-road/#73aa68de5039. Accessed 23 July 2020.

$43 billion in (some say questionable) green bonds (Zhang 2020). The CDB participates, offering certified green bonds as a means of funding the BRI. The CDB has also been singled out by the civil society financial watchdog, BankTrack, for engaging in several 'dodgy deals' (that is, projects identified as damaging to the environment or society), including a pulp and saw mill in Russia, coal power plants in Vietnam and Turkey, and pulp and paper projects in Indonesia.[17] Still others point to the environmentally problematic CDB support for the Sino-Myanmar oil and gas pipelines (Barone and Spratt 2015). If there is a green 'floor' to CDB lending, it is subterranean, maybe even asthenospheric.

For the Nordic Investment Bank (NIB), there is the need for further research as there is little to no English language academic or civil society literature in general about the bank, let alone in reference to the NIB's green credentials. For example, BankTrack does not list any NIB 'dodgy deals' (probably a good thing). The financial and popular media make no reference to NIB scandal or crisis (again, likely a good sign). For example, while the *Financial Times* reported on the China Development Bank's problems with corruption, over-indebtedness, and greenwashing, it reports nothing on the NIB. It would be nice to say that the NIB does not generate the same contradictions, but it is not certain.

In practice the NIB tends also to privilege growth over green. In 2016, for example, the NIB states that 96 per cent of all new loans achieved a good or excellent mandate rating (that is, in relation to either mandated productivity or environmental or both) (2017, 1). In 2019 this mandate rating improved to 98 per cent of new loans (NIB 2019, 4). The NIB thus demonstrates very strong recourse to its institutional mandate. This is, from an accountability and governance lens, significant. But from a 'green' decarbonisation lens we know that sometimes only 20 per cent and at other times at most 46 per cent of

---

[17] See www.banktrack.org/bank/china_development_bank#dodgy_deals. Accessed 6 March 2020.

NIB loans achieve only a good or better environmental rating (Table 4.5). This means that for the NIB to achieve mandate-compliant lending of 96–98 per cent, most loans (that is, from 54 to 80 per cent) only meet the bank's *productivity* mandate. Not to lightly dismiss its achievements, but the NIB overwhelms on productivity and under-whelms on environment. This links back to the bank's founding mandate, which was to spur economic growth, which remains the case, albeit modified by environmental concerns. It is also connected to the competitive pressures that the Nordic region faces as a whole within global capitalist markets.

Questions have also been raised around the Nordic green bonds. Research by Maltais and Nykvist (2020) show that for investors the Nordic green bond certification and de-risking structure make them an attractive product as 'sustainable finance'. Indeed, the green Nordic branding is a powerful draw (and sell) for NIB clients (Confidential Interview, HLM, February 2020). Maltais and Nykvist (2020) suggest that green bonds are a good way of educating financial investors about 'good' sustainable investments, a sentiment confirmed in NIB interviews. Yet the researchers conclude that green bonds are a 'quite conservative innovation ... [that] do not appear to be unlocking new sources of capital for green investment or making green investments financially viable when they otherwise would not be' (Maltais and Nykvist 2020, 15). That is, finance capital's search for credibility amidst the crisis of climate finance, rather than concern for substantive decarbonisation, may be driving investors' interest in NIB green bonds.

The contradictions of the CDB and NIB financing of decarbonisation are not isolated but rather endemic to 'sustainable development'. According to environmental scholar Michael Redclift, since coming of age in the 1980s sustainable development is a concept and strategy draped in contradictions as it becomes increasingly subordinated to neoliberal marketisation (2005, 2017). As popularised by the 1987 Brundtland Report, sustainable development encouraged society to conserve nature while pursuing relentless economic growth

(Redclift 1987). The pattern persists. Consider, for example, the title of the 2017 OECD report, *Investing in Climate, Investing in Growth.* Mainstream interpretations uncritically accept neoliberal faith in market-based coordination, individualistic consumption-based choices, and self-interest as capable of restructuring society to re-produce itself ... sustainably (Redclift 2017, 704–05). The logic is questionable, but insidious. As the editor of *The Banker* admits, financiers' commitments to combatting climate change are 'skin deep' yet he nonetheless sees self-interest as saving the day:[18]

> They could always do more. But in my conversations with senior bankers, sustainable finance is at the top of their agenda. Even if their motivation is as much about fear of having stranded carbon-heavy assets on the balance sheet as it is about saving the planet, the all-important outcome will be the same.

Without confronting the contradictions of financing sustainable development within neoliberal capitalism, the idealistic strategy of global investors and pro-market advocates is to create 'win–win situations for both business and sustainable development' (Weber 2014, 5). Others are more sceptical of Pollyannaish scenarios. Commenting on the nascent European 'Green Deal' in 2020, economist Daniela Gabor writes that the current financing for sustainable development strategy offers but a 'third-way approach that seeks to nudge the market towards decarbonisation' with the benefits of unrolling public funds to encourage private finance simply lining the pockets of the already rich and greenwashing their otherwise carbonising investments.[19]

---

[18] B. Caplen, 'How Fast Can Banks Be "Climate Change Ready"?', Editor's Blog, *The Banker*, 20 February 2018. Available at www.thebanker.com/Editor-s-Blog/How-fast-can-banks-be-climate-change-ready. Accessed 19 March 2020.

[19] 'The European Green Deal Will Bypass the Poor and Go Straight to the Rich', Opinion, *The Guardian*, 19 February 2020. Available at www.theguardian.com/commentisfree/2020/feb/19/european-green-deal-polish-miners. Accessed 19 March 2020.

Yet the win-win approach to sustainable development is constitutive of the UN 2030 Sustainable Development Goals, with little attempt to square the structural circle of contradictions between going green and going for growth. Recent empirical work demonstrates the incompatibility of aims within the 2030 SDGs. For example, a 2019 study asks whether the SDG aim of living in harmony with nature is compatible with the aim of annual global economic growth of 3 per cent, assessed in terms of resource use and carbon dioxide emissions. The study concludes that 'global growth of 3 per cent per year renders it empirically infeasible to achieve (a) any reductions in aggregate global resource use and (b) reductions in CO2 emissions rapid enough to stay within the carbon budget for 2°C' (Hickel 2019, 873). The evidence is that escalating growth-induced carbon emissions feed global warming, contradicting mainstream promises of going green through unrestrained growth (Hickel and Kallis 2019). This warning is applicable to both the CDB and NIB.

There is, as such, an unavoidable and underlying problem. In her book, *Carbon*, environmental scholar Kate Ervine writes that capitalism is a system of (re)production in need of continuous growth and profitability, and this growth and these profits depend on generating ever more carbon (2018, 31). For historian Ellen Meiksins Wood, capitalism itself is structurally 'incapable of promoting sustainable development, not because it encourages technological advances that are capable of straining the earth's resources but because the purpose of capitalist production is exchange value not use value, profit not people' (2002, 197). In such a system of social reproduction, self-interest demands that, for example, large auto manufacturers leverage their accumulated mass of capital and class power 'to ensure that the narrative of a green future is one that keeps us driving and consuming, with a minor tweak' (Ervine 2018, 121). Put otherwise, dominant technocratic and market-based approaches obscure how individual and collective human agents – like auto manufacturers, petroleum producers, global investment bankers, and of course some public banks, among others – are the protagonists of climate change

(Taylor 2014, 4). Indeed, much of capital accumulation today, be it in production or in finance, depends on carbonising growth strategies that accelerate human impacts on the environment (Magdoff and Williams 2017; Gerber 2020). As critical geographer David Harvey writes, the three most dangerous contradictions of our time are '[c]ompounding growth, environmental degradation, and widespread alienation' (Harvey 2015, cited in Gerber 2020, 1). For finance to not exacerbate but to mitigate these contradictions it needs to be commanded to do so.

By being located within the public sphere, public banks have the potential to meaningfully tackle the financing of decarbonisation by being commanded to do so. There is in the China Development Bank and the Nordic Investment Bank such material and institutional potential, and it is massive potential at that. But squaring the circle of competing green and growth imperatives within global capitalism remains an elusive and contradictory process. These two public banks persist as credible institutions, despite the neoliberal odds against it, because they tend to favour growth over green. The pull of private interests and of capital accumulation imperatives will need to be more directly confronted if the full decarbonisation potential of these public banks is to be bent disproportionately towards the public interest and in green and just ways. The future of financing decarbonisation will be anything but neutral, in carbon or class terms.

5   Definancialisation

The previous chapter looked at how public banks have acquired the financial capacity and standards to fund decarbonisation and also how these functions remain contradictory within global capitalism. Public bank decarbonisation is outweighed by carbonising activities. This chapter turns to public banks and 'definancialisation' in a post-global financial crisis world. I argue that the definancialisation functions of the Indian National Bank for Agriculture and Rural Development (NABARD) and the American Bank of North Dakota (BND) help these institutions persist as credible public banks in their class-divided societies. As with decarbonisation so too with definancialisation. Contradictions arise and struggles endure over who benefits from what public banks do. Public banks can shield workers, the poor and marginalised, micro-, small-, and medium-sized enterprises (MSMEs), the public sector, and spatial regions (rural/urban) from the discipline of financialised market imperatives. Public banks can similarly shield finance capital, the wealthy and privileged, large financial and non-financial corporations, and even the financial world market from these same financial imperatives, entrenching their unequal power over social reproduction.

Three premises support the argument. First, the problem of definancialisation arises from the instabilities and inequalities related to neoliberal 'financialisation'. Second, the NABARD and the BND have acquired functions that enable these banks to operate in pro-public ways that counter financialisation. These functions have an often distinctly 'spatial' character. Third, contradictions nonetheless arise as these two public banks also privilege private interests in the shadow of global capitalism.

5.1   THE PROBLEM OF DEFINANCIALISING FINANCE

The problem of definancialisation begins with the destabilising effects of 'financialisation'. Not unlike the proliferation of globalisation research in the 1990s, so too with financialisation research since the early 2000s. Financialisation is now seemingly applicable to nearly every contemporary socio-economic and political process as the causal force of change or degradation. There is a risk of stretching the concept too far. As Fine and Saad-Filho (2017, 691) warn 'In much of this literature, financialization is merely a buzzword reflecting the greater significance of finance in economic and social reproduction in recent decades, and the (closely related) growth and proliferation of financial assets.' The term is at risk of becoming an empty signifier. Anything dealing with money or credit can qualify. Yet such is the gravitational pull of 'financialisation' that even as you criticise the concept you must adapt it as your own (cf. Christophers 2015, 2018). There is no avoiding financialisation, in the literature as in everyday life. Nevertheless, the expanding field of research speaks to real issues of social reproduction, financial power, and class-based inequality that impact our lived experiences, future aspirations, and the nature of global capitalism.

Broadly speaking, financialisation refers to a historically specific type of economic logic. According to heterodox economist Gerald Epstein's widely cited definition, it involves the 'increasing role of financial motives, financial markets, financial actors and financial institutions in the operation of domestic and international economies' (2005, 3). This framing, largely based on the US experience, has influenced a generation of financialisation studies, with scholars tinkering with the wording often according to one's disciplinary frameworks (Aalbers and Pollard 2016). In its breadth, this understanding of financialisation has opened up new avenues of inquiry and allowed otherwise non-financial experts to investigate the phenomenon outside the narrow confines of financial economics.

Other heterodox economists have worked with this broad definition to highlight the specific economic forces pushing 'real' and 'financial' investments further and further apart. Özgür Orhangazi's (2008a, 2008b) close study of the United States argues that real investment is being crowded out by non-financial firm managers putting money into shorter-term and higher-return financial investments that, in turn, intensify economic uncertainty and instability. Changes to market-based corporate governance and shareholder value strategies since the 1980s and 1990s have given rise to these financialised accumulation strategies. More recent studies link such changes to reduced economic growth (Tomaskovic-Devey et al. 2015). In this line of research, financialisation is about the drive for maximising shareholder value with the consequences being economic instability and widening inequality due to the accelerating divergence between financial and real investments (see Onaran et al. 2011; van der Zwan 2014; Mazzucato 2015; Lazonick and Shin 2020). Financialisation is about using money capital to amass more money capital but without necessarily producing anything but greater social inequality.

Marxian studies have emphasised the structural, class-based, and exploitative dimensions of financialisation. Economist Costas Lapavitsas defines financialisation 'as a systemic transformation of mature capitalist economies' involving large non-financial corporations reducing reliance on bank financing and acquiring in-house financial capacities; banks in turn expanding activities in financial markets and to households; and, households becoming more tied to finance both as debtors and as asset holders (2011, 611–12). His work emphasises financial expropriation, wherein finance as a class of capitalists seeks to extract more and more wealth from the income of workers (Lapavitsas 2009; Lapavitsas and Mendieta-Munoz 2016). Researchers in developing countries show similar patterns of banks increasing profits through household financing in ways that disadvantage workers in particular, and that this transformation has been enabled by neoliberal restructuring and the commodification of public services such that households increasingly need to turn to consumer credit to survive (Karacimen 2014). Financialisation is thus distinctly class-based and class-divided.

Other critical financialisation studies have focused on everyday life and the social logics, disciplinary features, and cultures of finance in ways that benefit the interests and power of finance capital (Martin 2002; Langley 2008; Pellandini-Simányi et al. 2015; Konings 2018). Researchers too have exposed the intensifying role of financial markets and interest-paying financial transactions in social reproduction (Pollard 2012; cf. Soederberg 2013). One of the most pernicious ways this takes shape is through microcredit, which Adrienne Roberts argues represents 'the extension of credit as a means for the poor to pay for their reproduction' (2015, 113). Evidence suggests that microfinance involves transferring financial risks onto the poor in ways that augmented the chances of investors generating and retaining (often astronomical) financial returns (Aitken 2013; cf. Bateman 2017). In this sense, the private interests shaping microfinance are not dissimilar to those pro-market forces shaping the financing decarbonisation agenda. Financialisation is about bending the essence of life-making and societal reproduction to the interests of private financial accumulation.

Financialisation, it follows, involves the restructuring of the state. The state apparatus and role of state authorities are underappreciated features of contemporary financialisation (Karwowski 2019). I have argued elsewhere that finance capitalism (or 'financialisation') is made possible by the fusing of the interests of domestic and foreign financial capital into the state apparatus such that the actions of state managers and government elites benefit finance in ways often detrimental to labour and popular classes (Marois 2012; cf. Yalman et al. 2019). One of the sharpest expressions of this has been during post-financial crisis state-led rescues. At moments of crisis, state authorities tend to socialise private financial risks gone bad by passing the costs on to workers, popular classes, and the most marginalised in society through the state financial apparatus via austerity, taxation, reductions in essential services, privatisations, and so on (Marois 2011). By socialising private financial losses state authorities enable renewed financial accumulation in ways that reinforce the class-divided power of financial capital and the structural logics of financialisation (Marois 2014). Financialisation thus involves the institutionalisation of the power of finance capital within the state to the benefit of private over public interests (Muñoz-Martínez and Marois 2014; Marois and Muñoz-Martínez 2016; Ho and Marois 2019).

Financialisation further represents the intensifying interconnectedness of capitalist social relations and circuits of capital, and hence of social reproduction (cf. Chesnais 2016). Writing earlier than most of the topic, Elmar Altvater identified both the quantitative and qualitative dimensions to this historical shift: as financial contracts surpass real economic transactions, this leads to qualitative change in the real economy and social relations as both are subordinated to the financial system and disciplined via intensified credit relations (1997, 59). The financialisation of capitalism does not determine all that occurs, but it has imparted a new and significant logic of social reproduction and capital accumulation globally that is distinctly class-divided and inequality-reinforcing.

The dynamics and impacts of financialisation, nonetheless, remain open to debate across different disciplines (Bracking 2016; Maxfield et al. 2017; Christophers 2018). My intent is not to resolve 'financialisation'. Nevertheless, among critically minded scholars there is a shared sense that something is fundamentally wrong and that we need change (Epstein 2010; Marois 2015; Mazzucato 2018). There are massive economic imbalances, widening social, gendered, and class-based inequalities, financial instability, unaccountable power structures, and continued environmental degradation – all ostensibly to generate a more concentrated mass of wealth among capitalists and financiers (Tooze 2018). And this despite the recurrent and massively costly crises of finance. Between 1970 and 2011 there have been 147 banking crises, 211 currency crises, and 66 sovereign crises, with the lion's share occurring since the mid-1980s and with the deepening of neoliberalism (Laeven and Valencia 2013). Financialisation prevails not for its economic efficiency but for the unequal structures of power and privilege behind it – that is, for being credible in the interests of finance capital. Financialisation is, as such, an action that is produced by individual and collective agents (Aalbers and Pollard 2016, 368). It is made. So too, then, can *definancialisation* be made.

The gross class-divided inequalities, recurrent crises of finance, and the inability of financial markets to resolve the crisis of climate finance have given rise to demands for definancialisation. To date, academic calls have mostly been made as afterthoughts of critiques of financialisation, often couched in a short concluding section, as beyond the limits of the project, or as a call itself for further research (Roberts 2015; Chesnais 2016; Fine and Saad-Filho 2017). Most studies of financialisation do not lay out much of a strategic pathway let alone explore anything like promising or programmatic real-world alternatives from which to build on (see Castree and Christophers 2015, 378).[1] This lack of critical attention to actually existing definancialisation can generate a collective sense of disempowerment undermining the possibilities of change that many suggest are necessary for a green and just transition. The definancialisation literature should be as empirically rich and debated as financialisation and be understood to be as pressing as calls for decarbonisation. That it is *not* is a problem.

There are indications of a nascent definancialisation debate, however. The most active participants have been heterodox economists, who tend to call for definancialisation as a response to problems of too much finance and too little regulation (Sawyer 2017). Definancialisation means reining in the (excessive) role of financialised motives, markets, actors, and institutions as per Epstein's

---

[1] While pitched on different grounds, a study of east-central European countries seeking to 'definancialise' after the 2008–09 global financial crisis draws the following conclusions, notably that 'the willingness to (at least partially) engage in definancialisation and financial repression is dependent on how important the financial sector is for the growth model, how much domestic banks are able and willing to provide similar services as foreign-owned banks, and how strong the anti-finance stance of the respective government is. Further, willingness is not enough, as states need to have the institutional capacity to do so' (Ban and Bohle 2020, 19).

definition of financialisation (Karwowski 2019, 1001). For some, definancialisation can be achieved through incremental changes and regulatory reforms, with some potential for reigniting the public ownership of financial institutions therein (Sweeney 2019, 1068). For others, the democratisation of public financial institutions is needed (Epstein 2010; Block 2014; Sawyer 2016). By and large, however, definancialisation debates lack real-world case studies exemplifying their calls for definancialisation. As economist Ewa Karwowski stresses, 'more research into both theory and practice of definancialisation is required if deeper and more widespread definancialisation is to proceed' (2019, 1020). Definancialisation needs grounding, empirically and theoretically.

The definancialisation debate has not been restricted to academia. Some of the strongest calls come from civil society and independent research centres. A UK-based Institute for Public Policy Research report on definancialisation calls for re-regulating finance away from its more socially useless and speculative functions and towards greater democratic oversight (Lawrence 2014). Others point to the need for deeper structural changes. Recognising that private finance has politically mobilised its mass of concentrated wealth to escape and subvert economic and financial re-regulation, Thomas Hanna of the US-based Democracy Collaborative asks the following (2018b, 32): 'How might America's over-mighty and crisis-prone financial sector be fundamentally restructured and reimagined in the public interest?' The answer? 'Based on real-world experience, outright public ownership is the most immediately viable – and perhaps even the only – effective option' (Hanna 2018b, 32). Hanna continues in unambiguous terms (2018b, 45):

> Public ownership would convert rent-seeking concentrations of private financial power into public utilities that work for the common good. It holds out the prospect of a way to fundamentally restructure and reimagine the financial sector as something that no longer fuels financialization, speculation, and consolidation, but

instead works to allocate funds to real productive investment and decentralizes financial power to support prosperous and healthy local economies everywhere. It goes beyond simply breaking up large banks into smaller banks by changing the ownership structure, incentives, and market dynamics at the heart of the financialized capitalist system.

In not dissimilar terms, the Amsterdam-based Transnational Institute (TNI) calls for concrete public sector alternatives to financialisation (see Steinfort and Kishimoto 2019). Noting the failure of private finance to confront societal challenges like social inequality and climate change, the TNI argues that there is much greater potential to mobilise existing public financial capacity in the public interest than is commonly recognised. Definancialisation requires alternative public financial capacity.

This chapter responds to academic and civil society calls to confront definancialisation, conceptually and concretely. The concrete focus is on existing public banks. Conceptually, definancialisation is framed not as *shrinking* the total mass of finance capital or as simply re-regulating global markets. Rather, definancialisation is understood as having the pro-public financial capacity to democratically overwhelm the undemocratic and exploitative motives and practices of financialised capitalism over social reproduction. The public banks discussed below have not yet achieved this, but they offer important lessons on ways that this might begin to be realised alongside decarbonisation and democratisation.

5.2 THE WAYS OF DEFINANCIALISATION: THE NATIONAL BANK FOR AGRICULTURE AND RURAL DEVELOPMENT AND THE BANK OF NORTH DAKOTA

There is nothing inherent in public banks making them function in ways that definancialise economies and societies. There are public banks of all types, be they commercial, development, and universal banks, that pursue financial profits over developmental and social mandates, like the corporatised UK Royal Bank of Scotland; that engage in speculative activities that have harmed the public interest, like the KfW subsidiary IKB Deutsche Industriebank prior to the 2008–09 global financial crisis; that undermine bank worker collective organisation, as with Ziraat Bank in Turkey following the 2001 crisis; that use public funds to empower carbonising private corporations, as with Mexico's National Bank of Public Works and Services (Banobras); and that enable neoliberal marketisation by promoting privatisation and public–private partnerships, as with the new Canada Infrastructure Bank. Public banks can and do privilege and intensify private financialised interests and logics.

Yet because public banks exist in the public sphere, there is the *potential* for society to make them function in definancialising ways. Public banks can be made to slow financial flows, channel funds to public goods, prioritise public mandates over profits, collaborate rather than compete with other banks, support local development, amass knowledge of development, offer payment moratoriums, reduce interest rates, mitigate the impacts of crises, and so on. Public banks have credible historical legacies of doing this and much more. But definancialisation functions are only ever *potentially* so, and potentially fleeting at that. Definancialisation functions, like decarbonisation, are pulled between contending public and private interests in class-divided society.

In this chapter I explore two case studies of public banks that have acquired definancialisation functions, the National Bank for Agriculture and Rural Development (NABARD) and the Bank of North Dakota (BND). As elsewhere in this book, these two public banks are not meant to idealise public banking or the societies in which they exist and persist. Nor do the two cases pretend to speak to worldwide definancialisation (just as the paired cases of other chapters cannot speak to worldwide decarbonisation or universal democratisation). Instead, the chapter excavates the promising practices of these public banks' definancialisation functions, however imperfect and contradictory, that can counter financialisation in a given place at a given time.

5.2.1   The National Bank for Agriculture and Rural Development (NABARD)

Contemporary India has a population of over 1.3 billion people and is regarded as the world's largest democracy. According to World Bank data, its 2018 GDP was \$2.72 trillion and GNI per capital \$2,020. The National Bank for Agriculture and Rural Development (NABARD) is a unique national financial institution that operates as a development bank, providing development financing and on-lending to other development and cooperative banks, and as an 'apex' institution with financial regulatory and expert planning roles in India's rural economy. The NABARD is effectively tasked with 'fixing' otherwise mobile financial capital within rural India, exercising an explicit spatial function of channelling and slowing money flows from capital rich urban and foreign markets to capital poor regions in India. As such, the NABARD is an expression of state spatial strategy, realised through the public sphere in the form of a public bank (cf. Ho and Marois 2019).[2]

5.2.1.1   History and Current Structure of the NABARD

The post–1947 Independence Indian banking sector was reshaped by a dramatic turn to public banking. Previously, British colonial powers and private bankers had dominated the Indian economy. This would persist into the post–World War II, post-Independence period. However, little by little, the Government of India built up alternative banking capacity by founding a number of new public financial institutions meant to sustain economic independence by raising capital, funding infrastructure, and supporting national industrialisation and rural development. The Industrial Finance Corporation of India (established in 1948) was the first public financial institution created. The

---

[2] Clifton et al. (2021b) present a similar argument in terms of the Instituto de Crédito Oficial, Spain, forming part of a national spatial strategy, which was preceded by an argument in Clifton et al. (2018) about the (spatial) integration function of the European Investment Bank.

Industrial Credit and Investment Corporation of India (ICICI; established in 1955) followed as did the Industrial Development Bank of India and the Unit Trust of India (both established in 1964). However, the most decisive post-Independence transformation in the domestic credit system came in 1969 when the Government of Indira Gandhi nationalised fourteen large private banks. The stated rationale was that bank nationalisation was needed to sever India's colonial ties and to enable more socialist and state-led planning on a nationwide scale. Indian authorities subsequently continued to build capacity. In 1971, the government created the Industrial Reconstruction Corporation of India to assist failing industries and, in 1982, the Export–Import (Exim) Bank to fund international trade expansion. By this time, in 1980, the government had nationalised six more banks, bringing public control of banking assets in India to over 90 per cent.[3] Then, in 1988, the National Housing Bank (NHB) was set up as an 'apex' institution responsible for providing long-term housing finance and, in 1990, the Small Industries Development Bank of India (SIDBI) was established to support micro-, small-, and medium-sized enterprises (MSMEs) sector and to help coordinate other MSME-oriented institutions. The Indian credit system thus entered the neoliberal era largely constituted by public banks and financial institutions.

It was within this milieu of financial restructuring and capacity-building that the National Bank for Agriculture and Rural Development (NABARD) came into being in July 1982 (NABARD 1983, 74). This new public bank was to be an institutional pillar 'that would give undivided attention, forceful direction and pointed focus to rural development in the country' (Rao 2012, 28). The idea of a new *rural* public bank had gained prominence in 1979 when the government requested that India's central bank, the Reserve Bank of India (RBI), form the 'Committee to Review the Arrangements for

---

[3] As of 2019 there are twenty-seven public commercial banks in operation (see Indian Banks' Association. Available at www.iba.org.in/depart-res-stcs/key-bus-stcs.html. Accessed 10 April 2020).

Institutional Credit for Agriculture and Rural Development'
(CRAFICARD). The CRAFICARD, in turn, recommended that
NABARD take on the RBI's rural credit and oversight functions,
including inspections of India's cooperative and regional rural banks.
The NABARD would retain close structural ties with the RBI through
shared 50/50 per cent ownership with the government, better
allowing the new rural bank to draw on the financial resources and
expertise of the RBI.

With an initial capital injection of □100 crore (□1 billion) in
public funds and by also taking over the refinancing functions of the
erstwhile Agricultural Refinance and Development Corporation, the
NABARD was set to begin channelling finance into India's capital
poor countryside and agricultural sector. The significance of this
ostensibly spatial financial function should not be underestimated.
India has a heavily agriculturally oriented economy and agrarian society (cf. Lerche 2013). Since its founding in 1982, the NABARD has
developed a nationwide presence with twenty-eight regional offices
and has expanded its operations and capacities immensely. According
to Rao, the NABARD has evolved into one of the most unique financial institutions in the world because it integrated in a single public
bank the functions of a central bank, development agency, financial
institution, infrastructure funding agency, microfinance institution,
planning board, and apex-level policymaker (2012, 28). Therein the
NABARD constitutes one of four 'All-India Financial Institutions',
the other three being the Exim Bank, the SIDBI, and the NHB
(Sharma 2010, 29). While not without problems, on average, India's
development banks have functioned as stable, even profitable, financial institutions (Chakrabarti 2012, 258; World Bank 2012a). For its
part, the NABARD has averaged 0.86 per cent ROAA (2012–19),
which is in line with or even superior to other development banks
around the world (Table 5.1).

According to the NABARD, the sector's public and
collaborative character have been foundational. It writes that the
'[i]nstitutionalisation of rural credit was achieved to a large extent

Table 5.1. *The NABARD and Bank of North Dakota at a glance*

	NABARD	BND
Board of governors	Fourteen-member board of governors appointed by the government in consultation with the central bank, plus an advisory council.	Three-member Industrial Commission, plus a seven-member advisory board.
Mission	Promote sustainable and equitable agriculture and rural development through participative financial and non-financial interventions, innovations, technology and institutional development for securing prosperity.	To deliver quality, sound financial services that promote agriculture, commerce, and industry in North Dakota.
Type of bank (year established)	National Development/ Apex Institution (1982)	Commercial (1919)
Ownership	Government of India	State of North Dakota
Total assets	$70.54 billion (2019)	$7.02 billion (2019)
Return on assets (annual average)	0.86 (2012–19)	1.83 (2013–18)
Net profit after tax (annual average)	$391.1 (2012–19)	$129.3 million (2013–18)
No. of employees	3,793 (2018)	181 (2019)
No. of branches	32 (2018)	1
Credit rating	Baa2 (Moody's)	Aaa (Moody's)

Sources: BND 2018 (Annual Report); BankFocus (BND Data update 1717 – 01/04/2020) NABARD website 10 April 2020; BankFocus (NABARD Data update 1724 – 07/04/2020)

with the nationalisation of banks and making ubiquitous multi-agency institutional arrangements for socialised provision of credit for agriculture and rural development' (NABARD 2019, 80). Following the new economic policy of 1990–91, the rural sector would see the entry of new types of private credit institutions, including microfinance institutions (MFIs), non-bank finance companies (NBFCs), and small finance banks (SFBs). Covering both contemporary public and private financial institutions, the NABARD maintains an anchoring role nationwide in the financing of agriculture as well as MSMEs via India's 'multi-agency approach'. This approach means farmers and rural enterprises can access financing from an assortment of smaller and larger public and private financial institutions, which all benefit from NABARD refinancing and are subject to its oversight. In a country the size and scale of India, this is a mammoth task. The NABARD oversees 21 public banks; 26 private banks; 56 regional rural banks; 33 State Cooperative Banks; 13 State Cooperative Agriculture and Rural Development Banks; 11 small finance banks; 403 rural cooperative banks; 1,574 urban cooperative banks; 11,682 non-banking companies; and, 93,500 rural cooperative societies (Amalorpavanathan 2017b, 2; NABARD 2019, 90). Through its nationwide institutional ties and functions, the NABARD nevertheless maintains a role in grassroots and local credit planning through its district-level presence (Rao 2012, 28; NABARD 2017, 78).

Notwithstanding, important changes began to take place in 2012. For one, the government proposed changes to the ownership structure of the NABARD, notably to remove the RBI ownership stake (Rao 2012). Seven years later, in February 2019, the government acquired a 100 per cent ownership of the NABARD by purchasing the RBI shareholding. During this interregnum, the NABARD aggressively expanded its operations. From 2012 to 2019, NABARD's total assets doubled from $35 to $70 billion (Table 5.2). Indian authorities also started to promote a more market-oriented and neoliberal 'financial inclusion' approach, which penetrated the operations of the

Table 5.2. *NABARD operational data, 2012–19*

	2012	2013	2014	2015	2016	2017	2018	2019
Total assets (billion USD)	35.61	39.21	42.40	45.71	46.85	53.77	62.57	70.54
Net profit after tax (million USD)	321.8	335.8	321.3	389.7	384.8	414.8	464.1	496.3
ROAE	4.47	4.67	4.62	5.45	5.30	5.19	5.22	5.34
ROAA	0.97	0.92	0.83	0.90	0.86	0.82	0.80	0.77

Source: Orbis BankFocus (Data update 1724 – 07/04/2020)

NABARD. This structural reorientation can be linked to recommendations from the September 2013 RBI-constituted 'Committee under the Chairmanship of Dr. Nachiket Mor' (Member, Central Board, RBI) (NABARD 2014, 9). Nachiket Mor is a well-known US-educated economist who advocates for market competition and microfinance financial inclusion. His intent was to make the Indian financial sector more financialised, and indeed NABARD therein. We return to this below.

In terms of governance, the NABARD has a representative form. The Indian government appoints the fourteen-member board of directors in consultation with the RBI. The board is made up of a chair, a managing director, and twelve other directors. The twelve directors include three experts in rural economics, rural development, cottage and village industries, small-scale industries, or people with experience in cooperative banks, regional rural banks, or commercial banks; two members from the RBI; three Government of India officials; and four state government officials. The bank's board also has an advisory council, which consists of directors of NABARD and anyone else who NABARD feels is necessary to advise its operations (NABARD 2019, 119). While the board is representative, it is unclear to what degree it is democratic. Unlike the State Bank of India, the NABARD's board, for example, does not include formal representation from bank worker unions.

5.2.1.2   *The NABARD and Definancialisation*

In order to channel and 'fix' otherwise mobile capital into capital poor rural India, the NABARD has functioned in three ways that have 'definancialised' contemporary finance for development processes. These include NABARD's sourcing of capital, ways of lending, and building of public sector financial knowledge, expertise, and institutional capacity.

The sourcing of capital for the NABARD has a solidly public sphere character. In the first place, NABARD's core capital, reserves, and surpluses constitute about 9 per cent of its funds (in 2018, 9.42 per cent and in 2019, 8.96 per cent). This core capital is complemented by smaller combined allocations of 3–4 per cent of funds through the Indian government's National Rural Credit Long-Term Operations and Stabilisation Funds. Further contributions from the RBI add to NABARD's base sources of capital (in 2018, 3.95 per cent and in 2019, 3.3 per cent). Four other deposit-based schemes draw in additional sources of capital from India's public, private, and foreign commercial banks that have not met priority lending targets set by the RBI (Amalorpavanathan 2017a, 5). Three features stand out here. One, as India's commercial banks are disproportionately public, so too are these deposit contributions to the NABARD. Two, the bulk of commercial bank deposits are urban based, so the deposit contributions represent transfers from capital rich to capital poor regions in India. Third, the schemes constitute a structured and collaborative connection between India's deposit-taking retail/commercial banks and India's apex rural development bank, the NABARD. This institutional framework is formidable. In 2018 the deposit-based schemes accounted for 51.6 per cent of NABARD capital and 44.7 per cent in 2019 (NABARD 2019, 131–32). The four schemes are as follows:

(1) The Short-Term Cooperative Rural Credit Fund: A fund supplied by commercial banks that have not achieved their priority sector lending obligations and by central budget allocations (in 2018, 11.1 per cent and in 2019, 9.2 per cent of NABARD's capital).

(2) The Short-Term Rural Credit Fund for Regional Rural Banks: A fund set up in 2012–13, again supplied by commercial banks unable to meet their priority lending obligations but also by central budget allocations (in 2018, 2.5 per cent and in 2019, 2.1 per cent of NABARD's capital).

(3) The Long-term Rural Credit Fund: A fund set up in 2014–15 to support cooperative banks and rural regional banks, also supplied by shortfalls in commercial banks' priority sector lending. This fund can benefit from direct government allocations (in 2018, 9.4 per cent and in 2019, 8.8 per cent of NABARD's capital).

(4) The Rural Infrastructure Development Fund (RIDF): The largest fund by far, it is similarly supplied by commercial bank deposits and by government allocations (in 2018, 28.6 per cent and in 2019, 24.6 per cent of NABARD's capital).

Combined, these sources of capital constitute around 60 per cent of NABARD's loanable funds. The NABARD complements these sources of capital through additional market-based borrowings in corporate bonds issuance, commercial paper, certificates of deposit, term money borrowing, and commercial bank term loans, which represent a growing proportion of capital. In 2018, market sources comprised 26.6 per cent of capital and in 2019 35.2 per cent, with bond issuance accounting for about half of these sources of capital and commercial paper providing 5–7 per cent. The remainder of NABARD's sources of capital come from various funds, other liabilities, and bonds, with a very minor portion coming from foreign currency loans (about one-fifth of 1 per cent).

The bank's ways of lending are as important as the sources of funds. The NABARD acquires capital to supply rural and regional financial institutions more cheaply than otherwise possible. The rationale is that by augmenting flows of credit to the rural and agricultural regions, the NABARD (and the government by extension) can support growth, development, and poverty alleviation in India's agriculture and rural areas (see NABARD 2014, 35, 41, 65). The NABARD is, as such, an institutional arm of the government's finance for development policy and practice constituting an institutional conduit of central government support schemes. These include interest rate subventions for farmers and priority sectors, financial support to avoid distress sales of produce, financing for the marketing of products, and directed subsidies for green energy alternatives and organic farming (NABARD 2018, iv, 75, 86; 2019, 77–78).

The two ways of NABARD's lending stand out: medium- and long-term project loans and the Rural Infrastructure Development Fund. The medium- and long-term project loans constitute the single largest way of NABARD's lending, which account for just under a third of annual lending (in 2018, 30.2 per cent and in 2019, 31.3 per cent) (NABARD 2019, 135). This lending provides refinancing (on-lending) to rural commercial and development banks so that they themselves can provide credits for longer terms and at cheaper rates of interest. The second largest way of lending is through its RIDF, which accounts for about a quarter of all lending (in 2018, 27.1 per cent and in 2019, 24.7 per cent) (NABARD 2019, 135). The RIDF was created in 1995 in response to a shortfall in public investments in rural infrastructure and as a mechanism for channelling financial resources to state-level governments for rural infrastructure (NABARD 2000, 87). Over its twenty-five years, the RIDF has expanded lending dramatically, from ☐2,000 crore in 1995–96 to ☐28,000 crore in 2018–19 (NABARD 2019, 102). Lending is nation-wide, with loans going to state-level governments for the creation of rural infrastructure (agricultural sector, irrigation, rural connectivity, and social infrastructure) (Amalorpavanathan 2017a, 6). The logic behind these public lending programmes is that rural development projects in agriculture and irrigation will encourage farmers to invest more in technology and inputs, and this will lead to productivity gains and farm income growth. To this end, the bulk of resources (nearly half) goes to agriculture and irrigation, followed by about a third to rural 'connectivity' projects (that is, roads and bridges). Social sector projects, which include education, health, drinking water, and so on, account for about a fifth of RIDF lending in 2018–19 (NABARD 2019, 104–07).

The future of this way of lending in India appears stable, if moving in new directions. The deputy managing director of NABARD suggests that the bank needs to bolster support for rural non-agricultural job creation and for the manufacturing and service sectors, as well as for health, education, and social empowerment (Amalorpavanathan 2017a, 11). Over the last few years, NABARD's long-term financing has grown in this direction of non-farm and MSME lending, expanding from about 35 per cent in 2016 to 53 per cent in 2019. Agriculture-specific lending fell during this same period, from 34 per cent to 15 per cent, as microfinance financial support grew from 11 per cent to 14 per cent (NABARD 2019, 75–76). Indeed, 'scaling up microfinance initiatives' has evolved as a (potentially contradictory) priority of NABARD (2017, 90) (linking back to the financialisation preferences of Nachiket Mor).

Three additional destinations illustrate significant ways of NABARD's lending. In 2019, for example, the NABARD committed 13.7 per cent of lending to production and marketing credit accounts, 7.8 per cent to the purchasing of government securities and other investments, and 7 per cent to the Long-Term Irrigation Fund (NABARD 2019, 135). Beyond these, there are another dozen or so lending destinations, including the Infrastructure Development Assistance programme geared towards public sector entities, the Warehouse Infrastructure Fund and Food Processing Fund, and a social housing programme meant to respond to homelessness in India. Finally, climate change and decarbonisation have surfaced as a new mandated way of lending (see Mukhopadhyay 2016, 2–3; Amalorpavanathan 2017b, 4; NABARD 2017, 79). This lending cuts across several programmes, from the Natural Resource Management Initiative to the Participatory Watershed Development Programme and the Tribal Development Projects for sustainable livelihoods.

The state spatial strategy embodied in the NABARD is not only about financial intermediation and the 'fixing' of capital in poorer regions. The NABARD has also built up public sector knowledge, expertise, and institutional capacity on issues of rural finance and

development. For one, the bank supports research and the dissemin-
ation of knowledge around questions of rural and agricultural development, providing both large-scale empirical data and field-based
research (NABARD 2018, 68–69). Bank staff produce in-house studies,
whose research findings are published in journals and as internal
bulletins. The bank also supports and participates in relevant external
research projects. The NABARD shares its research with the government and in collaboration with other banks, with much of its work
freely available online for further academic and policy-based independent research. This 'knowledge' function is historical and set in
legal foundations and in accordance with the NABARD Act (1981)
that formally established the bank's Research and Development Fund
(cf. NABARD 1983, 109).

To fulfil this knowledge function, the NABARD nurtures long-
term partnerships with various research institutes (2019, 63–65, 93).
For example, the NABARD sponsors the Centre for Research in Agri-
Economics with the Indian Council for Research on International
Economic Relations, the Institute of Rural Management Anand, and
the Centre for Professional Excellence in Cooperatives at the Bankers
Institute of Rural Development in Lucknow. The NABARD supports
research-based chair units in university departments (as of 2019, there
are seven) and it offers student and research internships, as well as
providing support for seminars, conferences, workshops, and publications. These knowledge functions have been practised since the bank
first began operations in the early 1980s (see NABARD 1984, 59–61).

Internal knowledge capacity is related to its external coordination and development planning functions. As one of the four 'All-
India Financial Institutions', the NABARD is responsible for nationwide rural refinancing and credit expansion planning (2019, 67–68).
This involves setting refinance limits for the State Cooperative Banks
and for the Regional Rural Banks (RRBs), taking into account national
government-based incentive programmes. The NABARD works at the
local level through its 423 district development manager offices to
inform credit planning, monitoring, and coordination between various

initiatives. The NABARD is then tasked with preparing annual 'Potential-linked Credit Plans' for all districts across India. The performance of these mandated duties has underpinned the institution's internal capacity and expertise on rural development, which in turn serves as valuable resource for state planning.

Having acquired this knowledge capacity also means that the NABARD can respond to societal challenges from within the public sphere. In 2012, NABARD reported that the Adaptation Fund Board of United Nations Framework Convention on Climate Change (UNFCCC) accredited it as the only national implementing entity for India (that is, the only institution able and willing to take on AFB programmes) (NABARD 2014, 48). Since then the NABARD has created an Adaptation Fund and Green Climate Fund and is supporting sustainable farming and renewable energy projects (NABARD 2019, 35). Further in response to biodiversity challenges, the NABARD partnered with the Centre for Environmental Management of Degraded Ecosystems, University of Delhi, to organise a nationwide stakeholder consultation to inform new proposals on degraded forest and community wasteland management (NABARD 2019, 36). NABARD also supported the opening of the new Climate Change Centre (established in 2018) at the Bankers Institute of Rural Development, Lucknow. The Climate Change Centre is meant to support climate-related projects, to help build climate change capacity for NABARD officials, other banks, NGOs, farmers, and state governments, promote research, and to prepare policy documents and briefs (NABARD 2019, 37). Finally, as illustrated in the Epilogue, this too has allowed the NABARD to push forward with rural Covid-19 support mechanisms since early 2020. As significant as these acquired definancialisation functions are, the NABARD has also overseen otherwise exploitative financial practices, notably with India's microfinance revolution (addressed later).

5.2.2 The Bank of North Dakota

The United States is a global hegemonic powerhouse with a population of over 328 million people. According to World Bank data, its

2018 GDP was \$20.54 trillion and GNI per capita \$63,170. The Bank of North Dakota (BND) is the sole subnational state-level public bank therein, and it too has been built up around a distinctly state spatial strategy. By functioning through North Dakota's public sphere, the BND slows and 'fixes' otherwise mobile finance capital within its state's border. It is this institutional reproductive logic that tends to guide BND operations, not global financial mobility or shareholder value, even though it is located within the deeply 'financialised' society of the United States.

5.2.2.1   History and Current Structure of the BND

The BND exists and persists in an almost aberration-like situation within the archetypical 'liberal market economy' of the United States. Posed in opposition to 'coordinated market economies' like Germany and Japan, the American advanced capitalist economy is characterised by hyper-competitive and globally mobile institutions and corporations within a predominantly market-based financial system that has become extraordinarily significant, even world-defining, since the 1990s (Hall and Soskice 2001, 2009; Harmes 2001; Konings 2018). Therein, American finance capital is known for its giant 'too-big-to-fail' banks, including JP Morgan, Bank of America, Citigroup, Wells Fargo, Goldman Sachs, and Morgan Stanley that have combined assets of over \$10 trillion (cf. Panitch and Gindin 2012; Neuhann and Saidi 2018). Yet the American financial system also has a historically more fragmented banking sector made up of numerous smaller local commercial, community, savings, and development banks that function at nowhere near a global scale (Minsky et al. 1993). Each state has dozens, if not hundreds, of independent and cooperative banks. In the State of North Dakota there is one of the highest numbers of local banks per capita in the United States. Such is the context in which the BND exists persists today – a century-old state-level public bank that functions according to a unique mix of development (on-lending to local banks and development finance) and commercial bank functions (like personal savings, student loans, wire transfers, and so on) yet without an extended branch network.

Its historic foundations are important, and particular. The Bank of North Dakota was born out of an early nineteenth century progressive political movement. The socialist-influenced Non-Partisan League had built up strong popular support for its pro-public stance on the local economy and for its calls to democratise North Dakota's agriculture-based economy. The message connected with early settlers, many of whom were farmers and immigrants from Europe and who were familiar with cooperative and public service movements. A prime motivating political force behind the idea of a North Dakotan public bank, however, was the resentment the community had over the monopoly power of out-of-state banks, grain dealers, and large corporations that overcharged on interest and underpaid for grain (Kodrzycki and Elmatad 2011, 5; Lessambo 2019, 140). For decades, growing mortgage debts in the American Midwest had been pressurising farmers into increasingly marketised social reproduction, that is, having to produce more to sell in order to survive, transferring increasing proportions of their meagre wealth to financiers (McNally 2020, 186).[4] More and more, farmers and workers wanted to exercise economic control over local agricultural and banking matters. To them, the Non-Partisan League's idea of founding the Bank of North Dakota made sense. Within months of coming to power in late 1918, the Non-Partisan League had created the Bank of North Dakota in early 1919 and capitalised it with an initial $2 million bond sale. At the same time, the new government created the North Dakota Mill and Elevator Association (it, like the BND, continues operations as the only publicly owned mill in the United States). To govern the new public bank and mill, the Non-Partisan League established the Industrial Commission, a three-member board composed of the state

---

[4] It is important to also not over-romanticise early settler farmer communities. Undoubtedly, narratives of white yeoman farmers overcoming the travails of first settlement and then standing up to big city bankers can obscure the financing of 'accumulation by dispossession' by white farmers of indigenous peoples from their lands, a narrative returned to later in terms of recent oil and pipeline struggles in North Dakota.

governor (as chair), attorney general, and agriculture commissioner, which reports back to the North Dakota Legislature (this governance structure remains to this day).

The first years of BND operations, however, faced unyielding resistance from private banks and a Wall Street boycott (Hanna 2018a, that 21). The Government of North Dakota had planned on selling additional bonds as a means of funding the bank's early lending initiatives. However, the coordinated opposition by private bankers meant that the bonds went unsold and that the BND remained under-funded. During these first years opposition politicians, in coordination with the bankers, led a political campaign against the BND, charging it with favouritism. In 1921 the Non-Partisan League suffered a recall vote with the state legislature and the BND subsequently came under control of the opposition. Ironically, the change in government came just days after a tranche of BND bonds were finally sold, providing the BND with a much-needed $12.3 million capital injection. The incoming opposition party did not, however, shutter the nascent public institution. Instead, the new government opted to maintain banking capacity within the state's public sphere. The BND thus renewed lending to farmers. Between 1921 and 1932, it made 16,482 farm loans totalling $39.6 million (BND 1970, 15).

North Dakota then entered a period of difficult economic times. Regional drought and the coming 1930s Great Depression hammered the predominantly farming-based community. However, rather than making 'time' available for those farmers in distress, the opposition party oversaw Bank of North Dakota foreclosures on 6,500 farmers unable to repay their loans (BND 1970, 15). As economic crisis and foreclosures intensified, however, the Non-Partisan League came back to power. The new governor banned all new property foreclosures as long as the farmers were living on the land. Given the political will, the BND now allowed foreclosed farmers 'to stay on their land and repurchase it when *times* improved' (BND 2018, 13; emphasis added). Quite literally, the BND made 'time' available and gave farmers the chance to get their lives back in order, thus displacing the immediate impact of the economic crisis into the future (much like the Covid-19 pandemic emergency programmes; see Epilogue; cf. Konings 2018). US President Roosevelt's New Deal program (1933–39) and World War II would eventually lift North Dakota and the United States out of economic depression and into a period of expansionism.

In the decades following World War II, the Bank of North Dakota persisted but more quietly so. It functioned largely as a commercial public depository institution for the state and its public enterprises and services. In the late 1960s the BND initiated a student loan programme intending that 'no North Dakotan is denied further education because financial assistance is lacking' (BND 1970, 3). By the 1970s, it had evolved to include residential housing services, including support for specific, often vulnerable, communities (for example, for the elderly, retired, infirm, and veterans) (BND 1970, 2). Industrial development remained a core priority, as the BND provided both cheaper financing and technical expertise within the state (BND 1970, 10). Since the late 1950s, moreover, the BND began purchasing municipal and school bonds as a way of funding essential infrastructure (it also lent directly to public schools) (BND 1970, 11).

In 1979 the Volcker shock witnessed US prime interest rates extend to over 20 per cent alongside US President Reagan's turn to neoliberal marketisation (Strange 1994). The BND responded to the high-interest context and its disproportionate impact on farmers, businesses, students, and households by offering below prime interest rates and targeted subsidies (BND 1980, 9–13). That is, the BND mediated the space between national financial markets and local ones. The BND continued to lend to the public sector, including special loans programmes for nursing and old age homes as well as for community water facilities (BND 1980, 16). The coming neoliberal revolution, however, would affect how the BND institutionally reproduced itself within the public sphere. The BND began to rebrand its operations as in cooperation, not competition, with the private sector (BND 1980, 4). Since then, the BND has tended to emphasise its on-lending support for private local banks within North Dakota, facilitating and 'fixing' private money capital within the state's borders.

In its over 100 years of operation, the BND has retained the three-member Industrial Commission as the institution's highest decision-making body. The North Dakota Legislature (of which the Industrial Commission is a part), however, has deciding influence over the BND budget, staff, and salaries, major capital projects, and BND transfers to the state budget (Kodrzycki and Elmatad 2011, 9). In 1969 the BND incorporated a legally constituted advisory board of directors within its governance framework. The seven-member board is appointed by the governor, based on expertise in banking and finance. The board reviews BND operations and offers recommendations on management, services, policies, and procedures to the Industrial Commission. In this way, the BND has a representative democratic governance structure.

5.2.2.2   *The BND and Definancialisation*

Existing and persisting within the public sphere, the BND has a co-constituted and dynamic relationship with the State of North Dakota. This public sphere 'anchor' provides the material and institutional basis of the bank's definancialisation function of 'fixing' globally mobile finance capital locally. Notably, the BND benefits from public sources of capital and financial guarantees. Much like the NABARD, public sector deposits and receipts offer a recurrent supply of loanable capital, shaping the core reproductive strategy of the institution. In its own words, the BND is 'the depository for all of the state tax revenue. Upon receipt of tax revenues, the Bank exercises a variety of investment and loan strategies to enhance the Bank's profits' (BND 2016, 16). North Dakotan public assets thus directly support BND operations. In turn, this constitutes a material backstop to the BND's Aaa credit rating (S&P 2019). Ratings agencies expect that should the BND suffer financial difficulties, it will be supported by the North Dakotan state – a state that is backed by annual tax receipts and has access to US federal government support.

Table 5.3. *BND operational data, 2013–18*

	2013	2014	2015	2016	2017	2018
Total assets (billion USD)	6.87	7.22	7.41	7.30	7.00	7.02
Net profit after tax (million USD)	94.2	111.0	130.7	136.2	145.3	158.5
ROAE	18.56	18.43	18.64	16.76	17.09	18.80
ROAA	1.45	1.58	1.79	1.85	2.03	2.26

Source: BankFocus (Data update 1717 – 01/04/2020)

The State of North Dakota and the public sphere in turn benefit from the institutional and material persistence of the BND. Table 5.3 illustrates operational data for the BND from 2013 to 2018. As the ultimate owner, the government is paid annual dividends as a return on its investment (like the Nordic Investment Bank; see Chapter 5). For example, from 1971 to 2009, Federal Reserve (Boston) economists calculate that BND transfers of profits were equivalent to 0.75 per cent of state expenditures on average (Kodrzycki and Elmatad 2011, 9). This inflow of money into state coffers allows for greater flexibility in public policy and revenue management. BND President and Chief Executive Officer Eric Hardmeyer writes, 'Taxes are lower because the Bank's profits are returned to the general fund under the direction of the Legislature. Profits support infrastructure needs and disaster relief' (BND 2018, 4–5). Should legislators require it, moreover, the BND can pay-out higher dividends to the state to cover fiscal shortfalls or exceptional financial needs (BND 2016, 4). This public benefit builds with time. Since its first pay-out in 1945, the BND has earned cumulative returns of $1.8 billion and paid out over $1.02 billion in dividends (BND 2018, 11). The difference between what it has earned and paid out has allowed the BND to build up its own mass of financial capital and strengthen its institutional capacity to borrow externally and lend internally (BND 2018, 12). Whether BND returns stay in the bank or go the public purse, they remain 'fixed' within North Dakotan territory and subject to legislative oversight in very 'unfinancialised' ways.

The return profile of the BND is a result of many supportive factors, from its own management of its lending and investments to its lower cost of funds and operating costs. For example, the BND is tax exempt (federally and at the state level) because it is a governmental agency, that is, an entity located within the public sphere of North Dakota (BND 2018, 35). The BND business model is largely based on a classic intermediation role, with over 70 per cent of its balance sheet being loans, which provide a steady return on assets (Kodrzycki and Elmatad 2011, 8). Whereas the financialisation literature on the United States highlights the turn of banks to fee-generated income, this is not the case with the BND (cf. Lapavitsas 2009). In 2019, only about 3 per cent of revenue is fee based, with the other 97 per cent being based on interest rate spreads (S&P 2019, 6). Add to this that the BND resists exorbitant executive wage and bonus packages (Lessambo 2019, 148). In this way, the BND has been made to mitigate structural economic pressures within the US economy to maximise CEO remuneration, which has exacerbated financialisation (Hanna 2018a, 54; cf. Mishel and Bivens 2013; Mazzucato 2018).

In its way of lending, the BND loan portfolio is diversified but structured by its mandate and the historical economic context in which it reproduces itself. Commercial and business lending tends to account for over 40 per cent (this includes lending to public services), student loans around a quarter, followed by agricultural and residential lending averaging around 15 per cent each, give or take a few points (BND 2018, 18). About half of the BND loan portfolio consists of loan participations and loan purchases from local community banks (Kodrzycki and Elmatad 2011, 8). Much like the NABARD, the BND mandate facilitates the channelling and 'fixing' of finance capital into a defined geographical area, North Dakota.

A cumulative result is that North Dakota has one of the most diversified local banking sectors in the United States. The Institute for Local Self-Reliance reports that the state has more banks and credit unions per capita than anywhere else in the United States, and that the BND has been the key to sustaining such small-scale diversity

(Mitchell 2012). This is because the BND partners with local banks (Brown 2019, 145). The local banks can originate loans and then sell them to the BND or they can participate in tandem with the BND on a loan. The practice bolsters the viability of small local banks within an otherwise financialised US market, stemming the incursion of larger banking giants into the state's financial sector. That is, the centralisation and concentration of financial capital into larger and more powerful institutions, endemic to global financialised capitalism, is slowed or even halted by an 'originate and distribute' model mediated by the BND in the state's public sphere. In turn, local banks help to sustain the rural economy. Barry D. Haugen, President of the Independent Community Banks of North Dakota association, writes: '[c]ommunity banks are vital to the financial success of rural America, particularly as it relates to agricultural lending. Nowhere is that more true than in our state ... Critical to the ability to fund diverse needs is Bank of North Dakota's very important partnership with these local community banks' (quoted in BND 2016, 6). The BND mediates, slows, and fixes the flows of finance capital in the state.

It too has an important role enabling public infrastructure. Since the 1960s the BND has extended greater support to North Dakota's municipalities, public schools, hospitals, and municipal water facilities. The BND does so while providing an institutional conduit for other state, federal, and North Dakota Legislature loan programmes, including from the US Department of Agriculture Community Water Loan Program, the Infrastructure Revolving Loan Fund, and the School Construction Loans (BND 2017, 8). The BND has recently identified two strategic public interest initiatives: the expansion of municipal infrastructure financing and the provisioning of affordable housing support (2017, 14). Blake Crosby, Executive Director of the North Dakota League of Cities, writes on the BND that 'the ability to access capital for infrastructure projects such as water towers, water mains, sewer lines, street/road construction and medical and school facility construction has been vital' (quoted in BND 2016, 10). Jon Martinson, Executive Director, North Dakota School Boards

Association continues, 'Thanks to Bank of North Dakota, school districts have been able to access low-interest construction loans to address their facility needs that resulted from the dramatic rapid growth in enrollment over the past few years' (in BND 2016, 13). A 2019 independent report by the Northeast-Midwest Institute recommends that US states in the region take seriously the capacity of public banks to address critical investment gaps and to realign 'state resources with state interests' (Leder Macek 2019, 2). That is, public banks can play an important role in realising state development strategies. This can be done in ways contrary to financialised World Bank messages urging public finance to align with private investors' needs (World Bank/IMF 2015).

It is important to signal, if it were not already obvious, that alternative financial capacity cannot be built overnight. At critical moments and at times of emergency, public banks must already be in place and functioning. In North Dakota, residents have benefitted recurrently from the existing accumulated capital, institutional expertise, and culture of the BND. This began early on when facing systemic crises like the Great Depression. It extends to particular moments. For example, in the 1970s the private Pioneer State Bank of Towner collapsed, and the BND stepped in to provide emergency community financial services (BND 2018, 13). In response to the nationwide (and global) 1979 Volcker shock, the BND responded with the PACE (Partnerships Assisting Community Expansion) stimulus programme and the Beginning Farmer Loan programme (BND 1980, 2018, 13). When the 2007 US sub-prime crisis morphed into the 2008–09 global financial crisis and as private banks withheld lending and banking giants collapsed, the BND expanded loans and credit lines to local banks and businesses within North Dakota, helping the state to avoid the worst impacts of the crisis (Kodrzycki and Elmatad 2011, 4; Lessambo 2019, 146–48). The BND has also responded to unpredictable natural disasters. When North Dakota suffered a massive flood in 1997, the BND quickly extended emergency funding to support the state, farms, and families. It did so again during flooding in 2011, unrolling a low-interest, disaster loan programme (Industrial Commission of North Dakota 2011). When drought struck in 2017, the BND collaborated with the State Governor and the Department of Agriculture to create another disaster relief programme (BND 2017, 13). In the spring of 2020, as private banks struggled to support households and communities due to their risk-return constraints, the BND both facilitated federal government Covid-19 responses and provided its own bank-led support programmes (see Epilogue). Scholars and civil society organisations have pointed to such BND actions to substantiate the need for more alternative public and cooperative bank capacity within the American context (Hanna 2018a; Brown 2019; Leder Macek 2019; Marois and Güngen 2019). In effect, the BND has been made to 'definancialise' the otherwise destabilising tendencies of financialisation on North Dakotan society. This has not been without pitfalls and contradictions, but it does highlight how alternative and definancialised public bank capacity can exist and persist as credible even within financialisation.

5.3 CONTRADICTING DEFINANCIALISATION

The National Bank for Agriculture and Rural Development (NABARD) and the Bank of North Dakota (BND) persist as credible public banks within class-divided society but not without operational contradictions that need to be recognised and addressed. With the Indian public bank, NABARD, one of its most striking contradictions involves the role it has played since the early 1990s in the promotion of microfinance and financial inclusion (as basically interlinked strategies). Highlighting this paradox, researchers Premchander and Chidambaranatham asked in 2007 why advocates of microfinance do not invest in improving India's *already existing* financial institutions, that is, India's rural commercial, regional rural banks, cooperatives, and so on, many of which are public (2007, 1007; cf. Shetty 2009). The authors challenged NABARD's ostensibly *neoliberal* support for a market-oriented and competitive microfinance model, warning that continuing this trajectory will undermine India's advances in rural banking and women's empowerment. Within a few years in 2010, India suffered a dramatic microfinance crisis (see Taylor 2017).

The World Bank's 2014 *Global Financial Development Report* on financial inclusion framed the 2010 microfinance crisis in India in more frank than usual terms: 'Because of a rapid growth in loans, India's microfinance institutions were able to report high profitability for years, but this resided on large indebtedness among clients' (World Bank 2014, 2). The 2010 crisis stemmed from profit-oriented and profit-maximising microfinance institutions giving too much credit too fast as a strategy of financial accumulation concentrated on rural, poorer regions (Taylor 2012; Mader 2013). In effect, India's microfinance cum financial inclusion plan was (and is) a class-based strategy of financialisation that involves owners of money capital extracting wealth from the working poor. It is a strategy of accumulation premised on channelling money from the capital poor to the capital rich.

The NABARD, as steward of 'financial inclusion' in India, and the state authorities that made it do so hold responsibility. Since the 1990s, the NABARD has facilitated the making of the world's largest microfinance 'movement' (NABARD 2019, 49; cf. NABARD 2014, 2017). The Indian microfinance movement includes 100 million households, 8.5 million self-help groups, $2.5 billion in deposits, $6 billion annual credit flows, and $9 billion in outstanding loans (Amalorpavanathan 2017a, 7). The NABARD functions to offer 100 per cent refinancing to partner banks; give grant support to partner banks and to NGOs for training, capacity-building, and group promotion; train self-help group members in bookkeeping and micro-enterprise promotion; promote joint liability groups; and to help some private microfinance institutions to borrow from banks (Amalorpavanathan 2017a, 8). Building on its accumulated capital and expertise in rural finance, the NABARD has been catalytic to the rise of microfinance in India. This has entailed households internalising more marketised financial relations in order to survive (not unlike the build-up of farm mortgage debts in North Dakota).

The NABARD's flagship microfinance programme is the Self Help Group-Bank Linkage Programme (SHG-BLP), first piloted in 1992. According to the NABARD, the SHG-BLP organises the poor, mostly women, into groups and then links the groups to formal banks for credit facilities (NABARD 2005, 40; 2019, 49). The NABARD programme aims to help people avoid working directly with private microfinance institutions, which typically charge higher rates of interest and more strictly enforce repayment, sometimes brutally so (Premchander and Chidambaranatham 2007, 1006). Evidence suggests that, in comparison to dealing directly with private microfinance, the NABARD approach demonstrates tangible benefits that mitigate the worst of coercive market pressure (Rajeev et al. 2020). Whereas private microfinance providers charge no less than 24 per cent, often more, NABARD programmes charge 12 per cent. NABARD members nevertheless commit to paying a 24 per cent rate, but the additional 12 per cent becomes income for the group, not a private lender. Research also points to the non-economic social benefits attached to the NABARD SHG-BLP, such as enabling women participants to leave the home, visit banks outside their communities, and gain confidence speaking with officials, all of which enhanced their social status. This mirrors other claims of microfinance enabling women's empowerment and gender equity in India, particularly in terms of non-economic benefits (Kabeer 2005; Tiwari 2013).

Yet it may be the case that the NABARD programme does not go far enough in mitigating 'financialisation' and financial exploitation. Appropriate credit and lending programmes need to be stable and sufficient enough to enable the economic transformation desired (in a household, firm, or economy). Most NABARD-linked banks, however, tend *not* to lend sufficiently to cover the required demand of an individual (Rajeev et al. 2020, 177). This has had the contradictory effect of then pushing NABARD-linked borrowers into the hands of the more exploitative private microfinance institutions. As one perverse consequence, the burden of non-repayment then tends to fall back on to the formal, often public, NABARD-backed, and less exploitative lenders by virtue of not being as predatory and as coercive as the private micro-lenders that force borrowers to repay them first. This undermines not only the financial sustainability of public banks (bolstering neoclassical political view demands for privatisation), but it also paints a flawed image of private sector efficiency as households, especially women, cannibalise public sector resources for private profitability ends (public sector resources that otherwise disproportionately benefit women in the greatest need of public provisioning of essential public services; see Spronk and Miraglia 2015). The contradiction strengthens the hand of neoliberal reformers seeking the commercialisation and privatisation of the NABARD and other public banks in India.

So while the NABARD has facilitated microfinance across the sector, generating systemic problems, it has at the same time developed internal programmes that counter the most exploitative practices of for-profit private microfinance institutions. It is doubtful that NABARD's internal SHG-BLP will overcome the structural criticisms of microfinance and financial inclusion strategies in India and around the world (Weber 2004; Bateman 2010; Soederberg 2013). According to the 2011 Duvendack systematic review of the microfinance evidence, the developmental benefits of microfinance are based on 'foundations of sand' (see Duvendack et al. 2011, 75). Microfinance programmes, moreover, have tended to instrumentalise poor women to facilitate neoliberal capital expansion, justify profit-maximisation as a poverty alleviation plan, worsen class-based inequality, generate recurrent instability, and do remarkably little to overcome poverty and underdevelopment (Premchander and Chidambaranatham 2007; Duffy-Tumasz 2009; MacLean 2012; Bateman 2017; Taylor 2017). Within Indian households and communities, the push to make all women their own 'micro-entrepreneurs' has exacerbated competition over scarce resources and markets, causing women to have to work longer and harder to repay high-interest loans, with the impact being increased class- and caste-based inequality reinforcing the 'financiali-sation' of social reproduction in India (Morgan and Olsen 2011; Ghosh 2013). The NABARD SHG-BLP can mitigate but cannot elim-inate these problems of neoliberal financial inclusion strategies. While Rajeev et al. (2020) identify the public option as superior to the private, there remain structural problems of income, poverty, exploitation, and gender – all of which need strategic economic planning and democratic decision-making to overcome.

The contradictions of the US-based Bank of North Dakota (BND) are less researched. In many ways, the challenge of the BND is to persist as a credible public institution within a financialised American society (although the extent of privatisation of US public services is often exaggerated; see Hanna 2018a). This manifests in a particular narrative of institutional reproduction wherein the BND does not aim to compete with private commercial banks within North Dakota (although, it explicitly helps private banks within North Dakota outcompete out-of-state banks). In an interview given in the wake of the 2008–09 global financial crisis, President of the Bank of North Dakota, Eric Hardmeyer, responded to a question about the replicability of the BND in other US states:[5]

> Every state has their own particular needs. We've carved out a
> pretty good niche here and I think are well-respected by our peers in
> the banking industry. They look at us as partners and not
> competitors. That would be the key if you were to do this in any
> other state is to replicate that part of our model. That's where you
> really open yourself up for criticism, is state-owned businesses
> competing with the private sector.

In ways particular to its US context, the persistence and credibility of the BND depends on a conservative pact of non-competitiveness

---

[5] See www.motherjones.com/politics/2009/03/how-nations-only-state-owned-bank-became-envy-wall-street/. Accessed 3 June 2020.

with private banks (that is, on pure 'additionality' criteria in Keynesian terms). This has had influence outside of North Dakota. Perhaps like nowhere else in the world, the United States is home to a nationwide, grassroots, and bottom-up public banking movement. Alternative citizen and political movements have formed around campaigns of creating public banks in the public interest. Initially this was in response to the impact of the global financial crisis (Brown 2013). Increasingly, however, the public banking movement has adopted a more pro-active programme around public service financial support, affordable housing, municipal funding, financing a green new deal, and, as of spring 2020, responding to the Covid-19 pandemic. The movement builds off local activist traditions within the United States around financial alternatives. Since 2010, the Public Banking Institute (PBI) has been at the centre of demands for public banking alternatives, supported in large part by the work of its founder, Ellen Brown. As of June 2020, the PBI reports that there are at least twenty-five public banking initiatives underway, that thirty US states have proposed legislation in support of public banks, and that there are over fifty organisations promoting public banks.[6] The movement gained momentum after California Governor, Gavin Newsom, signed into law the Public Banking Act (AB 857) in 2019, which allows state authorities to create or sponsor public banks. The idea is that public banks will support public agencies with lower interest loans and better terms than those offered by private banks. A typical accompanying narrative has been one of non-competition for commercial services and partnership with private banks (see Schneiberg 2013, 297–98). It is not, however, universally accepted. A 2016 New York-based Roosevelt Institute report on municipal public banks

---

[6] See www.publicbankinginstitute.org/local-efforts-by-state/. Accessed 3 June 2020. See the City of Santa Fe, New Mexico, task force for an account of creating public banks in the United States (SFPBTF 2018, appendix A).

advocates public banks competing with private banks to generate public returns, a practice common among most public banks around the world.

The contradiction in the making is that after struggling to create new public banks in the United States, these public banks will be made subordinate to profit-making strategies of private banks. An important space for public banks servicing public entities will be potentially opened, but the potential of public banks to build up their own mass of capital and expertise will be constrained. The non-competitiveness strategy enables the fortification of private banks' financial and political power, which is often then mobilised in neoliberalism to undercut public sector priorities and services through public–private partnerships (PPPs) and outright privatisation.

The BND also illustrates how representative governance structures can endorse otherwise repressive state measures. In 2016 the BND provided nearly $10 million in loans to beef up North Dakota police and security force efforts to stamp out the indigenous Standing Rock protests and Sioux First Nations resistance against the construction of the Dakota Access pipeline by Energy Transfer Partners. How the partially BND-financed security forces treated the peaceful protestors was roundly condemned as 'inhuman' and 'degrading', including by the United Nations.[7] The finance support given by the BND is an expression of how public banks internalise contending public and private interests in class-divided society. According to one commentator:[8]

---

[7] M. Bearak, 'U.N. Officials Denounce "Inhuman" Treatment of Native American Pipeline Protesters', *The Washington Post*, 15 November 2016, Available at www .washingtonpost.com/news/worldviews/wp/2016/11/15/u-n-officials-denounce-inhuman-treatment-of-north-dakota-pipeline-protesters/. Accessed 21 July 2020.

[8] M. Stannard, 'North Dakota's Public Bank Was Built for the People – Now It's Financing Police at Standing Rock', *yes!*, 14 December 2016. Available at www .yesmagazine.org/democracy/2016/12/14/north-dakotas-public-bank-was-built-for-the-people-now-its-financing-police-at-standing-rock/. Accessed 21 July 2020.

North Dakota's leadership has bound the state's economy up so tightly in fossil fuels that it has forced itself to subsidize the security costs of energy companies. In fact, the energy industry has come to expect subsidization for its costs and easy externalization of its negative impacts.

Through the Industrial Commission, the BND became an instrument of North Dakota's fossil fuel strategy and in turn of private carbonising capital. Inadvertently or not, the BND also took on as its own the interests of the ten large private banks already funding the pipeline.[9] The incident points to the pitfalls of public banks being (more or less democratically) charged with enabling otherwise repressive political measures. Neoliberals would no doubt draw from this the need to depoliticise public banks via privatisation. This is an absurd line of thinking since it would simply expand the mass of private and unaccountable bank capital free to fund pipelines and carbonising growth, thus solving nothing. It does, nonetheless, point to the need for *substantive* democratisation of public banks, including full transparency and meaningful accountability.

The NABARD and the BND are dynamic expressions of sociopolitical responses to the exigencies of class-divided capitalist development. Not without contradictions, the two cases demonstrate that public banks can be made to counter market imperatives and contemporary financialisation. States can build up material and institutional expertise within the public sphere, and deploy these within their borders in myriad ways that do not need to conform to market imperatives or 'failures' alone. Public banks can and do definancialise contemporary social reproduction by slowing and fixing capital. There are enormous benefits to be realised from maintaining and extending this

---

[9] Indigenous Environmental Network, '10 Banks Financing Dakota Access Pipeline Decline Meeting with Tribal Leaders', n.d. Available at www.ienearth.org/10-banks-financing-dakota-access-pipeline-decline-meeting-with-tribal-leaders/. Accessed 21 July 2020.

public financial capacity (not least of which is decarbonisation). But it is not without risks and contradictions. There is no essentially 'good' or 'pro-public' orientation to public banks as they are subject to contending and evolving public and private power dynamics. In order to maximise the definancialisation (and decarbonisation) potential of public banks in the public interest, these financial institutions must also be democratised.

6   Democratisation

The democratisation of finance stands alongside definancialisation and decarbonisation as one of the great challenges of our times. In the wake of the 2008–09 global financial crisis, in light of the global crisis of climate finance, and as we face the fallout of the global Covid-19 pandemic, civil society and non-governmental organisations have demanded, and must have, more say over the world's tremendously significant, but mostly unaccountable and obscure, public and private financial institutions and regulatory structures. Yet aside from general demands and laudable principles, there are few concrete, evidence-based, and actionable alternative strategies being put forward that diverge from mainstream corporate governance and financialised approaches. Much of this is the consequence of forty years of neoliberal marketisation and corporatisation processes seeking to expose all financial institutions to competitive profit imperatives and privatisation free of popular oversight. It is also the result, however, of the inability of social forces and organised labour to resist market-oriented restructuring. Critics of neoliberalism and financialisation have collectively fumbled the challenge of delivering viable and desirable financial alternatives.

How existing public banks are democratised can begin to address this lacuna. It is a topic, though, somewhat unlike that of definancialisation and decarbonisation. Democratisation is not about mobilising finance for any particular development project or strategy per se. Rather, democratisation is about the rights of citizens, workers, women, popular classes, and the most marginalised to *command* a representative, meaningful, free, prior, informed, binding, and accountable say over how public banks use public resources to tackle common challenges. It is about having the collective ability to bring societal needs to the foreground of economic planning (Lefebvre 2016 [1972], 132). It means combining economic power with political power, democratically. Democratisation is the opposite of neoliberal governance and corporatisation frameworks, which promote ideals of market discipline to prevent 'the people' from having a say over how the economy and banks function. It runs counter to the practices of global 'financialisation', which, as political economist Servaas Storm observes, is 'difficult to reconcile with any acceptable definition of democracy' (2018, 309). The democratisation of public banks is an existential challenge to neoliberal market-based discipline as unquestionable best practice. It is a challenge whose time has come.

Through the lens of democratisation, this chapter continues to examine how public banks can function in the public interest, if not without contradictions. Looking at the cases of Germany's KfW and Costa Rica's Banco Popular, I argue that their ways of democratisation support their institutional credibility, and hence persistence. In distinct but meaningful ways, the KfW and Banco Popular enable their societies to have a meaningful say over how these public banks function. In contrast to decarbonisation and definancialisation, however, democratisation has a more disproportionately and self-evident public interest and purpose effect. Yet it is not a completed act wherein these public banks are democratised once and for all. Democratisation, too, is pulled between contending public and private interests in class-divided society. The chapter proceeds as follows. It first relates the problem of democracy within the finance for development literature. The chapter then turns to the German and Costa Rican cases, which make up the bulk of the chapter. This is followed by some reflections on the contradictions of democratisation in global financialised capitalism.

6.1 THE PROBLEM OF DEMOCRATISING FINANCE

The finance for development and economics literature has been largely uninterested in exploring expressions of public bank democratisation. Instead, inquiries into the ways of decision-making are almost always limited to prefigured and technical understandings of corporate governance, which are steeped in ideological commitments to orthodox market discipline (Shirley 1999). Governance therein is meant (a) to improve market-based financial performance and returns and (b) to ensure that public bank mandates do not drift away from targeting 'market failures' or towards the crowding out of private banks (Scott 2007). This neoliberal narrative prefigures public banks as best being subjected to market competition in order to impose 'discipline on the management' (Rudolph 2009, 3).

Emblematically, orthodox political view adherents and neoliberal advocates dismiss even the possibility of effective democratic control, believing that public ownership and popular control distort otherwise efficient markets and just allocations of resources (Fama 1970; Shleifer 1998). It is claimed that public banks (without ever really assessing their democratic structures) inevitably lead to the 'politicization' of economic decisions, governmental abuse, and systemic inefficiencies (Shleifer 1998; La Porta et al. 2002; Marcelin and Mathur 2015; see Chapter 2). The underlying ideological framework builds upon an a priori faith in the self-serving and self-maximising behaviour of individuals (Buchanan 1999; see Arnsperger and Varoufakis 2006). In a political view, corruption is embedded in the essence of public ownership (Barth et al. 2006; Calomiris and Haber 2014). Over the last thirty to forty years the World Bank and IMF have shepherded finance for development policy and practice in this orthodox direction (World Bank 2001, 2012a; Mishkin 2009; IMF 2020). It is now neoliberal common sense that political interventions within economic institutions are to be avoided and that economic democracy is an impractical and naïve policy unworkable in the real world. To read the finance for development debate, you would think it even unspeakable.

It is hard to underestimate the powerful influence of this neoliberal logic of governance. In 2007, just as the 2008–09 global financial crisis was about to explode, former US Federal Reserve Chair Alan Greenspan responded to a question about his preferred presidential candidate by saying that we 'are fortunate that, thanks to globalisation, policy decisions in the US have been largely replaced by global market forces. National security aside, it hardly makes any difference who will be the next president. *The world is governed by market forces*.[1] While Greenspan exaggerates the case, it is important to understand that this is the idealised goal of neoliberal idealism, which advocates attempt to put into practice. For example, when World Bank economist, Kemal Derviş, was brought in as an unelected minister of the economy to spearhead Turkey's response to its 2001 financial crisis, his policy goal was to 'separate the economic from the political' (see Marois 2012, 168). The problem of democracy within neoliberal worldviews and finance for development debate is not how its practiced but that it is.

Keynesian economists and heterodox development views on public banks have tended to be more ambiguous on economic democratisation. It is common to advocate for growth-oriented political interventions as part and parcel of state-led development. On average, though, statist strategies of development need not be related to democracy to be desirable (Selwyn 2014). The main concern is economic growth and capitalist stability. This framework is influenced by Weberian conceptions of elite state authority that has tended to accept top-down and authoritarian political interventions as an effective growth mechanism (Rostow 1971; Johnson 1982; Öniş 1991; Erdoğdu 2004; cf. Mazzucato 2015, 47). It is not that democratisation is an inherently naïve ambition, as per orthodoxy, but that it is not necessary. Any number of 'second-best' governance arrangements might reasonably achieve comparable or superior developmental ends (cf. Rodrik 2008). Critics, however, point out that such elitism has resulted in anti-democratic and socially repressive developmental regimes (Boyd and Ngo 2005; Pringle 2011; Chang 2013).

---

[1] Quoted in Adam Tooze, 'Beyond the Crash', *The Guardian*, 29 July 2018. Emphasis added.

Since the 2008–09 global financial crisis, heterodox views have exercised growing influence within development finance policy forums (see Griffith-Jones and Ocampo 2018; UNCTAD 2019; FiC 2020; Griffith-Jones and te Velde 2020). This is despite having little to contribute on public bank governance and democratisation. In general, heterodox economists acknowledge that there is 'no literature [that] specifically aims to address the problems of the governance of public banks' (Levy Yeyati et al. 2007, 246).[2] Rather, the tendency has been to accept and reproduce neoliberal corporatisation maxims around the necessity of institutional independence, depoliticisation, and non-political appointments to boards of governors. This stance, however, never really accounts for the dozens of public banks with political appointments enabling democratic representation and accountability.

We can see this within the important contributions of Keynesian economist Marianna Mazzucato. Mazzucato has extended her 'entrepreneurial state' and 'mission-oriented' innovation framework to call for increased support for and by public development and investment banks (see Mazzucato 2015; Mazzucato and Penna 2016, 2018; Mazzucato and Semieniuk 2017). The framework fuses ideas of Keynes and Schumpeter, emphasising the importance of state interventions and the potential of public development banks to contribute not only to overcome market failures but also to market-making. Mazzucato's work has become very influential in economic policy-making circles, internationally and nationally. Yet her work on public banks has yet to engage substantively with democratisation or the governance of public banks. This gap prevails despite earlier work stressing the importance of democracy to finance and development. In a 2013 article, for example, Mazzucato writes that 'precisely because *publicly* funded patient capital is so important, it is

---

[2] There are notable exceptions. Researchers linked more closely to institutional political economy and historical institutionalism have delved more into the case study dynamics of public bank governance and issues of democratisation (for example, von Mettenheim and Del Tedesco Lins 2008; von Mettenheim and Butzbach 2014; Scherrer 2017).

important to make sure that the direction of that funding be *intensely* and *democratically* debated' (2013, 857; emphasis added). This important warning, one of Mazzucato's strongest statements on democratisation, does not appear to be elaborated on further in subsequent publications on public banks. A 2017 article, based more broadly on mission-oriented innovation and the public sector, raises issues of governance and democracy (Kattel and Mazzucato 2018) and a 2018 policy report describes the basic governance frameworks of a few state investment and development banks (Macfarlane and Mazzucato 2018). In the latter, the authors move little beyond corporate governance messages, arguing that while 'political representation can help to maintain alignment with government policy and maintain a path of democratic accountability, steps should be taken to prevent undue political interference or capture by interest groups' (Macfarlane and Mazzucato 2018, 50).[3] The challenge of interrogating public bank democratisation in practice is one yet to be taken up by most heterodox researchers (see Griffith-Jones and Ocampo 2018).

Heterodox economists are not alone here among critical scholars on finance. Marxian economists and historical materialist scholars have likewise mostly avoided the question of public bank democratisation (and even more so the study of existing public banks) (see Harvey 1999; McNally 2020). Following the global financial crisis, interest resurfaced in public banks as a possible solution to the crises of financialisation. For example, leading Marxian scholar of financialisation, Costas Lapavitsas, writes that 'public banks ought to be democratically run and fully accountable to society as a whole. The boards of public banks ought to have full representation of popular interests, including trades unions and civil society organisations. Their remit ought to be set socially and collectively, their decision-making ought to be transparent, and their activities ought to be

---

[3] That said, recent work by Mazzucato on the importance of engaged citizens informing the missions of public banks holds enormous promise for fostering democratisation (see Mazzucato and Mikheeva 2020).

accountable to elected bodies' (2010, 191). Yet the case study research has not followed. Scholars are in a state of remarkable ignorance around the different ways, for better or worse, that societies and governments govern their public banks – a fact acknowledged even by World Bank economists (De Luna-Martínez and Vicente 2012, 2).

This is not for lack of broad-based demand, concern, or necessity. Debate has been intensifying in civil society around democratising public banks and, in particular, how this relates to equitable public service provisioning and green and just transitions (see Tricarico 2015; Hanna 2018b; Steinfort and Kishimoto 2019). At issue, as Ben Tarnoff of *The Guardian* writes, is that 'public services offer a more equitable way to satisfy basic needs. By taking things off the market, government can democratize access to the resources that people rely on to lead reasonably dignified lives'.[4] Similarly, María José Romero of Eurodad, a Europe-based finance-related civil society organisation, writes on public development banks that 'it is important to recognise that institutions governed on the basis of a truly democratic governance structure should find ways of including other actors – not just governments – in the decision-making process' (Romero 2017, 21). A report by the Civil Society Reflection Group on the 2030 Agenda for Sustainable Development also directly links democracy to public banks and to the realisation of the 2030 UN Sustainable Development Goals (SDGs) (Martens 2017). Through these civil society interventions there is a growing sense of urgency around the democratisation of the public sphere and finance as involving, in the words of geographer David Harvey, substantive means for people to command of the state 'public goods for public purposes' (2012, 88). Public banks, with their combined mass of $49 trillion dollars in capital and over 900 institutions globally, occupies a powerful, if largely underappreciated, potential place therein (see Chapter 1). As Harvey again points out, 'the raw money power wielded by the few

---

[4] 'How Privatization Could Spell the End of Democracy', 21 June 2017, www
.theguardian.com/technology/2017/jun/21/privatizing-public-services-trump-
democracy. Accessed 10 February 2020.

undermines all semblances of democratic governance' (2010, 220). Public banks are in a unique position to offer material and institutional counter-power, if made to do so, wherein the amassed and raw *public* money power and acquired institutional legacies wielded by many societies can provide the foundations of economic democracy for a green and just transition. The ways of public bank democratisation below illustrate how two different societies have crafted their own responses. While imperfect, the cases should be a catalyst for future research into this vital, but under-studied and under-theorised, topic.

6.2 THE WAYS OF DEMOCRATISATION: THE KFW AND THE BANCO POPULAR Y DE DESARROLLO COMUNAL

Democratisation is not a natural way for public banks to be run. There is nothing in public ownership, in and of itself, that offers anything like a guarantee of meaningful representation or accountability. This much should be obvious. There are public banks made to be legally firewalled from direct political involvement (like the state-rescued Royal Bank of Scotland), ones made open to political abuse (like Halkbank in Turkey), and others made to succumb to market rationalities, putting capital accumulation before public interest mandates (like the German IKB and the Spanish *Cajas*). There are also public banks made to operate nothing like this, ones which have rules and regulations that provide meaningful representative oversight and accountability (Butzbach and von Mettenheim 2014; Marois 2016; Scherrer 2017; Vanaerschot 2019). The examples are many. The French Bpifrance Group board features representation from its owner, the French public bank Caisse des Dépôts, alongside representatives from national and regional governments, employees, and other independent representatives. The State Bank of India's board of directors includes not only government appointees and shareholders as directors, but also bank workers, bank management, and up to six other directors that are specialists in cooperatives, the rural economy, or in business, banking, or finance. The Nordic Investment Bank has eight members in its board of directors, each one appointed by its respective member states. The Brazilian

BNDES development bank operates under private law but is supervised by a government minister, has a board dominated by government representatives, and one elected worker representative. There are dozens of examples, with some more and some less democratic representative practices. Admittedly, though, we know little of them. What we do know is that public ownership per se guarantees nothing but that being located within the public sphere nevertheless opens up the possibility of democratisation within democratic societies.

The German KfW and Costa Rican *Banco Popular y de Desarrollo Comunal* (BPDC) illustrate different approaches. Table 6.1 provides a brief overview of these two banks. As with every public bank in this book, I have no wish to idealise either bank or to imply that they exist without contradictions. There are problems, pitfalls, and room for improvement. The aim is rather, from a dynamic view, to situate their democratisation functions as a pro-public element of their institutional credibility and persistence within class-divided society.

6.2.1   Germany's Kreditanstalt für Wiederaufbau (KfW)

Forged at a time of national emergency, the KfW (Kreditanstalt für Wiederaufbau or 'Credit Institute for Reconstruction') is a public development bank, or 'promotional' bank in European Union terminology, whose way of *representative* democratisation contributes to the institution's credibility and persistence within German society and amidst neoliberal financialisation. Democratisation has helped to do so by enabling the KfW to respond to popular demands and to catalyse societal aspirations, including contemporary challenges like climate change and public service provisioning, in the public interest if not independently of the pull of private interests.

6.2.1.1   History and Current Structure of the KfW

The Deutschmark already exists, the Federal Republic is still some months away, as KfW first sees the light of day in Frankfurt am Main. 'Wiederaufbau' [Reconstruction] – a word that from now on will remain part of KfW's name 'Kreditanstalt für Wiederaufbau' – reflects our corporate mission. The National Socialists have left a trail of destruction in their wake. A quarter of the housing stock and a fifth of all industrial and commercial enterprises lie in ruins. Eight million German displaced persons and refugees are living in the three western occupation zones alone. A new and democratic state is now to emerge whose prime task will first of all be to reconstruct the economy and integrate the refugees.[5]

The history of the KfW is important. Founded in 1948, the KfW was conceived of within post–World War II reconstruction efforts. Rather than directly spending the incoming US Marshall Plan funds, the German government created the KfW as a public bank designed to hold the incoming capital, magnify it, and then to redirect it towards post-war economic reconstruction and the refugee crisis. The decision had foresight. Since then, the KfW has become institutionally significant within Germany and, in the process, emerged as one of the largest and most stable national development banks in the world (Hubert and Cochran 2013; Moslener et al. 2018). The global scale of the KfW reflects its position within Germany – an advanced capitalist state at the centre of Europe, politically and economically, with nearly 83 million inhabitants. World Bank data places German 2018 GDP at $3.95 trillion with a GNI of $47,111 per capita. It is a high-income democratic country. Positioned near the apex of the international hierarchy of states, German authorities and capital can project their financial and economic power into the world market. The KfW has evolved and reproduced itself within this position of global political and economic privilege.

The KfW is firmly situated within the German public sphere. It is a fully publicly owned and controlled development bank whose

---

[5] Statement on the foundation of the KfW, as presented on the KfW website to celebrate the bank's seventieth anniversary in 2018. Available at www.kfw.de/KfW-Group/About-KfW/Identit%C3%A4t/Geschichte-der-KfW/KfW-Jahrzehnte/. Accessed 21 March 2019.

Table 6.1. *KfW and BPDC at a glance*

	KfW	BPDC
Institutional form of democratisation/ board of governors	Representative oversight in a thirty-seven-member governing board, co-chaired by two ministers of government; cooperative relations between bank and government ministries	A 290-member Workers' Assembly constitutes the highest decision-making body followed by a seven-member national board (four assembly and three government representatives)
Mission	To promote the sustainable improvement of the economic, social, and ecological conditions of people's lives	To serve the social and sustainable welfare of Costa Rican inhabitants
Type of bank (year established)	Development/ promotional (1948)	Universal (1969)
Ownership	Federal Republic of Germany 80%; German federal states 20%	Working class of Costa Rica 100%
Total assets	US$569 billion	US$6.24 billion
Return on assets (average 2012–19)	0.35%	1.35%
Net profit after tax (average 2012–19)	US$2.10 billion	US$61.96 million
No. of employees	6,705	3,872
No. of branches	80 offices (no branch network)	107

Source: Annual Reports; Orbis (24 July 2020). Bank websites

existence is inscribed in German public law. Ownership rests with the Federal Republic of Germany, which holds 80 per cent of KfW shares, and with the German federal states, which hold 20 per cent. Its existence belies hardcore orthodox faith in the need of separating the political from the economic. As researchers Hubert and Cochran write, KfW activities 'continue to be tied with the political priorities of its two shareholders', that is, the German federal and state-level governments (2013, 1). Its government-led mandate to support the 'sustainable improvement of the economic, social, and ecological conditions of people's lives' has a clear public interest character. Yet the wording allows the KfW to champion pro-public demands *and* capital accumulation – that is, to function in both the public and private interest. As elaborated later, this is not without contradictions.

As a development bank, the KfW functions differently from public commercial and universal public banks. The KfW does not accept personal deposits or lend directly to individuals. In certain cases, however, it can lend directly to large corporations (for example, Airbus). Mostly the KfW specialises in programme-based on-lending to other institutions – be they other public and private banks, government authorities, or developing country governments.

Early in its history the KfW relied on public sources of capital for its lending (upwards of 90 per cent of its capital was of public origin in the mid-1950s). Having built up its own mass of capital reserves, nearly all new KfW capital is sourced via bond issuances in financial markets and from retained earnings (Naqvi et al. 2018, 681–82; KfW 2019a, 12–13). Consequently, its position within the public sphere is enormously significant. The KfW is formally backed by the German state's sovereign guarantee, which in turn supports the bank's very strong credit rating (S&P AAA). The KfW can therefore access finance capital globally at the cheapest interest rates possible. For financial investors, KfW debt is 'as good as gold', backed as it is by the German state.[6] In turn, and because the KfW operates according to a public mandate not driven by profit maximisation, it passes on lower interest rates and more favourable credit conditions to its clients.

---

[6] For a fascinating account of the historical evolutions of public debt, gold, and money, particularly in the cases of the United States and Great Britain, and the eventual break in the dollar–gold standard in the 1970s, see McNally 2020.

The KfW also stands within the formidable German finance and credit system characterised by powerful banks, both public and private, which include the privately owned Deutsche Bank and Commerzbank as well as the extensive German public savings association, the Sparkasse (Tilly 1998; Deeg 1999; von Mettenheim and Butzbach 2017). In contrast to the US economy (Chapter 5), the German economy is regarded within comparative political economy as an archetypal bank-based 'coordinated market economy' able to provide patient and long-term capital (Hall and Soskice 2001; Röper 2018). The KfW made its mark (pun intended) by leading Germany's post-war reconstruction, indeed transformation, efforts. The political and economic exigencies of the moment meant that idealistic market-based mechanisms and 'market-failure' frameworks were unsuitable, even in the imagination. Long-term, stable, and fixed-rate loans below market rates with favourable repayment terms were needed to bolster the war-torn economy, to assist with the humanitarian crisis (notably via housing assistance), and to rebuild destroyed energy networks. The post-war conjuncture was thus foundational to the KfW as a public bank.

As Germany moved past the immediate post-war crisis, KfW operations expanded. By the late 1950s the KfW was financing small- and medium-sized enterprises (SMEs) and export production. SME lending was geared to supporting full employment and industrial innovation and growth within Germany. Relatedly, KfW infrastructure financing aimed to further ramp up domestic energy capacity, a pre-requisite for industrialisation. Consequently, an interdependent relationship formed between the KfW and German SMEs and domestic industrialisation. By the mid-1980s over 10 per cent of SMEs in the Deutsche Mark (DM) 5 million to 10 million range and over 30 per cent of SMEs in the DM 50 million to 100 million range had received KfW financial support (Deeg 1999, 117). This pattern of SME lending had the effect of integrating the KfW into the socio-economic fabric of Germany's domestic economy and social reproduction, particularly given the high numbers of workers employed by German SMEs. Put otherwise, the economy, workers, and society at large developed a material stake in the reproduction of the KfW. This would come to be represented within the KfW board and in how it is governed.

Within a decade of its establishment, moreover, the KfW began international development operations, first offering foreign loans to Iceland, Sudan, and India in 1958. Within a few years German state authorities mandated the KfW to commence with development cooperation, aid, and project financing. These typically large-scale infrastructure loans abroad were often tied to German economic priorities at home. The national interest was perceived as served by public banks financing German companies abroad, albeit within a shifting global context. Much as American post-war reconstruction financing in Europe facilitated the flow of American capital abroad, so too was German public aid a force for the internationalisation of Germany's industrialising economy, albeit in the shadow of and as pressurised by US Pax Americana global ambitions (Schmidt 2003; cf. Panitch and Gindin 2012). The public and private interest thus meshed within the KfW via the expansion of capitalist markets at home and abroad.

German reunification drew German society and the KfW into new material relationships after 1990. Given the sudden and substantial need for finance for development capacity and expertise, the KfW assumed the lead in post-reunification East German housing refurbishments. The KfW literally 'built' on its accumulated post-war reconstruction expertise to help modernise nearly half of the former East Germany's housing stock (Moslener et al. 2018, 72–73). KfW bank staff influenced the process, making the case that if refurbishments were to be done then the KfW should ensure that they be energy efficient.[7] Notwithstanding the contradiction that KfW refurbishments spurred gentrification in the east (cf. Nipper 2002), the KfW evolved as a national leader in financing housing energy efficiency. If a

---

[7] Confidential interview, high-level KfW management member, Frankfurt, 26 February 2018.

house is now a 'KfW Efficiency' house then it is recognised as having met the highest environmental standards available (Hubert and Cochran 2013, 25–26) (the experience would also prepare the KfW for its coming energy transition role). German reunification, moreover, magnified the KfW's mass of financial resources and, by extension, its ability to intervene in the economy. Because the KfW was already active in the former East Germany since 1990, the government believed it was well-positioned to absorb the Staatsbank Berlin – the institutional legacy of the former East German central bank. In 1995 the government merged the Staatsbank with the KfW, effectively tripling KfW's equity and significantly bolstering its financial capacity (Deeg 1999, 205). By facilitating the political project of German reunification, German reunification in turn bolstered KfW technical expertise, financial capacity, and geographical reach across Germany.

The KfW at this conjuncture would also evolve with Germany's transition to neoliberalism within the European Union and amidst an increasingly financialised global capitalism (cf. Lapavitsas 2013). Researcher Nils Röper argues that German society was never immune to the market freedom promises of neoliberalism: a 'widely shared political consensus emerged that saw the deregulation of the financial sector as a factor of competitiveness, source of economic growth and employment and essential in bringing "equity culture" to German households' (2018, 378). At the same time, however, the subjective experiences of citizens with German public services provided an important counter-narrative mediating and mitigating the neoliberal desire to privatise all things public (Schweizer et al. 2016; Sidki and Boll 2019). A relatively positive culture of public provisioning and public consultation includes the KfW and other public banks in Germany, notably involving Germany's history of local public banks undertaking charitable operations, lending to households, supporting SMEs, and collaborating with other public entities (Röper 2018, 382). There is, as such, a legacy of public banks functioning in the public

Table 6.2. *KfW operational data, 2012–19*

	2012	2013	2014	2015	2016	2017	2018	2019
Total assets (billion USD)	675	641	594	548	534	566	556	569
Net profit after tax (billion USD)	3.24	1.84	1.95	2.51	2.11	1.71	1.87	1.54
ROAE	12.37	6.18	7.19	9.28	7.66	5.12	5.54	4.43
ROAA	0.47	0.26	0.32	0.44	0.40	0.29	0.34	0.28

Source: Orbis BankFocus (24 July 2020)

interest, which has translated into a resilient basis of broad-based popular support for these public institutions (AGPB 2014). Consequently, bank privatisation never seriously garnered much societal credibility or governmental backing. Well into the consolidation of neoliberal financialisation, both before and after the 2008–09 global financial crisis, public banks persist as an important pillar of the German financial system (Schmit et al. 2011; von Mettenheim and Butzbach 2017; Naqvi et al. 2018). This has translated into higher expectations for democratic accountability by virtue of being located within the German public sphere (cf. Greiling and Grüb 2015). Table 6.2 below provides an overview of KfW operational data from 2012 to 2019.

In the case of the KfW, its governance and democratic accountability is structured by a robust and representative institutional framework set out in public law, specifically in Article 7 of the *Law Concerning KfW* (the 'KfW Law'). Therein the KfW's highest governing body is the Board of Supervisory Directors, which functions like a shareholders' forum comprising thirty-seven members (see KfW 2015, 174–79). The German federal minister of finance and federal minister for economic affairs and energy hold the chair and deputy chair positions on the board in alternation. Board membership is filled out by an additional thirty-five members from across German politics, economy, and society. These members include seven appointments each by the German Bundestag (Lower House) and Bundesrat (Upper House); five additional federal government ministers; one representative each from the mortgage banks, savings banks, cooperative banks, commercial banks, and business credit institutions; two industry representatives; one representative each from municipalities, agriculture, crafts, trade, and housing; and four trade union representatives. The KfW board thus draws together, by law, political and societal representation, internalising rather than erecting a false ontological divide between the state and the economy. Democratic representation facilitates the integration of societal will, insofar as board members can meaningfully shape the KfW's operational ethos and mandated direction. It also offers a forum of accountability for how the KfW functions and for what the bank does. Transparency is mandated by the KfW being legally subject to the Public Corporate Governance Code and by requiring the KfW to have its annual financial statements audited independently.

The diverse composition of the KfW board is substantive, positioning it among the most representative banks, public or private, in the world. This remarkable governance framework should not be treated lightly, though it regularly is. Heterodox contributions on public banking, for example, regularly make only passing reference to elite ministerial actions vis-à-vis operational direction in the KfW (Moslener et al. 2018; Naqvi et al. 2018). This is not to suggest such high-level collaboration within the public sphere is insignificant. KfW programme strategies bring KfW staff into regular and direct contact with government ministries and state authorities (Moslener et al. 2018). Most decision-making is indeed bi-lateral, made between KfW management and specific government ministries.[8] This routinises daily public sector practices in ways that are largely cooperative. Nevertheless, high-level interactions should not obscure the

---

[8] Confidential interview, high-level KfW management member, Frankfurt, 26 February 2018.

representative and democratic functions of broad-based governing boards. Should conflict arise between the KfW mandate and its actual lending operations, the KfW board can hold the bank to account. In turn, society can hold the KfW board to account, which in turn holds the ability to shift the bank's institutional orientation in line with societal priorities (such as 'lending without limit' in response to the 2020 Covid-19 pandemic; see Epilogue). It is the means by which German society can command a say over the bank, linking the political and the economic.

The institutionalised linking of the KfW to German society has enabled the bank to confront societal challenges in ways that have dynamically reshaped the institution, notably via Germany's post-1990s 'Energiewende' (energy transition). Researchers Haas and Sander argue that the Energiewende initiative has 'strong roots within civil society based on energy cooperatives, private investors, farmers, and a broad consensus on the advantages of a renewable-energy regime' (2016, 125). Support for (and struggles over) German energy transition emerged historically through a cross-class consensus that developed in the 1970s and through the environmental struggles of the time (cf. Lauber and Jacobsson 2016; Paul 2018). These environmental struggles found political expression within the German Green Party, which was latter to be included within the 1998 Federal coalition government. Since then a series of 'green' laws have reconstituted German energy efficiency strategies. Notable legislative milestones include the Renewable Energy Act (2000); the Integrated Energy and Climate Programme (2007); the Climate Initiative (2008); and the Energy Initiative (2010). The political and cultural basis of Germany's environmental shift thus arose from within society, but by virtue of its legal and institutional structure the KfW board translated the Energiewende initiative into a new environmental mandate *for* the KfW. This triggered changes in the bank's lending practices (Hubert and Cochran 2013).

KfW 'green' lending, defined as lending that leads to a reduction in greenhouse gas emissions and to increased energy efficiency, has become a pillar of KfW institutional reproduction. Internationally, these changes have led to the KfW being widely regarded as an industry leader in green lending (Ervine 2018, 149–51). On average, 40–45 per cent of all KfW lending is dedicated to environmental and climate protection projects (KfW 2017, 2; 2019a, 3). In the KfW's Development Bank division (which is linked to the government's foreign aid and development programmes), the percentage of green lending is closer to 60 per cent. Since 2014 the KfW has also begun to issue green bonds, which allows financial investors to direct capital towards projects that promote environmental and climate protections. There remains unfinished business, so to speak, since more than half of all lending presumably contributes to carbonising growth and to climate change (much like the Nordic Investment Bank, Chapter 4). Nevertheless, the KfW facilitates energy transition as an expression of German collective will.

There are knock-on public interest effects from the Energiewende changes. KfW programme lending strategically connects energy transition priorities with public infrastructure necessities. For example, the KfW Energy-Efficient Urban Rehabilitation programme supports the greening of German municipalities, local authorities, municipal companies, and non-profit organisations via energy-efficient building refurbishment loans (Bach 2017). Barbara Hendricks, Federal Minister for Building, highlights that the programme was established by the Federal Ministry for the Environment, Nature Conservation, Building and Nuclear Safety in a collaborative effort 'to improve the energy efficiency of entire districts in towns and cities'.[9] The KfW in turn provides long-term, low interest-rate loans. The terms are enhanced by repayment bonuses linked to the energy efficiencies realised by local authorities. Loan maturities may be up to thirty years, with a fixed interest rate for ten years, but repayment bonuses can be as high as 12.5 per cent of a loan's amount, subject to

---

[9] KfW Press Release, 'From the building to the district: fifth anniversary of the KfW "Energy-efficient Urban Rehabilitation" programme', 21 June 2016. Available at www.kfw.de/KfW-Group/Newsroom/Latest-News/Pressemitteilungen-Details_361280.html. Accessed 10 January 2020.

expert verification of efficiency gains. The KfW programme also provides repayment-free start-up periods of up to five years, which boosts the immediate liquidity of communities and municipalities. KfW programme lending like this is not just a top-down venture, but one that aims at broad-based, locally appropriate, and *definancialised* public financial support for a green and just energy transformation in Germany. In 2016 the Energy-Efficient Urban Rehabilitation programme accounted for nearly €750 million in public bank–public sector collaborative financing for municipal energy efficiency retrofitting. By being located within the public sphere and as a consequence of political decision-making priorities, the KfW thus shields public authorities and local communities from financialised market discipline (such as private financial investors' short-term, high-profit imperatives) in order to support public interest initiatives and climate mitigation efforts. The KfW's governance framework is the avenue by which the bank's accumulated mass of financial capital and institutional knowledge can be *made* to function in accordance with democratically determined economic and environmental ends.

The KfW democratisation framework illustrates how public banks can respond to working class and popular demands for effective public service provisioning that is green and attentive to local needs (cf. Angel 2017; Sidki and Boll 2019). The political link between public banks and the public interest is openly recognised and acknowledged in Germany. In the words of the president, Gunther Dunkel, and vice president, Otto Beierl, of the Association of German Public Banks, 'Acting on behalf of public authorities they [public banks] perform tasks that support political goals' (AGPB 2014, 3). The KfW presents itself as providing seventy years of 'financing with a public mission' (KfW 2019b, 4). Its representative structure allows it to internalise political goals, which in turn constitute a public interest element of the KfW's institutional credibility and persistence. This has not occurred without contradictions and operational pitfalls, which we return to below.

6.2.2   Costa Rica's Banco Popular y de Desarrollo Comunal

Costa Rica's Banco Popular y de Desarrollo Comunal (Popular Bank and of Community Development, or 'Banco Popular') is a public universal bank that combines retail/commercial and development functions in its overall operations and corporate structure. The Banco Popular's way of bottom-up, working class, and *substantive* democratisation contributes to the bank's credibility within Costa Rican society. Democratisation has done so by enabling the Banco Popular to internalise popular demands and operational oversight in legally binding and public interest ways (for example, by adopting new green, social equality, and gender mandates).

6.2.2.1   History and Current Structure of the Banco Popular

The Banco Popular operates within Costa Rica, a geographically small, Central American country with about five million inhabitants. According to World Bank country data, its 2018 GDP is $60.13 billion and its GNI per capita is $11,520. It is classified as an upper middle-income democratic country. In the context of Central America, these are impressive national achievements in and of themselves given the region's historic levels of poverty and experience with social upheavals (Robinson 2003).

Costa Rica's post–World War II history, like Germany's, provides insight into the Banco Popular as a dynamic institution. The country's 1949 Constitution followed from a period of national unrest, marked by the July 1947 working class and peasant strike 'Huelga de Brazos Caídos' and the short-lived 1948 civil war (Lehoucq 1990). The result was a domestic class compromise, which enabled Costa Rica's post-war era to be shaped by agricultural export production and state-led development initiatives, marked by extensive nationalisations and the expansion of the public sector (Booth 1998). A Costa Rican social consensus formed around institutionalising and managing social conflict through the state apparatus, which stabilised Costa Rica's peripheral transition to capitalism (Lehoucq

1996; Goss and Pacheco 1999). Therein peasants and workers struggled to fashion a relatively more egalitarian and democratic society, politically and economically (Edelman 1999). In particular, organised labour carved out an important and influential space within the organisation of society, even if state authorities tended to repress the more radical expressions of working class solidarity (Wilson 1998, 68–70). Relative inequality persisted, nevertheless, even as state-led developmental capitalism took root as the dominant strategy for economic growth in post-1960s Costa Rica.

In the process, Costa Rican society achieved relatively robust workers' rights, decent public sector services, and a nationwide cooperative movement. Formal banking services, however, remained largely out of reach for much of the labouring poor and peasantry, who fell victim to usurious financial practices that exacerbated poverty. Labour unions and social sectors reacted in the 1960s by demanding a genuine workers' bank (Cortés 2014, 60). The government responded by transforming an existing financial institution, the Monte Nacional de Piedad, which had been engaged in usury and exploitation of the poor, into a new bank for the poor and 'working class' of Costa Rica.

The Banco Popular y de Desarrollo Comunal was legally constituted on 11 July 1969. Its founding ethos was for the institution to combat usury against and to democratise credit for Costa Rican workers. This was inscribed into public law – the 1969 Ley Orgánica del Banco Popular y de Desarrollo Comunal No. 4351 (the 'BPDC Law'). Then Costa Rican President José Joaquín Antonio Trejos Fernández supported the new bank, but it was a woman, Deputy Cecilia González de Penrod, who championed the initiative within government (and who perhaps provided inspiration for the Banco Popular's impressive gender equity commitments).

The Banco Popular at first functioned to encourage household savings, offer credits, and to finance developmental and community organisations (hence the 'community development' aspect of its name). It has since grown into a full-fledged *universal* bank that provides retail operations (savings, payments, and so on) and developmental programmes, including infrastructure support. The public interest link between its financial functions and working-class base is protected in law. Article 34 of the BPDC Law specifies that its capital must be used to offer loans to workers, artisans, small producers, communal development associations, municipalities, cooperatives, and unions as well as for specific community and regional development projects that benefit 'collective welfare'. The Banco Popular thus works with those socio-economic groups often excluded from formal financial services, like small cooperatives and micro-, small-, and medium-sized enterprises (MSMEs), as well as with larger cooperatives, community and social developmental organisations, and even state institutions.

The Banco Popular has a unique ownership and control framework that positions it within the public sphere. It is an institution governed by public, not private, sector law. Yet the Banco Popular is not formally state-owned. The BPDC Law defines the bank as a *public non-state institution* that is 100 per cent owned by the workers of Costa Rica (BPDC 2012, 7). It is a worker-owned public bank situated within the Costa Rican public sphere. A worker's right to share ownership in the bank depends on having a mandatory savings account in it for at least one year. This is a defining feature of the Banco Popular, which in turn provides the bank with a unique source of recurrent, broad-based, and 'popular' capital contributions. Article 5 of the BPDC Law states that all public and private employers must contribute 0.5 per cent of paid monthly wages to the bank's capital base. Additionally, workers must deposit 1 per cent of their monthly wages in the bank. These combined monetary contributions (termed 'obligatory savings') are deducted by the employer and deposited into the Banco Popular. After one year, 1.25 per cent of this combined 1.5 per cent worth of obligatory savings are transferred to each worker's own pension fund. This pension fund can be kept in the BPDC or moved elsewhere. The Banco Popular, for its part, retains the remaining 0.25 per cent as a form of permanent capitalisation. This feature provides economic stability to the Banco Popular while structurally connecting its institutional reproduction to Costa Rican workers.

Unlike Costa Rica's other national public banks (like the Banco Nacional de Costa Rica or Banco de Costa Rica), the Banco Popular does not enjoy explicit sovereign backing against default. Senior BPDC staff, however, suggest that the bank benefits from implicit state backing.[10] That is, staff in the bank, but most importantly others in society and in financial markets, believe that the Banco Popular would receive state backing should the bank face economic troubles (as occurred in the 1980s at which point the government did back the bank). Banco Popular staff also suggest that this belief, matched with the fact that the Banco Popular is governed by public law (to which it must abide), supports societal trust in the bank and, by extension, in its credit rating in financial markets.

The Banco Popular, like the KfW, has also fostered substantive links to Costa Rica's public sector. For one, the Banco Popular accepts over 40 per cent of public sector payroll deposits (BPDC 2012, 42). That is, as a deposit-taking universal bank, much of its customer base is made up of public employees. For another, the Banco Popular is not required to hold capital reserves in the Central Bank of Costa Rica because the bank is governed by public law. This frees up capital reserves for its lending and helps to reduce funding costs. Additionally, the Banco Popular benefits from long-term deposits and loans made from other public development banks, such as the multilateral Central American Bank for Economic Integration, to support its domestic lending operations. In this way, the Banco Popular has a diversity of sources of capital that connect the Banco Popular to workers and to other public sector institutions even as it competes within domestic financial markets. At the same time, Banco Popular management and staff unequivocally recognise the

---

[10] Based on a series of confidential interviews in San José, Costa Rica, with BPDC high-level managers and senior staff, 3–7 April 2017.

bank's historic ties to Costa Rican workers and the public sector as defining characteristics of the institution and its ongoing operating strategy.[11]

As a universal bank, the Banco Popular maintains and fosters a nationwide branch network, operating within a competitive domestic market comprised of private domestic, foreign, and public banks. As such, the Banco Popular functions, like all the other public banks in Costa Rica, in ways that bear little resemblance to heterodox views that suggest public banks are meant to function only in 'addition' to those activities that private banks refuse to do (Griffith-Jones et al. 2018). It instead competes directly with public and private banks alike. Therein, the Banco Popular reproduces itself by charting a middle road between profitability and social lending. In the process, and especially over the last twenty years, the Banco Popular has developed into a financial conglomerate and the third largest bank in Costa Rica. It offers not only retail and development banking services, but also pension, stock market, investment, and insurance services. The bank's returns are in line with other commercial and universal banks in developing countries, public and private, averaging around 1.35 per cent ROAA (return on average assets) (Table 6.3).

Therein, the ways of democratisation in the Banco Popular have become more representative and substantively connected to citizens and the working classes of Costa Rica. It was not always so. When the Banco Popular was first developing its institutional capacities in the 1970s, the control and direction of the bank rested with the board of directors and a small management cohort (Cortés 2014, 62). However, in the late 1970s and early 1980s, Costa Rica entered a period of severe economic crisis (corresponding with Latin America's debt crisis) from which neoliberal structural adjustment emerged (Marois 2005). The Banco Popular faced severe financial difficulties and the government intervened, assuming temporary control over the bank.

---

[11] Various interviews, San José, Costa Rica, 3–7 April 2017.

Table 6.3. *BPDC operational data, 2012–19*

	2012	2013	2014	2015	2016	2017	2018	2019
Total assets (billion USD)	3.76	4.30	4.62	5.19	5.56	6.10	5.89	6.24
Net profit after tax (million USD)	84.29	61.11	59.55	64.39	69.70	63.44	35.17	58.01
ROAE	12.09	8.64	7.15	6.88	6.79	5.77	3.21	4.76
ROAA	2.43	1.72	1.38	1.31	1.32	1.10	0.61	0.93

Source: Orbis BankFocus (24 July 2020)

Subsequent neoliberal restructuring impacted the Banco Popular in two significant and contradictory ways: democratisation and neoliberalisation. In terms of democratisation, this can only be considered as an unintended consequence from the perspective of neoliberal reformers. In Costa Rica, the debt crisis gave rise to a broad-based consultative process over the Banco Popular, which included organised labour, government, and Banco Popular representatives. The outcome was the institutionalisation of more substantively democratic processes. Most remarkably, this entailed the formation of the Banco Popular's Asamblea de los Trabajadores y Trabajadoras (Assembly of Working Men and Women, or Workers' Assembly).[12]

The Workers' Assembly was formalised in public law in 1986 as the highest representative decision-making body of the Banco Popular. Fifteen years later, the Banco Popular reaffirmed and reinforced the importance of the Workers' Assembly. In 2002 an extraordinary reform was passed, enhancing the original BPDC Law. The reform is titled the *Ley de Democratización de las Instancias del Decisión del Banco Popular y de Desarrollo Comunal* (Law of the Democratisation of Decision-making Processes of the Popular Bank

---

[12] See www.bancopopular.fi.cr/AsambleaTrabajadores/Paginas/default.aspx. Accessed 27 June 2019.

and of Community Development, or the Democratisation Law).[13] Article 14 of the Democratisation Law, for example, specifies that the Workers' Assembly is to give general direction to the bank's activities – an important feature in and of itself. The law goes on to identify the further responsibilities of the Workers' Assembly, which include appointing four Workers' Assembly representatives to the bank's seven-member National Board of Directors; accrediting new representatives to the Workers' Assembly; knowing and reviewing the bank's annual and general audit reports; integrating the economic and budgetary content from the Permanent Commission for Women; and integrating the Vigilance Committee supervising and monitoring recommendations vis-à-vis all discriminatory practices based on ethnicity, religion, gender, sexual orientation, economic condition, or physical disability. In short, the Workers' Assembly is charged with providing meaningful democratic direction and accountable oversight, and this is legally enshrined in perhaps the most socially progressive and democratic banking law in the world.

The Workers' Assembly thus represents an authentic achievement of economic democratisation insofar as it institutionalises the participation of Costa Rican workers and society within core bank decision-making and strategic processes. By law, the Workers' Assembly is constituted by 290 representatives from ten social and economic sectors. These sectors include the artisanal; communal; cooperative; self-managed; independent; teachers; professional; as well as the confederated, non-confederated, and solidarity syndicates (trade unions). This translates into the Workers' Assembly representing about 1.2 million savers within the bank, which is equal to about 20 per cent of Costa Rica's population (BPDC 2017, 13). In the words of one Costa Rican writer and researcher, the Workers' Assembly is the foundation of the bank's contribution to

---

[13] See www.pgrweb.go.cr/scij/Busqueda/Normativa/Normas/nrm_texto_completo
.aspx?param1=NRTC&nValor1=1&nValor2=49559&nValor3=53016&strTipM=
TC. Accessed 27 June 2019.

the *democratisation* of Costa Rica's economy, development, and financial system (Cortés 2014, 62).

The Banco Popular has institutionalised even more representative decision-making by inscribing gender equity into the governance structure of the bank. The BPDC Law and the 2002 Democratisation Law stipulate that women must constitute at least 50 per cent of members and delegates in the bank's most significant governing and decision-making bodies. This requirement extends not only to the Workers' Assembly and the National Board of Directors but also to each of the local/regional Banco Popular Credit Boards (there are twenty-two such boards across Costa Rica that help to also decentralise decision-making processes). To monitor and ensure action on gender equity across the bank, the Banco Popular has a Permanent Commission for Women (Article 14).[14] The Workers' Assembly, for its part, must act on direction given by the Women's Commission, making the commission's role substantive, not ornamental. The practice of gender equity and representation has earned the Banco Popular an important marker of democratisation, namely that it became the first public entity in Central America to establish at least 50 per cent of women in their decision-making bodies (BPDC 2017, 13).

Effective control over the day-to-day operations of the Banco Popular are, like most complex institutions, overseen by a National Board of Directors (NBD). This is the Banco Popular's highest administrative unit. It is subordinate to the Workers' Assembly, and so it too is democratised. The NBD is composed of seven members. The Workers' Assembly designates four representatives (at least two must be women) and the Government Executive of Costa Rica names three (at least one must be a woman). In 2017, four women and three men constituted the NBD; in 2018, the opposite, as there are four men and three women. Both scenarios fulfil the Article 15 requirement that women make up at least half of the board's seven-person membership

---

[14] See www.bancopopular.fi.cr/AsambleaTrabajadores/Paginas/Organos-que-la-Integran.aspx. Accessed 27 June 2019.

given a stipulation that the majority can alternate between men and women.

The Banco Popular's democratisation structures play a formative role in the direction of the bank. In 2008, for example, the Banco Popular initiated a nationwide consultative process. This is itself remarkable for any bank, public or private. The results then informed and gave rise to five new guidelines for the Workers' Assembly (BPDC 2010). The new guidelines reflect both the Banco Popular's competitive market operations and its social developmental role. They include (1) the promotion of the social economy; (2) a quality offering of services by the conglomerate; (3) the competitive management of the institution; (4) regional and local development; and (5) the conglomerate as an entity for development.

Costa Rica's socio-political context is important here. The 2008 consultation took place as society sought out deeper engagement with the ideas of a 'social economy' (that is, an economy geared towards collective good rather than individual enrichment, to the public, not private, interest). As an expression of this, the left-leaning social democratic Partido Acción Ciudadana was elected in 2014 and then again in 2018 (albeit in both cases facing stiff opposition from the conservative right wing) (Colburn and Cruz 2018). Banco Popular's staff affirm that the PAC government, via its government representatives on the National Board of Directors, has encouraged the bank to move in a more social economy and 'green' developmental direction.[15] As one expression of this broad trend, the Banco Popular became the first Central American bank to affiliate with the UN Global Compact in 2009. The affiliation committed the Banco Popular to producing an annual 'Sustainability Report' that follows the guidelines and methodology of the Global Reporting Initiative (GRI) (www.globalreporting.org). Since 2010, the Banco Popular tracks its own consumption of energy and its carbon impact as a way of thinking strategically about how to reduce its carbon footprint. The

---

[15] Various interviews, San José, Costa Rica, 3–7 April 2017.

BPDC Pensions division, for example, was certified as 'carbon neutral' since 2013 and awarded a Five-Star climate change award three years running (BPDC 2017, 72). The GRI process has the knock-on effect of internalising a green ethos within the operations and among staff.

This was not the end of democratic self-reflection for the Banco Popular. In 2014 the bank's NBD launched a new three-year nation-wide consultation to garner popular input into its 2017–20 strategic plan and into how the Banco Popular could further support a social economy in Costa Rica. This, too, signals a remarkable commitment to outreach by a bank. Social sector leaders in the Workers' Assembly and senior management participated in the consultative forums, which connected with nearly 1,500 participants from across Costa Rica's eleven different regions. Three strategic axes emerged to guide banking decisions, including gender equity, accessibility, and environmental responsibility (BPDC 2015, 25). These axes were then translated into what the Banco Popular refers to as its *triple bottom line*: the economic, the environmental, and the social. Through democratised structures and transformative consultative processes, the environment, the public good (including gender equity), and financial sustainability have become defining features of the bank's institutional credibility. These achievements stand out within the banking world, but they have not come without challenges.

6.3 THE CONTRADICTIONS OF DEMOCRATISATION IN GLOBAL FINANCIALISED CAPITALISM

The democratised structures of the KfW and the Banco Popular make them democratically representative but not free of contradictions or independent of the pull of contending public and private interests within class-divided society. In the case of the KfW, as much as it reproduces itself within the German public sphere so does Germany exist within the European Union (EU) and in global capitalism. The EU context is particularly significant. In 2001–02 private German commercial banks complained to the European Commission of unfair market treatment because the German government supported its public banks, including the KfW (cf. Naqvi et al. 2018). The subsequently negotiated 'Understanding II' allowed German public banks to continue functioning but pushed them into more restrictive market conditions and out of more areas of the economy (AGPB 2014, 7). Private banking interests compelled EU competition law to restrain KfW state aid operations, driving institutional change and bending the KfW towards more market-based determinations. The KfW had to respond by splitting and fragmenting its corporate operations into four divisions, organised along domestic and international lines. The SME Bank (Mittelstandsbank) and the Municipal and Private Client Bank (Kommunal- und Privatkundenbank/Kreditinstitute) took on domestic operations, which accounts for about two-thirds of KfW lending. The KfW IPEX Bank and Development Bank (DEG) took on international operations, which accounts for the other third of lending. A fifth charitable division, the KfW Stiftung, was created in 2012 for not-for-profit operations (KfW 2015, 13–14). Then in October 2018 the KfW opened KfW Capital as another separate division that focuses on innovations and entrepreneurs (KfW 2019a, 9).

During this period the crises of global finance posed challenges for the KfW. As the US investment bank Lehman Brothers failed in 2008, pushing the global financial system to the brink of collapse, the KfW (apparently unwittingly) transferred €300 million to Lehman's as part of a currency swap, raising ire among German public and private sector representatives alike. For example, the conservative German Taxpayers Association took aim at KfW democratisation, laying blame on KfW's 'unwieldy' thirty-seven-member board.[16] This

---

[16] N. Kulish, 'German Bank Is Dubbed "Dumbest" for Transfer to Bankrupt Lehman Brothers', *The New York Times*, 18 September 2008. Available at www.nytimes .com/2008/09/18/business/worldbusiness/18iht-kfw.4.16285369.html. Accessed 21 June 2019. Such arguments are ideologically committed to 'political' views of public bank inferiority. It is hardly the case that solely public banks make errors. In August 2020, for example, 'Citigroup accidentally wired $900m of its own money to creditors' and then could not get it back (see S. Indap, E. Platt and R. Armstrong, 'Citi's $900m Blunder Was Culmination of Months of Drama', FT, 27 August 2020. Available at www.ft.com. Accessed 27 August 2020).

critique followed on from one of KfW's subsidiaries, the IKB Deutsche Industriebank, suffering massive losses from speculative bets on mortgage-backed securities (KfW bailed it out, and then sold the IKB off in 2008).

Internally, the KfW has at times operated at odds with its own mandate and with other divisions within the bank. Despite its institution-wide decarbonisation mandate, for example, the KfW continues to finance coal-fired energy abroad through its export financing division – if German technology is used. The KfW is also 'a leading provider of aircraft finance on all of the world's key aviation markets for over 40 years'[17] – hardly a climate finance banner for decarbonisation and for reducing greenhouse gas emissions. Lending operations like this explain why around 60 per cent of KfW lending still carbonises the environment. Indeed, KfW industrial lending has remained largely stable over the last few decades and oriented towards accelerating domestic growth (Naqvi et al. 2018). KfW remains credible among German industrialists.

The ability of the KfW to persist and reproduce itself has meant responding to contending private and public interests, industrial development versus green transition. This is a tension already in play in Germany, and it is reflected in the country's waning renewable energy advances (Lauber and Jacobsson 2016). Civil society organisations have criticised KfW's 'corporate capture', especially vis-à-vis the orientation of conglomerate-oriented 'green' lending and preferential support for global carbonising corporations (like Airbus). German industrialists want to retain access to KfW lending that bolsters their industrial and competitive capacity and profitability (cf. Haas and Sander 2016). Finance capital, to the extent KfW persists, wants to keep the bank squarely within a lending 'additionality' framework. To date the KfW has managed to balance the pull between public and

---

[17] See KfW IPEX-Bank, 'Global Aircraft Financing'. Available at www.kfw-ipex-bank.de/International-financing/KfW-IPEX-Bank/Business-Areas/Aviation/. Accessed 27 June 2019.

private interests, persisting amidst financialisation albeit with more modest advances on decarbonisation than perhaps could be achieved.

So too with the Banco Popular. It too cannot avoid operational contradictions within class-divided Costa Rican society. This was expressed in a 2017 interview. A long-time Banco Popular senior staff member explained that in its early days generating returns via profit-oriented activities was less important to the Banco Popular, but that this has since changed. Archival evidence supports the observation, documenting that in the 1990s the Banco Popular began moving away from its founding 'solidarity' focus and towards more profit-oriented financial ends (see Botey n.d.). This was made possible via reforms to the BPDC Law that allowed for more commercial activities. Further interviews confirmed the point: by the late 1990s generating returns had become an overarching concern for the Banco Popular, over-shadowing the bank's worker-oriented mandate. Its reason for exist-ence and its institutional credibility began to erode as the Banco Popular started to function as if it were like any other bank. It was becoming corporatised. In the pull between profitability and social mandate, profitability was winning out, and this generated social contestation over the bank's future.

One effect was mounting pressure to privatise the Banco Popular. Private banks wanted to take over its national networks, thousands of clients, nationwide portfolio, and, by extension, profit-making opportunities. The Banco Popular would not be sold off, however. Instead, the Workers' Assembly reasserted its governing authority, demanding a return to the bank's core mandate and to servicing the working class of Costa Rica (and later the social econ-omy). This would not come without internal conflict between the Workers' Assembly and senior management. Compromise between the two internal forces led to institutional restructuring, namely a splitting of the Banco Popular into three operational divisions: per-sonal banking (Banco de Persona); business and corporate banking (Banco Empresarial and Corporativa); and social development banking (Banco de Desarrollo Social). The first two divisions would emerge as relatively market-oriented while the Banco de Desarrollo Social division would be relatively shielded from the market. Through this 'Social Development' arm of the bank, 25 per cent of the entire conglomerate's profits are channelled into a series of 'special funds', which are intended to meet the social and developmental needs of those Costa Ricans typically excluded from the banking system (BPDC 2017, 58). Importantly, the Social Development arm has no formal profit mandate. The institutional compromise retained a profit-orientation for the Banco Popular as a whole, but it also defended a public interest orientation.

The compromise remains a source of tension.[18] For some Banco Popular management, the financial returns generated by its market-oriented operations are crucial to maintaining the Banco Popular's otherwise concessionary and socially oriented lending. It could not achieve one without the other. For other senior staff, however, the whole of the institution would be better geared towards social solidarity and concessionary lending. Presently, it charts a middle road with an aim to enhancing the social, economic, and environmental role of the Banco Popular on average. In doing so, the Banco Popular functions well beyond Keynesian 'additionality' prescriptions, directly competing to increase its market share. The Banco Popular's public ethos, moreover, continues to have material effect. As the Covid-19 pandemic reached Costa Rica in early 2020, the Banco Popular rapidly extended favourable lending terms and assistance across the country (see Epilogue). According to a Banco Popular branch manager, the bank moved to assist everyone facing the 'first impact of the crisis' as well as those with greater capital needs and vulnerable resources, notably micro enterprises, women, and local water providers.[19]

To date, many economists working within the financing for development field are uninterested in or unaware of the concrete

---

[18] Various interviews, San José, Costa Rica, 3–7 April 2017.
[19] Confidential email communication, Banco Popular Branch Manager, Costa Rica, 26 May 2020.

expressions of democratisation in public banking. There are many reasons why this could be. But one reason surely reflects the difficulty of matching ideological commitments to pro-market additionality with the indeterminacy of democratic decision-making. What if a democratised public bank decides to compete with private banks, capture market share, and to veer past just correcting for market failures? Within the economics literature, the response has been to best leave sleeping dogs lie.

Yet the democratisation of public banks holds enormous potential for realising the public interest. One of the most astute scholars of public banking identified the public interest potential (and pitfalls) of public banks to democracy more than a decade ago (von Mettenheim 2010, 2):

> Unless government [public] banks are part of the complexity,
> diversity and contestation involved in citizenship, political parties,
> interest groups, social movements and transparent government
> that reflect the separation and diffusion of power true to
> democracy, then government banks will fall short of their
> potential.

The representative and substantive ways of democratisation found in the KfW and Banco Popular are means by which public banks can be made to help realise economic democracy, and credibly so. Democratisation has not ruled out contestation over who benefits in class-divided society nor has it eliminated the internal contradictions over how these banks function in capitalism. But democratisation can shift the terrain of struggle within the public sphere and state. Democratisation can also tilt the pull of contending public and private interests towards public banks being made more pro-public and hence more responsive, accountable, and transparent in their decision-making processes to society. In doing so, democratisation magnifies the possibility of public banks being made to catalyse a green and just transition disproportionately in the public interest. Nowhere is this struggle complete or without complications. But it is necessary. Social forces need to systematically demand the right to democratically command that public banks confront a green and just transition in public interest. Chapter 7 advances a proposal of what that type of public bank might look like.

7   A Democratised Public Bank for a Green and Just Transition

A Proposal

There is widespread consensus that global financialised capitalism is the wrong dream. It neither functions to reproduce society effectively nor fairly. It generates gross social inequalities and economic inefficiencies. 'Sustainability' too often means protecting the future of private financial accumulation. Financialised capitalism is not fit for humane purposes. But what is to be done? The task of change in the public interest seems insurmountable at best. It is not.

In this chapter I develop the book's fifth and final premise, namely that there are sufficient existing pro-public public banking functions (and resources) to synthesise what a democratised green and just public bank can and should look like. Much of the content is drawn from evidence already provided on the decarbonisation, definancialisation, and democratisation of public banks. Here I pull these varied functions together in order to provide a floor for debate.[1] I do so to illustrate how public banks can be *made* to function in pro-public green and just ways otherwise impossible under the short-term, high-return regime of corporatised and private financiers. I do not suggest that public banks can do so alone or in isolation. The potential of democratised green and just public banks can only be realised within grander strategies of progressive socio-economic transformation, such as envisioned in the Green New Deal.

This chapter thus sets out a proposal for what such a public bank could look like. It revolves around pursuing a triple bottom line mandate aimed at (1) a green and just transition; (2) financial

---

[1] This chapter is based on the work of Marois and Güngen (2019b), *A US Green Investment Bank for All: Democratized Finance for a Just Transition*, written for the US-based Next System Project/Democracy Collaborative.

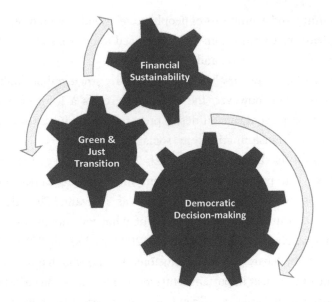

FIGURE 7.1 A triple bottom line: democratised, green and just, and sustainable

sustainability; (3) and democratic decision-making (see Figure 7.1). It is based on the principle that in the absence of a legally binding and accountable triple bottom line mandate forged in the public interest, any green transition will be socially unjust – hijacked by private interests, financial capital, market imperatives, and governing elites that, if left to their own devices, only promise more concentrated wealth, greater social inequality, and accelerated environmental devastation. Just as the neoliberal revolution has been as political as economic, so too must alternative strategies strive to politically reshape the future of economic and social reproduction.

I elaborate on this proposal in four sections. The first section looks at the possibility of creating new public banks; the second, their sustainable design; the third, connecting national public banks to local banks and communities; and the fourth, democratisation. Each function is drawn from existing public banks, and so this proposal is an evidence-based synthesis of persistent and credible functions performed by public banks in time- and place-bound contexts.

The ingenuity and aspirations of people have already given us enough working features to learn from – we only need to put these together in new, appropriate, effective, and credible ways.

Evidently, the proposal as yet exists in any single public bank. By synthesising them, however, the chapter exercises a form of praxis. While based on present capabilities, it prepares for the future and envisions possible transformations in social reproduction for a better common good (cf. Lefebvre 2016[1972], 26). Pro-public social forces should take this proposal to help them make public banks better, incorporating and modifying the features as relevant. This chapter therefore constitutes a narrative not about what we should resist but about what we should be for (cf. Ferguson 2009; McDonald 2016b). It is meant to inform debate, not set conclusions. The hope is that it contributes to one of the most important struggles of our time – the struggle to democratise public banks and finance for a green and just transition.

7.1   THE POSSIBILITY OF CREATING NEW PUBLIC BANKS

Public banks exist and persist as dynamic financial institutions around the world, with over 900 institutions controlling assets of $49 trillion. Public banks have a long historical legacy, having acquired important political and economic financial and knowledge functions. These functions offer important legacies, for better or for worse, that can help to build better public banks that are democratised, green, and just.

The making of new public banks and the remaking of old ones will depend disproportionately on political will. Many early neoliberal barriers have faded. Internationally, the opportunity for public banks to resurge within the global sustainable development agenda has already been opened. The 2015 United Nations Addis Ababa Action Agenda on Finance for Development recognised that national public banks should play an increased role in achieving the 2030 Sustainable Development Goals.[2] The 2019 United Nations Conference on Trade

---

[2] See www.un.org/esa/ffd/wp-content/uploads/2015/08/AAAA_Outcome.pdf. Accessed 13 June 2019.

and Development Report recommends that public banks be at the core of a global Green New Deal. Nationally, governing authorities have begun to command the public banks within their borders to respond to new climate change and social justice demands. Others have begun to create new public banks. The Finance in Common initiative reports that of the 450 public development banks it identified, 30 per cent, that is, some 135 institutions, were created since 2000 (FiC 2020, 5). For example, in the year 2000 state authorities created the Development Bank of Kazakhstan and since 2000 Germany has created at least nine new public regional and municipal investment banks. In the United States, indigenous tribal nations and the Alaska native corporation opened the Native American Bank in 2001 as a community development institution geared to provide financial services to native communities. In 2007, China created the new commercial public bank, the Postal Savings Bank of China. There are, of course, the new multilaterals, the Asian Infrastructure Investment Bank (AIIB) and the New Development Bank founded in 2015. In France, authorities have both made new public banks and remade old ones: the Bpifrance (established in 2012) and the Caisse des Dépôts (established in 1816) are leading on France's climate mitigation strategy, guided by national legislation like the National Low Carbon Strategy (SNBC) and the Multiannual Energy Plan (PPE). The point is that there is not just the possibility of creating new public banks, but the distinct reality of it. The extent to which any existing or new public bank is democratised and green and just will depend on how social forces shape or reshape the institution.

7.2 DESIGNING A PUBLIC BANK THAT IS FINANCIALLY SUSTAINABLE

A democratised green and just public bank will need to be financially sustainable. However, the meaning of financial sustainability, that is, the way an institution can reproduce itself over time, is as much political as it is economic. Contrary to neoclassical views, financial sustainability has no necessary relationship to profit or 'return' maximisation. In fact, financial sustainability can involve loss-making operations and highly subsidised programme lending – so long as the losses generated are covered by other return-generating lending within the bank or by direct government injections. There is no evidence that public banks must prioritise maximising returns to be financially sustainable and to persist. Designing a public bank's approach to financial sustainability thus requires consideration of the sources of the public bank's capital and the ways the bank will lend out capital. The type of public bank, be it development, commercial, or universal, will also affect the options available to it as will the public bank's location within a society's credit system and the financialised world market.

7.2.1 Financial Sustainability

The design of any public bank must secure its financial sustainability, that is, its ability to reproduce the institution indefinitely in ways that allow the public bank to fulfil its mandate. While this does not necessarily mean maximising returns, it does mean securing sufficient and recurrent income or capital transfers to fulfil its mandate indefinitely. It is important to underscore here that financial sustainability can and must be pursued on par with the aim of enabling a green and just transition and democratic decision-making. To pursue profits first would throw a spanner into the works of the bank's triple bottom line. This approach to financial stability as but one of three functional pillars contrasts with corporatised public and private banks whose shareholders (which may include public authorities) demand a short-term focus on increased returns, whether or not this damages the environment or upholds democratic decision-making.

Chapter 2 reviews the contrasting and inconclusive economic evidence on public banks. Here it is enough to signal that public banks, in particular development banks, around the world commonly function sustainably without having to prioritise earning high returns. The German development banks KfW and NRW earn less than a third of 1 per cent ROAA (return on average assets) while France's SFIL brings home less than one-tenth of 1 per cent ROAA. The Nordic Investment Bank, the China Development Bank, and Mexico's Nacional Financiera tend to earn around a half to three-quarters of 1 per cent ROAA. Commercial public banks often earn higher returns, such as the Bank of North Dakota (BND) and Banco Popular of Costa Rica, of around 1.5–2.0 per cent ROAA. By contrast, private banks like Wells Fargo, HSBC, or Citibank will often have ROAA levels in the range of 1 per cent, as do many public commercial banks. Public banks can function sustainably with either very low or high returns. There is no objective or universal limit one way or another. The more important political questions are around what a public bank does to function sustainably at low rates of returns or what it does with returns generated at a higher rate of return.

Here too there is no single pattern. What a public bank does with its returns depends on context and its legal framework. In cases like Germany's KfW, as set out in public law, all returns go back into the bank's capital reserves to enable further lending. By contrast, the Bank of North Dakota can send returns back to the State of North Dakota Legislature's General Fund, use them for mandated loan programmes, or add them to its reserve capital. In yet another example, the Banco Popular y de Desarrollo Comunal (BPDC) of Costa Rica uses higher-return activities to cross-subsidise the bank's loss-making social lending activities. The Turkish universal public bank, Halkbank, has done likewise in support of public services. Any one of these strategies can be financially sustainable and be consistent with a triple bottom line.

Public banks can and do generate annual losses in the fulfilment of their mandated activities, by extending lending at times of economic crisis and natural disasters, or through any number of public good operations (although cases of public banks with annual losses are now the exception than the rule) (see De Luna-Martínez et al. 2018, 33). In such cases, the responsible public authority covers the losses incurred due to such lending activities. When performed in line with mandated or publicly authorised activities, this too is a form of financial sustainability. The bank can reproduce itself indefinitely in the fulfilment of public good activities. This is an important point not to be overlooked. In response to the Covid-19 pandemic, for example, governments have injected direct capital support into public banks not to maximise returns but to support healthcare efforts and economic recovery. It is also inevitable that large-scale capital injections and other forms of financial support will be required for any global green new deal and decarbonisation ambitions given the scale and timeline of investments envisioned. Governments will need to support public banking activities to accomplish green and just transformations. Whether or not a public bank turns a profit will most likely be beside the point, as it should be. The more important 'key performance indicators' should reflect how the public bank confronted the challenge according to its mandate and specific missions.

The point is that financial sustainability means having sufficient annual income and capital resources – be it from a public bank's own earnings or from government transfers – to cover annual expenses, including any losses – nothing more, nothing less. When public banks generate returns, these can be used to bolster the bank's capital reserves, paid to its government owners, or some combination therein. When they generate losses, either internal or external sources must cover them for the institution to persist. The narrow focus of 'political' view economists on public banks maximising profits is based on ideological preferences and a related methodological error of universally grafting private firm profitability imperatives onto public banks.

An important political and economic decision in making public banks, then, is on the balance between concessionary lending (that is, not-for-profit and loss-making operations) and non-concessionary lending (that is, for-profit) (cf. Cochran et al. 2015). Moreover, who and what benefits, or not, from such concessionary lending? There are no natural answers. A public bank's public interest mandate and triple bottom line should provide a legal 'floor' for these operational decisions. But public banks are contested entities in class-divided society. They are subject to the pull of contending public and private interests.

While this pull cannot be avoided, it must be managed. As discussed later, operations will need to be democratically held accountable to be green and just.

This proposed approach to financial stability breaks from conventional economic thinking. For example, international institutions like the World Bank, World Economic Forum, the OECD, and certain UN bodies want public banks to socialise the investment risks of private finance in order to drive green transformation (WEF 2006; World Bank 2012a; OECD 2017; UN IATF 2019; see Chapter 5). Therein, mainstream narratives demand that public banks fund 'bankable' projects, that is, projects expected to earn enough money in the future to repay their debts plus the full costs of borrowing that include profit imperatives. This mainstream strategy empowers private financial capital by privileging market-based outcomes and capital accumulation. It bolsters financialised capitalism. It also undermines public bank capacity to push forward with green and just transitions by subordinating their potential to private sector profit imperatives. While socially responsible, sustainable finance, and environmental, social and governance (ESG) narratives show promise in the direction of sustainable futures, because they are subordinate to the 'bankable' business case they lack the potential to meaningfully and democratically command societal financial resources be deployed for and held accountable to a green and just transformation.

7.2.2 Sourcing Bank Finance Capital for a Green and Just Transition

The design of public banks for a green and just transition must consider its sources of finance capital so that democratisation is not undercut. Two matters need considering: (a) its initial capitalisation and (b) future recurrent sources.

7.2.2.1 Initial Capitalisation
The initial capitalisation of a public bank, or how much capital will need to be injected into the new bank to get it up and running, must

be decided in relation to the scope of activities planned for the bank. The initial injection should neither be too small that the public bank cannot achieve its short- to medium-term targets nor too large that money sits idle and ineffective, ultimately undermining the financial sustainability and credibility of the public bank.

There are two common strategies for the initial capitalisation of equity capital. First, a public bank could issue a start-up equity tranche for a specific amount (say, for example, $50 billion, depending of course on the country in question) that would be bought by the government (hence, injecting capital directly into the public banks). Or, second, the public bank could mirror strategies adopted in Europe and with the new multilateral development banks (the AIIB and New Development Bank) where public banks have a mix of paid-in capital (actual cash in hand) and 'callable' capital. Here the government's actual cash injection is a fraction (anywhere from 10 per cent to 50 per cent) of the total subscribed capital (say, again for illustration purposes, a total of $50 billion). That is, the government would inject $5 billion to $25 billion and guarantee as 'callable' by the new bank's board of directors the remaining $25 billion to $45 billion as and when needed. The advantage of the second approach is that the public bank can kick off operations while drawing less from government resources. For example, the North American Development Bank (NADB) is capitalised in equal parts by the governments of the United States and Mexico. The NADB has $6 billion in total capital subscribed equally by the United States and Mexico. Contributions in 2019 totalled $415 million in paid-in capital and $2.35 billion in callable capital.[3] Much of these combined resources go towards funding sustainable water infrastructure and renewable energy projects along the US–Mexico border. Another option could involve governments authorising an initial equity stake followed by bond issuances to provide new funding. There is a risk here that private investors may resist funding a new public bank, undermining its

---

[3] See NADB: www.nadb.org/about/capitalization. Accessed 6 June 2019.

sustainability (see Chapter 5, Bank of North Dakota). There is an opportunity here to foment cooperation within the public sphere. Public investors, like sovereign wealth funds, insurers, and pensions, could purchase the bonds as a means of public solidarity funding (the Epilogue illustrates such examples; cf. Barrowclough and Gottschalk 2018). No doubt there are other possible forms of innovative capitalisation strategies. The important point is that the choice of funding should enable and not undercut the bank's triple bottom line.

7.2.2.2 Recurrent Sources of Bank Finance Capital

Once established, public banks require recurrent flows of incoming fresh capital to fund ongoing and new operations. The potential sources of recurrent incoming capital can have different impacts on a public bank's ethos, its integration within the public sphere, collaborations with other public entities, its ability to fulfil its mandate, and its capacity to pursue a triple bottom line.

As a principle of pro-public design, a public bank must ensure, whatever its sources of recurrent capital, that the incoming capital enables rather than undermines the bank's democratic ability to fulfil a green and just transition mandate in the public interest. One strategy is to ensure that the bank's primary sources of finance capital are public in origin or mediated through the public sphere (Romero 2017). Recurrent public sources can include direct government allocations, types of permanent capitalisation from public institutions and workers, household and public sector deposits, and domestic and foreign public borrowing (see Box 7.1). For permanent recurrent capitalisation, it is also necessary to think creatively about potential public sources of capital that need not all involve borrowing at all (cf. OECD 2017, 4). For example, non-borrowed sources of public capital can come from transfers linked to a dedicated percentage of tax revenues received by various levels of government (local, state, and national); official grants; and regular injections from other public sector entities. Some less conventional but more innovative 'green' sources include carbon levies and taxes; emissions trading revenues; and utility bill or

---

BOX 7.1   **Recurrent sources of finance capital**

Direct government allocations: Various government funds for public banks; includes initial capital allocations; annual allocations from the government budget. Special government funds for development priorities (e.g., SMEs; farmers; trades; 'green' transformation; Covid-19 relief funds) that are managed and administered by the bank. Promotional and discounted facilities for targeted bank loans supported by the government. Government guarantees for programme lending. Quasi-equity capital: involves long-term government loans that are highly-subsidised (e.g., at zero or low rates of interest) and whose repayment may involve grace periods.

Permanent public capitalisation: State, municipal, local authority contributions; 'green' contributions from essential services and infrastructure (water, electricity, energy, transportation); worker pension and payroll services; proceeds from combatting illicit finance and tax avoidance.

Household and business savings: Public universal and commercial banks can accept current savings as part of their regular retail financial services, savings that can then be redirected to development projects or to public development banks.

Foreign and domestic public borrowing: Sources include the international financial agencies (World Bank Group; regional development banks), foreign governments, foreign development agencies, as well as between domestic development and commercial banks.

Private borrowing: From domestic and international capital markets; bond markets, including green, blue, and social impact bonds purchased by private institutional investors.

Source: Author's compilation

---

energy efficiency surcharges. Strategies of recurrent capitalisation can be linked to structures of class-divided inequality within capitalism. For example, public authorities can ratchet up coordinated efforts to end corporations' and wealth individuals' illicit financial flows and tax dodging strategies, channelling proceeds into transparent green and just funds within public banks.[4] These can all contribute to the cumulative build-up of public banks' financial capacity – that is, to amassing public banking capital within the public sphere – in ways that support its pursuit of a triple bottom line. In short, there are multiple, credible, and sustainable pro-public ways for channelling capital into public banks well beyond narrow marketised worldviews designed only to bolster private investors' power and profitability.

While never eliminating potential conflicts and contradictions in what public banks do (as evidenced in each of the book's case studies), public sources of capital can better enable long-term horizons and reduce short-term demands for higher returns. Indeed, it is precisely the failed neoliberal financialisation model that has supported resurgent interest in public banks. A recent European Commission report acknowledges that private investment is driven first and foremost by expected returns on investment (profits), and thus favour investments with high-return, short-term opportunities that neither support carbon efficient technologies nor help to realise sustainability objectives (let alone social equity) (EPSC 2017, 12). Public banks that have access to public money to generate stable, low-cost, and long-term forms of finance in the public interest can significantly reduce or eliminate neoliberal marketised pressures to maximise profit over mandated priorities and the public interest. For example, publicly owned funding agencies in Nordic countries, such as Kommuninvest (Sweden, established in 1986), Kommunalbanken (Norway, established in 1927), Kommunekredit (Denmark, established in 1898), and MuniFin (Finland, established in 2001), have emerged as innovative pioneers of green lending and vital supporters of municipalities, local development, and public infrastructure projects based on renewable energy, sustainable buildings, waste management, and

---

[4] See R. Kozul-Wright and K. P. Gallagher, 'The Fierce Urgency of Now: Toward a New Multilateralism', 24 June 2019. Available at https://unctad.org/en/pages/newsdetails .aspx?OriginalVersionID=2135. Accessed 16 June 2020.

environmental management. Regardless of lower ratios of return on assets (ROAA), their ways of pooling finance and distributing it to local communities are sustainable. Such a push for green lending is no longer specific to Nordic public banks and investors. As of 2018, 80 per cent of the members of the European Association of Public Banks have provided finance to green projects (EAPB 2018). There is nevertheless an urgent need to decarbonise the bulk of public banks' portfolios, as most funding continues to be carbonising. The curtailing of private interest profit-maximising imperatives is a necessary, but not sufficient, element of any long-term green transformational strategy conceived of in the public interest and as socially just.

Public–public funding collaborations, once formed within the public sphere, can assist public banks in protecting and realising their green and just mandates, in helping to advance a broader public ethos in society, and in reclaiming public sector knowledge, expertise, and capacity. That is, collaborations within the public sphere can help to generate a new breed of effective, just, sustainable, and democratically responsive public service providers (see Hanna 2018a, 2018c; McDonald 2018). In line with the triple bottom line, public sources of finance capital have the right to participate in how the bank operates. That is, no public monetary contribution without meaningful public sphere representation (that is, without economic democracy).

Private borrowing can also provide important sources of recurrent finance capital. This involves public banks tapping into global and domestic financial markets. This can provide near limitless access to finance capital, albeit with differential access depending on where a public bank is situated within the international hierarchy of states. For example, the KfW, Nordic Investment Bank (NIB), and China Development Bank (CDB) are better able to access financial markets than the Costa Rican Banco Popular. Sovereign state guarantees nonetheless help public banks access financial markets at the most favourable rates and terms available to the country.

Public banks can access financial markets by issuing regular, green, blue, social impact, gender, or any number of project-defined bonds domestically and internationally. The green bond market is already well underway. The volume of bonds aligned with climate change reached $1.45 trillion in 2018 and green bonds are estimated to have reached the volume of $389 billion (Climate Bonds Initiative 2018). The United States, for example, is among the countries dominating the issuance of climate-aligned bonds (Weber and Saravade 2019). Nordic countries are also leaders in this area (see Chapter 4). Indications are that green finance will continue to expand and that public banks are well-positioned to benefit from opportunities to borrow cheaply in financial markets. As a principle of pro-public design, however, it must be enshrined in the bank's operations that any sourcing of private capital does not undermine the public bank's mandate, public ethos, or triple bottom line. Rather than 'financialising' a public bank's balance sheet (that is, intensifying the logic of capital accumulation and bending the institution to align itself with private interests), public banks must structure private borrowing and bond issuances in ways that 'definancialise' the capital borrowed (that is, sanitise and eliminate the direct influence of private interest short-term, high-return imperatives) (see Tricarico 2015; Chapter 5). It should be noted that ostensibly public bank borrowing via bond issuances may in practice take the form of public–public funding and sustainable solidarity-based financing (UNCTAD 2019). The Epilogue illustrates this as the NIB and CDB explicitly connect with other public financial institutions to raise capital to support pandemic responses.

This is an important principle because if a public bank is dependent on short-term, return-maximising, and volatile private sources of capital, this dynamic could undermine the ability and autonomy of the public bank to pursue its public interest mandate, especially if private interests conflict with a triple bottom line. Private finance can engage in 'capital strikes' (withholding new capital or calling in existing loan commitments) and are structurally pro-cyclical in their lending behaviour. The effect would be to structurally undermine a public bank's capacity to fulfil its mandate or to bend its green and socially just mandate so that it is more aligned with or subordinated to private interests and capital accumulation. By contrast, a good foundation of public capital and sovereign backing places a public bank firmly within the public sphere and enables it to be aligned with a pro-public framework and democratic accountability.

The point is not that public banks must avoid sourcing capital from private financial markets. Not at all. There are very good reasons for public banks to draw capital from financial markets. By doing so, public banks can build up their own mass of capital over time while also definancialising contemporary financial markets by channelling private capital into public interest projects (offering a form of 'patient' capital, see Mazzucato and Semieniuk 2017). Nevertheless, public banks must be strategic in sourcing capital so that the public interest is fostered and the triple bottom line protected. Public banks must also be strategic in their ways of lending.

7.2.3   Ways of Public Lending for a Green and Just Transition

The design or remaking of a public bank must consider how it will lend for a pro-public green and just transition. Financial institutions, public and private, lend money for a price, which is the cost of borrowing. The cost or price of borrowing for clients involves several factors. How much interest does the bank itself have to pay to access sources of loanable capital? What risks of non-repayment are involved? What are the operating costs of the bank (staff, IT infrastructure, real estate)? What level of return is required? These will be reflected in the interest rate, as well as in any fees or commissions charged by the bank. Yet what a bank actually demands in return for providing a loan or financial support can be concessional or nonconcessional. The price of lending may or may not fully reflect the actual cost of providing it.

It follows that no lending strategy is ideologically or socially neutral but is instead deeply political in its economic and classdivided social implications. Whereas private and corporatised financial institutions lend only to 'bankable' projects and thus have a single 'bottom-line' based on expected returns, a pro-public public bank can have more options. Projects may or may not be 'bankable' per se. Returns may form but one of several considerations. It is a matter of design and political (not just economic) imperatives. It will depend on how societies make their public banks. There are, nevertheless, many ways of lending conducive to a triple bottom line mandate (see Box 7.2). These include offering a variety of repayable loans, facilitating directed funds from third parties (public agencies, official donors,

---

BOX 7.2 Ways of lending for green and just transitions

Standard loans: Must be repaid by the borrower, at concessional or non-concessional rates.

Development loans: Often are concessional and repayable but may blend sources of government or donor funds as well as other public and private investor capital.

Official donors: Provide directed funding that is channelled through the public bank as an intermediary.

Grants, transfers, and subsidies: Do not need to be repaid, and may be tied to government or donor programming or official targets (e.g., carbon reductions).

Equity: Involves taking a direct ownership stake in a project or company.

Public–public collaboration: Involves public sphere collaborations in undertaking projects where ownership, debt risks, and expertise are shared.

Technical assistance: Involves agreements to provide expertise and assistance at little or no cost to the recipient (e.g., project preparation, sectoral expertise).

Bond issuance: Involves providing financial instruments for investors who want to specifically channel their funds directly into certified sustainable development and social impact projects.

Source: Author's compilation

or green investors), offering targeted grants, taking a direct ownership stake (equity investment), providing technical assistance, or engaging in public–public sector collaborations (cf. I4CE 2018, 13). Subject to democratic oversight and scrutiny, these ways of lending and channelling of money can be consistent with and indeed empower a pro-public public bank, thus catalysing rather than undermining green and just transformations.

There are, however, lending instruments that are clearly inconsistent with a pro-public triple bottom line design. For example, any financial strategy that involves project risk sharing agreements where the public bank *guarantees* private investor profitability above all other considerations (which is the strategy advocated by the World Bank's Billions to Trillions SDG agenda in World Bank/IMF 2015) is inconsistent with a triple bottom line and the public interest. It is a dead end to begin a green and just transition by first socialising the risks of investment by ensuring the privatisation of profits. A second closely related and inconsistent strategy involves the promotion of public–private partnerships (PPPs). Here public authorities facilitate infrastructure and essential service provisioning by the private sector. Public banks do so by taking on investment risks and helping to guarantee profitable returns for private and unaccountable corporations. Yet these PPPs are fraught with problems, typically driving up infrastructure costs to the public sector while eroding any sense of democratic decision-making and accountability (Eurodad et al. 2018; McDonald et al. 2021). Lending for a green and just transformation must, and can, do better.

7.3   CONNECTING PUBLIC BANKS WITH COMMUNITY

It is of no small significance that a core commitment of the proposed US Green New Deal legislation was that it 'must be developed through transparent and inclusive consultation, collaboration, and partnership with frontline and vulnerable communities, labor unions, worker cooperatives, civil society groups, academia, and businesses'. These are recurrent themes within global justice movements and with those concerned with economic democracy for green and just

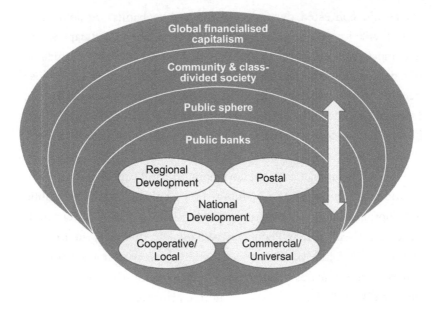

FIGURE 7.2 Envisioning a democratised public banking solidarity structure

transitions.[5] Public banks, by virtue of being located within the public sphere, can be made to reflect these societal concerns. It means institutionalising ways of functioning and coexisting *collaboratively* and *inclusively* with different types of commercial, universal, development, and postal banks vis-à-vis national, regional, and local communities in class-divided society (see Figure 7.2).[6] Therein, formal democratised and solidarity structures should institutionally connect the functioning of public banks to the public sphere, to other public services, and to communities. There is no avoiding that as historical

[5] As of late 2020, the Green New Deal Agenda has increasingly shifted towards the new 'Thrive' (Transform, Heal, and Renew by Investing in a Vibrant Economy) Agenda. See online at www.thriveagenda.com/.

[6] The figure is illustrative not definitive. It builds off of the book's theory of dynamic public banks (see Figure 2.1). There are of course variations beyond the types and scales proposed. The regional category might reasonably include municipal and state-level public banks of any type. Cooperative banks need not be local but may be national scale. Supra-national regional banks might also be integrated. And so on.

social and contested dynamic entities public banks are subject to class-divided power relations within global financialised capitalism. The most realistic response to this is democratisation. The structure of a democratised solidarity system need not be complex, but it does need to enable, not undermine, the fulfilment of a triple bottom line. Neither is the democratisation of public banks hypothetical, borrowing on existing aspects of structures found in North Dakota, France, India, Germany, and Costa Rica.

Quite simply, a national development bank can sit at the hub of a national system of regional (and/or state-level and municipal) public development banks that in turn work collaboratively with communities and their local and cooperative banks. In this way, the funding of a green and just transition can benefit from working within and across different scales of society while benefiting from (and respecting) local knowledge and socio-economic priorities.

There are significant functional benefits to this interconnected solidarity system. The national development bank can access large amounts of cheaper finance capital in national and international markets, in turn supplying regional banks with stable and affordable loanable capital. This in turn is passed on to local municipal banks and communities. As a national hub, a national development bank can tackle the largest investment projects that are beyond the capacity of smaller regional and municipal banks. It is also capable of taking responsibility for being the central knowledge hub of expertise, capacity-building, and training around the vast complexities of financing a green and just transition. This would include organising internal capacity-building and advancement opportunities for staff as well as coordinating external higher education staff training programmes alongside regional programmes. The national hub would be the scale to locate a national public banking association designed to represent and defend the public interest benefits of public banks to government and society. This would need to be matched by a national bank workers union capable of defending and representing the rights of staff. As environmental scholar Laurie Adkin (2019, 3) recognises,

'Institutional change, citizen involvement, planning exercises, and educational work ... will also be needed to transition our societies to post-carbon futures.' Public banks can be the pro-public repositories of this citizen involvement, planning, and expertise.

Regional development banks, as well as state- and municipal-level banks, can work within a smaller geographically defined space, drawing on national public banks (development, commercial, universal, postal) financial and technical resources to fulfil regional investment priorities (cf. Clifton et al. 2021a). Being closer to the projects on the ground, the regional banks can facilitate respect for the full spectrum of the triple bottom line. As the middle-level bank, the regional banks can also facilitate dialogue and decision-making between local banks and communities and the national development bank hub. In turn, local and cooperative banks, as well as municipal banks, are responsible for everyday financial services and for rolling out green transition programmes for the community and for households. As retail banks, these banks will specialise in understanding the needs of the community and then representing these needs to the regional and national levels. Importantly, as deposit-taking institutions, people and communities can decide to hold their savings here knowing that these sources of capital will be secure in a public bank 'safe-haven' and will go towards supporting a green and just transition in the public interest.

The design of this solidarity structure must be armoured in representative, accountable, and democratic processes across and through the different public banks, the public sphere, and in community. More is said on this later. What needs to be emphasised here, however, is that finance in this structure can be a force for definancialised societal integration and the public interest, rather than a source of financialised community disintegration and a driver of grotesque private fortunes and dead-end carbonising investment strategies. Evidence shows that public banks, like other public institutions, can be made to practice non-competitive cooperation as a matter of mandate and good practice in ways that promote common efficiencies and the public interest over private accumulation (see Marois 2013, 2017; Butzbach 2016; Kishimoto and Petitjean 2017; Périlleux and Nyssens 2017; Steinfort and Kishimoto 2019). They can also be made otherwise, a reality against which democratisation can armour public banks. The proposal here can enable the efficiencies and resources available at the national scale to appropriately support 'community-defined projects and strategies' in ways consistent with a Green New Deal, a pro-public future, and other solidarity-based green and just transitions.

7.4   DEMOCRATISING PUBLIC BANKS FOR A GREEN AND JUST TRANSITION

> Yet without explicit, democratically formulated and publicly 'owned' rules, the ruling elite is left to interpret unwritten rules and conventions more or less as it likes. Neither the public nor their representatives have an adequate basis, beyond party manifestos, on which to call the executive to account.

Hilary Wainwright,[7] Feminist Scholar

For public banks to be anything other than just another financial institution captured by neoliberal logics and the interests of wealthy elites, they must move beyond corporatised 'governance' models to being meaningfully democratised. Only through purposively designed and legally binding democratisation can public banks be held to account and be able to fulfil a green and just transition for all.

Democratisation means internalising and acknowledging the already existing connections and disparities between classes, society, politics, and economics in institutional decision-making in ways that are transparent and accountable to the affected community. In the case of public banks, one key democratisation challenge is to strategise how to align national operations with regional and local representatives within national and local development plans (see Romero

---

[7] Wainwright (2020, 204).

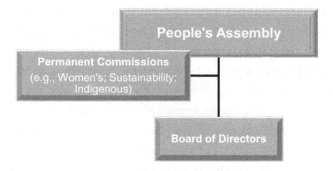

FIGURE 7.3 Democratisation structure of public bank

2017, 15). It is useful to apply the principle of subsidiarity, or the aim to devolve decisions 'to the smallest political unit capable of discharging them' (Basu 2019), while also designing binding means of multi-scalar representation across the public banking structure. Democratic forces must be able to protect against public banks being abused by powerful public or private sector elites for their own interests. In this, neoliberal corporate governance models have not proven effective, as efficiency and profitability imperatives have served as trojan horses for subordinating the public sector to private capital accumulation interests (notably, the World Bank's blending agenda). Substantive democratisation, therefore, is the only viable strategy able to armour public banks against undue and undemocratic abuse and capture for private interests or personal gain.

The design need not be overly complex, but it must be well-crafted and robust (see Figure 7.3). Drawing from existing public banking practices, a democratisation structure should combine both inclusive and representative elements in its institutional structure (I discuss this here in terms of a general type of public bank, so the ideas and principles need to be modified according to different contexts, scales, capacities, and institutional types).

Public banks can be designed with a two-level but hierarchical democratisation structure formally composed of a people's assembly and a board of directors. The people's assembly forms the highest decision-making body and the bank's most inclusive forum. While its precise responsibilities must be debated openly and spelled out in law, the people's assembly is meant to provide the overall vision and mandate for the public bank and to guarantee democratic oversight and accountability over the bank's operations with respect to its mandate. The people's assembly would, for example, review and approve annual reports and undertake strategic planning and consult-ations, but it would not involve itself in more technical and manager-ial operational decisions – unless requested to do so by the board of directors. This enables professional autonomy within the public bank as well as overarching democratic accountability.

There is no pre-set number of people's assembly representatives required. This must be determined in the make-up of the public bank and in light of country context. However, as a matter of democratic principle and to enable broad-based representation of the people, assembly member numbers should presumably begin in the dozens. All people's assembly members would be elected by designated con-stituencies and social sectors representing, for example, trade unions, teachers and educators, environmentalists, SMEs and cooperatives, public services, economic associations, and community anchor insti-tutions (hospitals, universities, and so on). To enable bottom-up repre-sentation and dialogue across the public banking structure, the people's assembly would include designated representatives from the regional, postal, and local public banks (as applicable) and from the bank workers' union.

The people's assembly would be the legal location for permanent commissions to reside. Permanent commissions are specialist bodies responsible for ensuring that public bank operations are consistent with mandated priorities and transformative missions, such as social justice, women's equality, indigenous rights, and green transitions. Permanent commissions are responsible for reviewing core mandates and oper-ational decisions according to their specialisation. Members of commis-sions would be based on expertise but nominated democratically by the people's assembly. The inputs of the commissions must have a mean-ingful impact on the decisions of the assembly and the board.

A public bank's second highest decision-making body would be the board of directors. Unlike the people's assembly, the board is tasked with managing and coordinating daily operations and with implementing the vision of the people's assembly and recommendations of the permanent commissions. It is more likely to require monthly meetings. As with the people's assembly, there is no pre-set number of board members, but as a matter of principle it should be sufficient to ensure substantive representation and to guard against institutional capture by any particular group of social forces or individuals. Therein board membership will need to be context relevant, but it should consider a tripartite model that includes government- and parliament-assigned delegates (national, state, and municipal); people's assembly delegates, and community delegates. This democratisation of the board should translate into substantive democratic control over the managerial, strategic, and operational direction of the public bank, while remaining subordinate to the people's assembly's vision and direction.

The design of democratisation should not be interpreted as 'depoliticising' a public bank's decision-making processes as per neo-liberal ideological commitments. Rather, democratisation should be seen as insulating the public bank from individual political and corporate capture by opening bank processes up to broad-based democratic deliberation – deliberation that internalises and openly acknowledges political differences in order to find common ground. Three additional principles should complement the bank's democratisation structure: the right to collective action, transparency, and accountability. As a matter of human rights and dignity, public banks must uphold a worker's right to self-organise into unions and to take collective action (that is, to strike). Presently, the right to strike for bank workers is not guaranteed by all banks, public or private, around the world. Yet any institution's public interest mandate is fatally undermined if its own employees cannot exercise their basic human rights, articulate their own collective interests, or hold management to account for violations of the bank's mandate.

Democratisation must also be backed by robust *transparency* and *accountability* mechanisms that guarantee open communication, feedback, and inclusive decision-making processes. This means directly challenging existing international financial practices that accept bank secrecy and executive impunity. What a public bank does must be held to account, openly. Transparency, in this case, means having the legal and substantive right to access information held by public banks and by public authorities on public banks (Romero 2017, 23). As best practice, public banks must be required to disclose all key documentation, to detail their clients, sub-clients, and end users, and to provide accessible and verifiable annual reports. To be meaningful, transparency needs to be written into contractual funding agreements. Burdensome administrative processes for accessing such documents must be eliminated by making key documents openly available online and to all. At the same time, affected communities must have regular access to open decision-making forums to be able to hold all public bank decision-makers accountable. Internally, public banks require a user-friendly and independent complaints procedure that protects complainants and whistle-blowers. To meaningfully link transparency and accountability, public banks have to formally allocate annual resources for regular and independent evaluations of the banks' operations. The public bank's green mandate must be included in these mechanisms, for example, by reporting externally to organisations like the Global Reporting Initiative,[8] which highlights sustainability criteria.

People *make* history, if never in the conditions of their own choosing. So too do people *make* public banks, if never independently of the pull of public and private interests in class-divided society. The evidence and analysis presented in this book underscores that it is not only possible but vital to have green public banks, to definancialise the economy, and to democratise finance in order to support the public good and social equity. Green transitions can be financed

[8] See www.globalreporting.org/Pages/default.aspx.

sustainably and justly without the burden falling disproportionately upon the working, the poor, and the marginalised in society. Public banks can leverage alternative sources of finance, channel resources effectively, stabilise social reproduction, learn from successful green lending projects, and be models for collaborative pro-public initiatives to green the economy justly. The aim, then, is to build the pro-public and democratised financial capacity capable of 'overturning the socio-economic relations that constitute the armature' of today's class-divided, unequal, and environmentally devasting society (cf. Lefebvre 2016[1972], 102). To do so public banks must be themselves constituted by and accountable to communities. By democratising public banks, it is possible to have green and just financial institutions that are both commanded by and working for the public good. The path is not without historical precedent or future necessity. It is here that we must be the most ambitious, bold, and creative.

8 Epilogue

Public Banks in a Time of Covid-19

> Public banks ready to step in to help shield economies from the impact of the Coronavirus outbreak.
>
> Press Release, European Association of Public Banks, 31 March 2020[1]

The histories of many public banks have been forged in times of national distress, emergency, and crisis. The crisis of the Covid-19 pandemic holds that possibility, but crisis cannot determine the ways that public banks will respond or for whom. The pandemic itself does not make or remake a public bank. Individual and collective agents do so in a context of class-divided societies grappling with the pandemic. In those societies with public banks, many are mobilising them to confront the crisis. Yet at this early stage, but months into the pandemic, it is impossible to say with certainty what the long-term effects might be of this resurgence. We can only sketch out what their functions have been based so far based on their immediate responses to the pandemic. Overall, the epilogue makes two interrelated points, points which have run through the book so far. First, it exposes the societal dangers of subordinating control of the financial system and its capacity to the private sector and to financialised profit imperatives. Second, it highlights the benefits of protecting public banking capacity in order to make *time* available when needed.

The chapter proceeds as follows. It first sets the stage by providing an overview of the problem of the pandemic in its early stages. Second, the chapter offers an alternative theorisation of public banks'

---

[1] Available at https://eapb.eu/media-corner/press-releases/209:public-banks-ready-to-step-in-to-help-shield-economies-from-the-impact-of-the-coronavirus-outbreak.html. Accessed 10 May 2020.

interventions, one focused on 'time', which moves beyond mainstream economists' 'counter-cyclical' and 'market failure' narratives. Third, the bulk of the chapter details the ways public banks have responded to the pandemic by looking at the six public banks already discussed in this book. Unlike previous chapters, little detail will be given by way of institutional background. Readers are invited to refer to the earlier chapters for context. The purpose here is to map out their different responses.

But first an important caveat. This epilogue is not an in-depth study of the banks' motivations or an assessment of the impacts of their intervention. That is beyond the scope of the chapter and beyond the timeframe of this publication. In the coming years, both must be subject to scrutiny. It is already evident that in most countries there are valid criticisms over government responses and public bank programmes are being pulled by contending interests, public and private. At the time of writing, relatively little has yet been said on public banks and the pandemic (cf. McDonald et al. 2020). Yet where public banks have responded it has been by leveraging their accumulated mass of capital, geographic networks, and financial expertise to make time available – that is, to displace the immediate economic crisis into the future.

8.1 THE PROBLEM OF THE COVID-19 PANDEMIC

According to the World Health Organisation (WHO), initial indications of the pandemic appeared in Wuhan, China, as a pneumonia of unknown cause, first reported on 31 December 2019. Within a month, on 30 January 2020, the WHO declared the outbreak as a Public Health Emergency of International Concern. Within two weeks, on 11 February 2020, the WHO tagged the new coronavirus disease as COVID-19. Within a month, Italy had followed China's lockdown, but the virus had already gone global. Country lockdown after country lockdown followed, to lesser and greater degrees. When first drafting this epilogue in mid-May 2020, there were more than 4.5 million confirmed cases (and climbing by nearly 100,000 per day) and 300,000 deaths (with more than 4,000 more per day). By late summer

2020, total global cases had surpassed 24 million and the numbers of deaths tripled.

The early impact of the pandemic and attempts to stem its spread to save lives were dramatic, immediate, and unprecedented. At the end of March 2020 British economist James Meadway[2] cautioned that society is not simply facing a recession or a financial crisis, but a 'profound dislocation of the essential components of economic and social life itself' that requires not a wartime but an 'anti-wartime' economy where governments must demobilise much of the economy through social isolation and self-distancing. This has had profound economic effects for global capitalism. The World Trade Organisation expects global trade to fall by between 13 per cent and 32 per cent in 2020.[3] The IMF grasped that the 'unprecedented circumstances require unprecedented actions', responding in myriad ways, including doubling access to its emergency facilities, providing debt service relief for twenty-five low-income countries, and providing a new quick-disbursing financing facility to manage 'liquidity pressures for countries with strong economic policies'.[4] Critics, like Eurodad, have begun to detail how this is, nevertheless, far too little for developing already indebted societies.[5]

Workers have been disproportionately impacted. As development scholar Alessandra Mezzadri writes, 'Thousands of factories

[2] J. Meadway, 'The Anti-Wartime Economy', *Tribune*, 19 March 2020. Available at https://tribunemag.co.uk/2020/03/the-anti-wartime-economy. Accessed 24 March 2020.

[3] 'Trade Set to Plunge as COVID-19 Pandemic Upends Global Economy', Press Release, 8 April 2020. Available at www.wto.org/english/news_e/pres20_e/pr855_e.htm. Accessed 12 May 2020.

[4] 'The Managing Director of the IMF and the Heads of the RFAs Emphasize Their Readiness to Cooperate to Mitigate the Impact of COVID-19 on the Global Economy', Press Release No. 20/177, 21 April 2020. Available at www.imf.org/en/News/Articles/2020/04/21/pr20177-imf-managing-director-heads-rfa-readiness-cooperate-mitigate-impact-covid-19-global-economy. Accessed 12 May 2020.

[5] D. Munevar, 'COVID-19 and Debt in the Global South: Protecting the Most Vulnerable in Times of Crisis I', Eurodad blog series covering the impact of COVID-19 on vulnerable countries in the global south. Available at https://eurodad.org/covid19_debt1. Accessed 14 May 2020.

are shut entirely, and the production of most non-essential goods and services has halted in many countries .... The pandemic has irrefutably shown the centrality of human labour to the production of all value.'[6] For many precarious workers, the lockdown and containment measure translate into immediate poverty and desperation. For workers in accommodation and food services, manufacturing, wholesale and retail trade, farmers producing for the urban market, among others, the ILO estimates 'lost labour income will result in an increase in relative poverty for informal workers and their families of more than 21 percentage points in upper-middle-income countries, almost 52 points in high-income countries and 56 points in lower and low-income countries'. No doubt informal workers will be the worst hit, with lockdown generating social tensions and even survival strategies that are at odds with government strategies to contain the crisis.[7] ILO figures point to 1.6 billion informal economy workers losing 60 per cent of their already poverty-level earnings by staying at home.[8] They are damned if they do not stay at home, and damned if they do.

Public services and public sector workers have been especially hard hit, with the public sphere being at the heart of pandemic responses. Public services expert David McDonald argues that with neoliberalism policymakers have orchestrated sustained budget cuts to public services matched by sustained outsourcing of essential service provisioning. This has sacrificed the coherency of service provisioning because it is fragmented between contending public and private operators. Covid-19 exposes this deadly incoherency and

[6] A. Mezzadri, 'A Crisis Like No Other: Social Reproduction and the Regeneration of Capitalist Life during the COVID-19 Pandemic', *Developing Economics*, 20 April 2020. Available at https://developingeconomics.org/2020/04/20/a-crisis-like-no-other-social-reproduction-and-the-regeneration-of-capitalist-life-during-the-covid-19-pandemic/. Accessed 13 May 2020.

[7] 'COVID-19 Crisis and the Informal Economy: Immediate Responses and Policy Challenges', *ILO Brief*, 7 May 2020. International Labour Organization. Available at www.ilo.org/wcmsp5/groups/public/—ed_protect/—protrav/—travail/documents/briefingnote/wcms_743623.pdf. Accessed 10 May 2020.

[8] www.ilo.org/global/about-the-ilo/multimedia/video/institutional-videos/WCMS_744256/lang–en/index.htm. Accessed 9 May 2020.

fragmentation. McDonald writes: 'Frontline workers are showing the stress of insufficient resources, while coordination across services and regions is weakened by the competing mandates of profit-seeking firms and legal contracts that limit our ability to respond flexibly to a crisis.'[9] Political economist Adam Hanieh concurs: 'One clear example of how this disaster is human-made is the poor state of public health systems across most countries in the South, which tend to be underfunded and lacking in adequate medicines, equipment, and staff .... [pointing to a] much larger set of issues including a widespread lack of basic resources (e.g. clean water, food, and electricity), adequate access to primary medical care.'[10]

Feminist scholar Tithi Bhattacharya connects the Covid-19 pandemic to a crisis of social reproduction, that is, to the activities and institutions that are required for making, maintaining, and generationally replacing life.[11] Everything from giving birth to other life-necessary activities, such as cleaning, feeding, cooking, washing clothes, and physical institutional requirements, like housing, public transport, and public spaces like parks, schools, and hospitals are implicated. Through a lens of social reproduction, we can thus 'locate the source of wealth in our society, which is both human life and human labor' and recognise that most social reproduction activities and jobs are done by women workers that, under exploitation-, productivist-, and profit-oriented capitalism, systematically undervalues these activities and workers.

This view jars with those of the world's wealthiest who want the world to go back to business as usual as rapidly as possible. The

---

[9] 'COVID-19 and Our Public Way to Safety', Rabble.ca., 17 April 2020. Available at https://rabble.ca/blogs/bloggers/views-expressed/2020/04/covid-19-and-our-public-way-safety. Accessed 20 April 2020.

[10] 'This Is a Global Pandemic – Let's Treat It as Such'. Available at www.versobooks.com/blogs/4623-this-is-a-global-pandemic-let-s-treat-it-as-such. Accessed 13 May 2020.

[11] S. Jaffe, 'Social Reproduction and the Pandemic, with Tithi Bhattacharya'. Available at www.dissentmagazine.org/online_articles/social-reproduction-and-the-pandemic-with-tithi-bhattacharya. Accessed 12 May 2020.

political faces of this 'non-response' include Trump, Bolsonaro, and Putin. Corporate capitalists and CEOs like Elon Musk of Tesla/SpaceX even threatened to sue governments (in his case, the State of California) for preventing them from producing and accumulating more capital (there is a radical-right lineage to this line of 'thinking' linking back to anti-organised labour and anti-union movements like the 'right to work' movement).

There are, nevertheless, widespread and more hopeful calls for rebuilding better. At the multilateral level, UN Secretary General António Guterres argued that 'we must commit to building back better by using the recovery from Covid-19 to pursue a more sustainable and inclusive economy and society in line with the Sustainable Development Goals'.[12] This is but the tip of the iceberg, as other UN institutions, NGOs and CSOs, activists, and academics urge policymakers and governments to press forward with needed environmental and democratic reforms of the economy and global capitalism. Early indications are that much of this are just words. Social forces will need to force action in order to drive a green and just recovery within their societies out of the global Covid-19 crisis (see Macfarlane and Brett 2020). Public finance and banking will occupy a central role in any future, be it business as usual or building forward greener and more equitably (Cochrane and Pauthier 2020). To ensure the latter, it is important that we understand what and how public banks have first responded to help ensure that the future is better, greener, and more just.

8.2 PUBLIC BANKS: MAKING TIME IN RESPONSE TO THE COVID-19 CRISIS

So far economists have tended to employ traditional conceptual tools to frame public bank interventions and the pandemic. In this

---

[12] www.un.org/sg/en/content/sg/statement/2020-04-16/secretary-generals-statement-the-effect-of-the-covid-19-pandemic-children-scroll-down-for-french-version. Accessed 10 May 2020.

narrative, the raison d'être of public banks, albeit largely restricted to development banks, is to respond to 'market failures'. Presumably, private banks have or will fail to respond to the Covid-19 crisis adequately, so public banks must function counter-cyclically, that is, to provide large-scale funding to protect jobs, the economy, and so on from the crisis. This Covid-19 crisis is discussed, for example, in reference to the 2008–09 global financial crisis as a way of underscoring the need for public banks to do more (Griffith-Jones and te Welde 2020; Griffith-Jones et al. 2020).

While such framing has the benefit of underscoring the capacity of public banks to lend into and against the prevailing economic curve, it does so at the high cost of subsuming much more complex socio-political realities into narrowly economic tropes on the essence of public banks – it is as if the Covid-19 pandemic was just another economic cycle or market failure wherein public banks respond by offering 'additionality' to private finance and by lending 'counter-cyclically'. The limits to these economic concepts, often derived from fixed understandings of 'publicly' owned bank, are discussed earlier in the book (Chapter 2) and need not be further reviewed here. Suffice it to say the argument of this book has been for a more historically open and *dynamic* conceptual approach. Rather than responding mechanically to economic cycles, public banks' pandemic responses are better understood as being made to make time available. What public banks are doing is not a timeless reflection of an essential 'reason to be'. Rather, public banks have acquired a diversity of functions and built up material capacity in ways that enable them to respond, without determining it to be so.

As a reflection of the strategies of state and political authorities, the immediate impacts and longer-term costs of the Covid-19 crisis are being displaced in time and space across class-divided society (cf. Marois and Muñoz-Martínez 2016; Ho and Marois 2019). Banks are adept at this process of transforming current money and credit obligations into future ones. Above all, public banks can do this effectively because they are located within the public sphere and because they have the ability to do so *not* based on profit but based on public mandates. Here I draw on work around state spatial temporal strategies and theorisations of how public financial institutions can bend time. Political economist Bob Jessop has discussed state spatial strategies in the following terms (2016, 23–24):

> These strategies refer to the historically specific practices through which state (and imperial) institutions and state managers (and the social forces they represent) seek to reorder territories, places, scales, and networks to secure the reproduction of the state in its narrow sense, *to reconfigure the sociospatial dimensions of the state in its integral sense, and to promote specific accumulation strategies, state projects, hegemonic visions, or other social imaginaries and projects.*

The mobilisation of public institutions like public banks offer a concrete vantage point into such state strategies at times of crisis, particularly in terms of Jessop's related articulation of a temporal 'institutional fix', which is (2016, 25)

> a complementary set of institutions that, via institutional design, imitation, imposition, or chance evolution offer (within given parametric limits) a temporary, partial, and relatively stable solution to the coordination problems involved in securing economic, political, or social order. Nonetheless, *it is not purely technical* and, rather than providing a post hoc solution to pre-given coordination problems, it is *partly constitutive* of this order.

As I have argued elsewhere, this conceptual framework is useful for interpreting the responses of state financial institutions to crises as a condensation of class-divided social forces pursuing contending socio-political and spatial strategies (Ho and Marois 2019). Through public banks, social forces attempt to manage 'space' and create 'time' to help protect contending public and private interests in light of the contradictions and crises that arise in capitalism. Spatially, public banks can respond by combining, mobilising, and channelling resources from capital rich to capital poor locations, that is, from wealthier cities, regions, countries, and institutions that have capital surpluses to those with shortfalls, both domestically and internationally. Temporally, state strategies can attempt to 'fix' economic crises *now* by pushing and displacing them into the *future* (Marois 2014; Sgambati 2019). Through lending, 'banks command a power to make available time', as expressed in the elegant wording of political economist Martijn Konings (2018, 79). By combining state spatial and temporal strategies, authorities combine and mobilise finance capital in ways that displace economic crisis now into the future.

The successes of state's spatial-temporal strategies in the present are not without potential complications and contradictions in the future. Jessop cautions that 'current zones of stability imply future zones of instability' (2016, 25). This is subject to power relations. Crises are managed or 'fixed' in the present context but within class-divided society: 'the ways in which minor and major crises are resolved, or not, is historically contingent on domestic social affairs, state institutional capacity, relative balance of power between capital and labor, and global pressures' (Marois 2012, 36). Consequently, it is at times of crisis like this that more democratic, accountable, and transparent public banks are needed to push responses towards the public interest.

8.3   THE WAYS OF PUBLIC BANKS CONFRONTING THE PANDEMIC

There are, of course, no guarantees that public bank mandates will serve the public interest or even 'build back better' in anyone's but private interests within neoliberalism. Public banks can be made to do so, but this requires organised political coordination. In the current conjuncture, there are indications that, given the severe impacts faced by public health and wage labourers, the public interest is tending to shape public banks' pandemic responses. As you will see, these responses are often in stark contrast to private corporate banking responses premised on protecting profits and future accumulation prospects.[13]

Some underlying assumptions frame this tentative analysis. First, it is unlikely that a Covid-19 vaccine will be available until late 2020. Producing sufficient quantities will take perhaps years longer. The Covid-19 'crisis' will therefore be prolonged, unpredictable, and ultimately deadly. Second, neoliberal financialisation has far from faded away, based as it is on corporate power, a mass of privately held capital, marketised social reproduction, the privileging of financial accumulation imperatives, and corporatised cum authoritarian governance measures. Third, neoliberal advocates and corporate capitalists will want to find common ground with statist Keynesians to keep capitalism afloat, and Keynesians will want to support renewed capitalist growth and productivity. The ascendancy of a pro-market additionality narrative around more or less 'public'–private partnerships is most probable in official circles. These will be confronted by more popular, public interest driven struggles to match pandemic responses with green and just transition strategies.

Consequently, public banks' pandemic responses will be variegated and shaped by the pull of contending public and private interests and by the ways they are integrated within global financialised circuits of capital. In other words, what public banks can do is tempered by 'the unequal credit conditions and fiscal abilities of their sovereigns' (Mertens et al. 2020, 8). Whereas the European Association of Public Banks highlights how its members have provided €1 trillion of the European Commission's total €3 trillion response package (that is,

---

[13] In the UK, for example, its financial watchdog, the Financial Conduct Authority, only asks that the banks take what *they* see as appropriate measures to support families struggling with mortgage payments (in terms of payment holidays). If and when the banks do so, however, they have decided to make any payment holidays taken count against a household's future credit rating (see M. Vincent, 'UK Banks Told to Offer Mortgage Support When Payment Holidays End', FT.com, 27 August 2020). That is, families' future creditworthiness will be impacted, a decision that is only to the benefit of the banks themselves. In most cases below, the public banks have explicitly excluded this punitive action.

a full third) by mid-summer 2020, the African Association of Development Finance Institutions cautions that its members' capacity to respond is hampered by constrained government support (see AADFI 2020; EAPB 2020).[14] The purpose here is to provide a sense of how specific societies have responded early on through the public banks. I focus on the cases already discussed in the book: the Nordic Investment Bank, the China Development Bank, the Bank of North Dakota, the NABARD, the Banco Popular y de Desarrollo Comunal, and the KfW.

8.3.1   Nordic Investment Bank (NIB)

Unique among the public banks studied in the book, the NIB is a regional development bank owned and controlled by eight different member countries (see Chapter 4). According to the regional organisational body, Nordic Co-operation, Nordic country members have adopted distinct approaches to confronting the Covid-19 pandemic. Within a broadly shared Nordic system of welfare provisioning, the countries have adopted different government strategies, with Sweden having a less restrictive approach than Finland, Denmark, and Norway.[15] Nevertheless, these Nordic countries and three Baltic countries (Estonia, Latvia, and Lithuania) made a shared request of the bank they control. On 27 March 2020 NIB member country ministers (the governors of the NIB) instructed it to ramp up and maximise lending to protect their economies from the economic hit of the pandemic. The statement reads as follows[16]:

---

[14] Between May and December 2020, the Municipal Services Project, SOAS University of London, Eurodad, and UNCTAD launched a website (https://publicbankscovid19 .org/) and co-produced a new book detailing the rapid responses of dozens of public banks around the world to the Covid-19 crisis (McDonald et al. 2020). In the summer of 2020, the IMF had also complied a rolling list of country-based Covid-19 policy responses. See www.imf.org/en/Topics/imf-and-covid19/Policy-Responses-to-COVID-19#U.

[15] www.norden.org/en/news/nordic-co-operation-covid-19. Accessed 13 May 2020.

[16] www.nib.int/who_we_are/news_and_media/news_press_releases/3471/statement_ by_the_nordic-baltic_ministers_on_nib_s_role_in_the_corona_crisis. Accessed 13 May 2020.

We expect the NIB to support sustainable businesses facing short-term liquidity problems due to the crisis. The NIB should be able to extend loans to financial intermediaries for on-lending to small and medium-sized companies as well as provide direct financing to larger businesses experiencing a downturn. It is also of utmost importance that the bank seeks out businesses under strain and assists them in bridging the effects of the current crisis. The bank should support member states' businesses to the widest extent possible to overcome the crisis.

Action was immediate, most likely coordinated even before the ministerial statement. Henrik Normann, President and CEO of the NIB, replied that the pandemic demanded a rapid revision of the NIB's annual plans, committing to substantial increases in lending to member countries. The bank's function at this moment was to help stem economic decline and counter threats to growth and employment. At the same time, the NIB acted to protect its own operations and staff by segregating the institution. Staff would work from multiple locations, but mostly from home.

The NIB's most immediate and dramatic response involved unveiling major governmental support packages for its Baltic state members, Estonia, Lithuania, and Latvia. On the same day as the above statement, 27 March 2020, the NIB signed a €750 million, fifteen-year loan package with Estonia.[17] Then, on 3 April it signed a €400 million ten-year loan package with Lithuania.[18] And, on 9 April 2020 it signed a €500 million ten-year loan package with Latvia.[19]

---

[17] www.nib.int/who_we_are/news_and_media/news_press_releases/3469/nib_provides_covid-19_mitigation_loan_to_republic_of_estonia. Accessed 13 May 2020.

[18] Available at www.nib.int/who_we_are/news_and_media/news_press_releases/3483/nib_finances_lithuania_s_covid-19_response_action_plan. Accessed 13 May 2020.

[19] Available at www.nib.int/who_we_are/news_and_media/news_press_releases/3479/nib_provides_covid-19_mitigation_loan_to_republic_of_latvia. Accessed 14 May 2020.

The NIB was extending massive public–public support in response to the Covid-19 crisis.

Speaking on Estonia's package, Normann specified that '[t]he purpose of this loan is to provide countercyclical financing, and to alleviate the immediate socio-economic consequences caused by the Covid-19 pandemic'. In the case of Lithuania, the fund would contribute to the government's €2.5 billion Economic and Financial Action Plan to confront the pandemic. Likewise for Latvia in terms of pandemic mitigation, though the Treasury would be responsible for redirecting the NIB funds to support municipal and local government projects on favourable credit terms.[20] In all NIB packages, the funds were used to cover increased and unanticipated expenditures related to healthcare and civil protection services (purchasing protective medical gear, testing kits and other medical equipment, ensuring additional social guarantees for medical staff and officers working in risk-areas amongst other measures); employee compensation and loss of income; liquidity support and payment relief for business, SMEs, tourism and transportation; business compensation losses and costs related to government restrictions (closures of sports and entertainment venues and imposed regional restrictions and border closures); and to provide general economic stimulus.

To fund this rapid increase in lending, the NIB issued its first 'NIB Response Bond' for €1 billion on 30 March 2020. According to the 'NIB Response Bond Framework' document,[21] loans derived from the bonds 'should support the provision of products and services contributing to health conditions and maintaining living standard for groups challenged by the Covid-19 virus'. Three categories of lending are targeted: to the public sector; to the financial sector (to on-lend); and to the real economy (healthcare and medical equipment

---

[20] Available at www.leta.lv/eng/home/important/A04FAD7E-9DCD-4F71-A029-1F9C3C857A37/. Accessed 14 May 2020.

[21] Available at www.nib.int/filebank/a/1585555664/59aa748f8c25ba29e2b145db6785d08e/10201-NIB_Response_Bond_Framework_30_March.pdf. Accessed 14 May 2020.

companies; infrastructure sector). The framework specifies that the NIB's Sustainability and Mandate Unit standard assessments will be suspended ('excluded' companies, according to the NIB's Sustainability Policy and Guidelines, will continue to be excluded). Instead, this unit will ensure the funds are used 'to finance projects aimed at alleviating negative socio-economic consequences of the Covid-19 pandemic in NIB's member countries', that is, according to Covid-19 mitigation priorities.

The rapid response and quality of the NIB bond issuance was widely praised within financial markets: 'The orderbook reached above EUR 3.2 billion with more than 80 investors in three hours, enabling the transaction to price 3bps tighter than initial guidance.' According to the NIB news release, it drew wide geographical interest[22]: 19 per cent to Benelux investors; 12 per cent to Nordics; 6 per cent to France; 4 per cent to the UK; 32 per cent to other Europe; 21 per cent to Asia; and 6 per cent to various other countries. Public financial institutions were major purchasers: Central Banks and other Official Institutions constituted the lion's share of investors, accounting for 58 per cent of the bond, followed by banks at 24 per cent, fund managers at 12 per cent, and pension funds, insurance, and corporates at 6 per cent. That is, the NIB drew money from capital rich spaces to fund pandemic responses in capital poor regions. These flows of capital had a public interest basis. Wilfried Bolt, Senior Investment Manager at PGGM (a Dutch cooperative pension fund service with combined pension assets worth €252 billion) writes[23]:

> PGGM is content to be an investor in the first Response Bond, on behalf of the Dutch healthcare sector pension fund. This bond provides an opportunity, at historical attractive valuation levels,

---

[22] Available at www.nib.int/who_we_are/news_and_media/news_press_releases/ 3476/nib_issues_inaugural_response_bond. Accessed 14 May 2020.

[23] Available at www.nib.int/who_we_are/news_and_media/news_press_releases/ 3486/nib_lists_eur_1_billion_response_bond_on_nasdaq_helsinki?utm_source= Newsletter&utm_medium=email&utm_campaign=Responses%20to%20Covid-19%20pandemic. Accessed 14 May 2020. Emphasis added.

not only to aim for financial goals *but also add to non-financial objectives* which we believe are achievable through allocating capital.

Within days the NIB issued a second NIB Response Bond for kr4 billion (€376 million) but raised over kr5 billion due to strong demand. Geographically, the SEK issuance drew from across northern European, and mostly Sweden-based, orders: 78 per cent to Sweden; 11 per cent to Denmark; 6 per cent to Finland; 4 per cent to Czech Republic; and 1 per cent to Latvia. Private banks led in this bond accounting for 40 per cent of purchases, followed by pension funds and insurance at 29 per cent, fund managers at 27 per cent, and central banks at 4 per cent. The NIB anticipates that its increased interventions will not have a significant long-term impact on operations, thus maintaining its triple-A credit rating (AAA/Aaa).[24]

8.3.2 China Development Bank (CDB)

The actions of the CDB in response to the Covid-19 outbreak in China were made in close correlation with the decisions of the Communist Party of China's (CPC) Central Committee and the State Council, which sit within the governance structure of the CDB (see Chapter 4).[25] On 28 January 2020 the CPC Committee of the CDB met and specified that the bank assume an organisational and leadership role in confronting the virus outbreak (which was not, as yet, a global pandemic). Subsequently, the CDB set up 'green' channels to rapidly decide on and allocate resources. The key target was emergency financing for epidemic prevention and control. State authorities directed the CDB to respond within twenty-four hours to requests from central and local leadership groups or command offices and

---

[24] www.nib.int/who_we_are/news_and_media/articles/3488/nib_s_first_responses_to_covid-19_pandemic?utm_source=Newsletter&utm_medium=email&utm_campaign=Responses%20to%20Covid-19%20pandemic. Accessed 13 May 2020.

[25] The following information is taken from CDB News, including the CDB Covid-19 Responses-Summary. The news releases are available at www.cdb.com.cn/English/xwzx_715/khdt/. Accessed 15 May 2020.

within forty-eight hours to epidemic prevention and control-related enterprises.

By early February, the CDB had established three internal policies: (1) for enterprises impacted by Covid-19, it would not demand early repayments or suspend/delay loans; (2) for small enterprises in Hubei Province it should provide favourable loan rates and terms; and (3) for education loans, there would be no interest penalties for delayed repayment and delays in repayments would not be considered as default. In these instances, making *time* available was of the essence. The government then reinforced the role of the CDB in wider economic recovery and counter-cyclical lending following decisions made at the CPC Politburo conference on 21 February. That same decision stated that this should be done while ensuring safety in the bank's workplaces and providing care for its employees.

Government direction was clear on the ways of CDB lending. In general, the CDB should provide the best rates and most favourable terms possible for requests related to epidemic prevention and control-related enterprises and institutions. Additionally, the CDB should support small enterprises and private businesses with support loans; provide special loans to farms; back newly launched projects; provide support for critical infrastructure, manufacturing, strategic emerging and high-tech industries; offer long-term financing for major industry development; support foreign trade and investment; and promote domestic consumption. Authorities also encouraged the CDB to help overcome poverty by offering loans and donations.

As with all the public banks, there is as yet little by way of impact analysis. However, the CDB highlights a few specific interventions. On 24 January 2020, the CDB issued an emergency ¥2 billion (€260 million) loan to support Wuhan in Covid-19 prevention and control. Reportedly, as of 10 February 2020, the CDB had committed to ¥35 billion (€4.5 billion) in Covid-19 emergency loans and provided ¥20.4 billion (€2.7 billion) to build hospitals and purchase of emergency supplies. By 20 February 2020 ¥69.9 billion loans (€9.08 billion) in support had gone to enterprises and the economy, though the public and private distribution is unclear.

To support CDB's lending capacity the People's Bank of China (PBC, the central bank) lent the CDB ¥7.6 billion (€990 million) in late January for coronavirus epidemic prevention. In doing so, the PBC specified a preferential lending rate to reduce financing costs. The CDB then issued ¥13.5 billion (€1.75 billion) in new bonds in early February (one-year maturity and a fixed interest rate of 1.65 per cent). Furthermore, through the domestic interbank bond market, the CDB issued bonds worth ¥8 billion (€1.04 billion). These were purchased by financial institutions within China, including many public commercial banks, such as Industrial and Commercial Bank of China, Bank of China, Shanghai Pudong Development Bank, CITIC Bank, Donghai Securities, Bank of Communications, Zhejiang Rural Credit Cooperative Union, China Merchants Bank, Nanhai Rural Commercial Bank, and China Bohai Bank. A second set of bonds worth ¥5.5 billion (€714 million) were issued and sold to the public through online banking of the public commercial banks, including the Agriculture Bank of China, ICBC, BOC, Industrial Bank, Bank of Nanjing, Shanghai Rural Commercial Bank, BOCOM, and Bank of Ningbo. In this case, the funding of the CDB has been distinctly public in character, drawing financial resources from the often public commercial banks in China to channel them into first public and then public and private sectors in government-directed response to the emergency pandemic.

8.3.3   *Bank of North Dakota (BND)*

In the United States, the lone state-level public bank, the BND (see Chapter 5), initially responded in March 2020 by administering a federal government programme on wage support, as any qualifying bank could do, and by providing bank-led loan relief for students. The first federal programme involved the US Small Business Administration (SBA) Paycheck Protection Act. Here financial institutions determined borrower eligibility and credit worthiness without going through standard SBA processes. The programme targeted support for small business of 500 employees or less; sole proprietors, independent contractors and self-employed individuals; and non-profit and veterans' organisations until 31 December 2020 for loans up to $10,000,000. The loans are to be used for payroll support such as employee salaries, paid sick or medical leave, insurance premiums, mortgage payments or other debt. Another federal BND-administered programme included the SBA Small Business Disaster Relief Program. This one is aimed at start-ups; individuals operating as a sole proprietor or independent contractor; cooperatives and employee stock ownership plans with fewer than 500 employees. The recipients need not have been operating for more than a year and loans are available up to $2,000,000 for a term of thirty years.

Within the BND itself, it announced on 24 March 2020 a bank-led Student Loan Relief plan to 'assist borrowers impacted by COVID-19' by allowing them to defer payments for six months. The BND also reduced variable interest rates by 1 per cent and fixed interest rates by at least 1 per cent. Over the next month, the BND internally developed two additional support programmes, announced on 24 April 2020. These programmes were aimed at assisting 'North Dakota businesses in obtaining long-term, low-interest loans to assist in the state's economic recovery from the COVID-19 pandemic'.[26] At base, the programmes help small and large businesses secure working capital and to fund the replenishment of depleted inventories. A joint statement from the Industrial Commission (the bank's governing board composed of the state governor, attorney general, and agriculture commissioner) clarifies the rationale (emphasis added):

> We understand and empathize with the challenging situation facing our business community. The Bank of North Dakota makes our state uniquely positioned to provide much-needed assistance *as federal programs are exhausted.*

---

[26] Available at https://bnd.nd.gov/industrial-commission-authorizes-bank-of-north-dakota-programs-to-assist-businesses-in-pandemic-recovery-efforts/. Accessed 15 May 2020.

The details of the two BND-led Covid-19 relief programmes are as follows.[27] In both programmes, the BND aims to provide low cost, long-term working capital and cash flow to restart business operations within the state. First, the Small Employer Loan Fund (SELF) works through local financial institutions or certified development corporations to connect with very small businesses (maximum ten employees) for loans up to $50,000 and for up to ten years at a fixed interest rate of 1 per cent. Loan payments can be deferred for up to six months to free up immediate liquidity. Second, the COVID-19 PACE Recovery Program (CPRP) also works through local financial institutions. This programme has a much higher loan limit, up to $5 million for businesses with less than 500 employees or up to $10 million for businesses with more than 500 employees, and likewise offers low-interest loans, up to ten years terms, and payment deferral for up to six months. In the CPRP programme, the BND subsidises (via 'buydowns') the interest rate to 1 per cent with a time-limited maximum subsidy of $500,000. The BND made $200 million available for interest buydowns and $50 million for low-interest loans, which will be leveraged to provide up to $2 billion in low-interest loans. In the case of the BND, its primary orientation in responding has been to provide the time needed for the private sector and businesses to maintain operations without closure as well as for students to retain 'creditworthiness' by not defaulting.

8.3.4 National Bank for Agriculture and Rural Development (NABARD)

Like many other public development banks, the NABARD first reacted as a government institution or agency to administer and facilitate government-led support programmes. On 27 March 2020, the Reserve Bank of India (RBI; the central bank) issued sector-wide re-regulations of current credit relations. As an apex institution involved across all aspects of rural finance in India (see Chapter 5), NABARD

---

[27] Available at https://bnd.nd.gov/business/. Accessed 15 May 2020.

has a central role in the regulatory and refinancing aspects of these measures as they relate to rural and cooperative banks and communities. The RBI re-regulations authorised India's banks to help 'mitigate the burden of debt servicing brought about by disruptions on account of COVID-19 pandemic and to ensure the continuity of viable businesses'.[28] The move embodied the essence of 'making time available', involving payment rescheduling for term loans and working capital facilities, granting banks the right to extend a three-month moratorium on payments (although interest continues to accrue). For working capital facilities, banks can defer interest payments of their cash credit and overdraft lending facilities. At the same time, the RBI re-regulated working capital financing, allowing financial institutions to 'recalculate the "drawing power" by reducing the margins and/or by reassessing the working capital cycle'. The RBI specified that because these measures are 'being provided specifically to enable the borrowers to tide over economic fallout from COVID-19', borrowers will not be penalised by asset classification downgrades (that is, their creditworthiness will be shielded). NABARD oversees this process for India's rural financial institutions.

The NABARD itself also began to increase its lending and refinancing operations. In March 2020 NABARD announced plans to extend ☐42,313 crore (€5.15 billion) for constructing rural infrastructure in 2020 (although just under half had already been disbursed).[29] While pandemic-relevant programmes like connectivity, water, and social housing were included, it was not clear that these were new pandemic-related funds. In April, however, the RBI announced an injection of liquidity into NABARD in direct recognition of the 'tightening of financial conditions in the wake of the COVID-19 pandemic', which has made it difficult to raise capital in financial

---

[28] 'COVID-19 – Regulatory Package', Reserve Bank of India Circular, RBI/2019-20/186. Available at www.nabard.org/auth/writereaddata/File/RBI%20circular%20dt% 2027.03.2020.pdf. Accessed 18 May 2020.

[29] www.nabard.org/news-article.aspx?id=25&cid=552&NID=286. Accessed 18 May 2020.

markets.[30] According to NABARD Chair, Harsh Kumar Bhanwala, the received □25,000 crore (€3.05 billion) is destined for refinancing India's regional rural banks, rural cooperative banks, and microfinance institutions to improve these institutions' liquidity situation amidst the crisis. India's public commercial banks provide over a third of rural short-term crop loans to farmers, and the RBI injection will reduce lending costs to farmers. In a CNBC TV18 17 April 2020 interview, Bhanwala underscored the timeliness of the cash injection, as more funds would be needed for seasonal agriculture demands. At the same time, the RBI injection helped to compensate for a fall in deposit savings held in India's rural banks due to the lockdown (as people draw down their savings to survive, in turn reducing the capital banks have available to lend out). Finally, in early May, the Indian government injected an additional □30,000 crore (€3.65 billion) into NABARD through the Emergency Working Capital Fund for farmers.[31] This fund will on-lend to the state cooperative and district cooperative banks and to the regional rural banks. It is anticipated to reach 30 million small-scale farmers. The NABARD reports that from when the lockdown began in late March to early May 2020, it had extended some □30,021 crore (€3.66 billion) to the rural banks in response to the Covid-19 pandemic.[32] As with all the banks, the extension of credits and the provisioning of additional resources is intended to help people survive the worst of the crisis, that is, to push the immediate impact into the future. This is unlikely to resolve the crisis, but displacement may help many overcome it. It is worth noting that in the case of NABARD there is a distinctly spatial strategy at work as national funds are channelled through NABARD

---

[30] www.nabard.org/news-article.aspx?id=25&cid=552&NID=285. Accessed 18 May 2020.

[31] www.nabard.org/news-article.aspx?id=25&cid=552&NID=290. Accessed 18 May 2020.

[32] www.nabard.org/news-article.aspx?id=25&cid=552&NID=282. Accessed 18 May 2020.

according to a specifically rural orientation. The NABARD thus mediates space and time in its government-led Covid-19 response.

8.3.5 Banco Popular y de Desarrollo Comunal (BPDC)

As a nationwide universal bank, the BPDC deals with daily transactions and customers as well as with wider development projects (see Chapter 6). Unlike the other public banks, the BPDC first reacted independently of government-led direction by unrolling two Covid-19 initiatives. In late March 2020 the BPDC National Board of Directors approved the bank's Solidarity Programme (delivered online or by phone so people can stay home).[33] Through it, clients could halt payments on credits for three months without it affecting their credit record or preventing them from accessing their financial resources held in the bank. The idea was to ensure people had liquid cash resources in order to meet urgent commitments and necessities. The programme applies to all BPDC credits, including business, mortgage, and housing credits. The unpaid amounts, however, will accumulate to the principal balance. As of mid-May 2020, Marvin Rodríguez, BPDC General Manager, reports that the Solidarity Programme approved 79,594 support operations nationwide.[34] Additionally, if you have a BPDC credit card and are enrolled in the Solidarity Programme, the bank will be flexible in making or delaying payments. The BPDC also temporarily eliminated bank commissions on cash advances and reduced or removed transaction charges for a wide range of online debit, credit, and transfer services to help promote electronic transactions and to reduce in-person visits to branches. The second BPDC-led initiative is called the Debtor in Arrears Programme.[35] For individuals or companies in arrears of payments for less than 120 days

---

[33] BPDC. Available at www.bancopopular.fi.cr/Documents/ARCHIVOS-COVID-19/BENEFICIO_SOLIDARIO.pdf. Accessed 16 May 2020.

[34] Available at www.crhoy.com/nacionales/plan-propone-salvar-empresas-con-utilidades-de-banca-publica/. Accessed 15 May 2020.

[35] BPDC. Available at www.bancopopular.fi.cr/Documents/ARCHIVOS-COVID-19/DEUDORES_ATRASADOS.pdf. Accessed 15 May 2020.

(on 31 March), the BPDC will not pursue legal collection processes during the next three months. Both BPDC programmes are fundamentally geared towards making time available for individuals, households, and businesses in Costa Rica.

Like the other public banks, the BPDC facilitated various government-led programmes, particularly in payments and financial supports delivery, across its various corporate arms. The BPDC Pension arm, for example, administers and delivers financial resources according to the new Costa Rican Law for the Delivery of the Labor Capitalization Fund (FCL) to people affected by the economic crisis. The FCL supports people whose jobs have been terminated, contracts suspended, or working days reduced in ways that have caused a loss of income. The BPDC deposits eligible government support payments directly into people's accounts held in the bank, which are then available for immediate personal withdrawal. In mid May 2020, Róger Porras, Manager of BPDC *Popular Pensiones*, stated, 'We were able to give an agile and effective response to the workers affected by COVID-19 and by the economic crisis that resulted from this health pandemic. Just four days after the new Law came into force, ₡274,837,893 million had already been delivered to individuals and families who need it so much right now.'[36] The BPDC will also distribute additional government support payments for lost income via the national *Plan Proteger* (Protect Plan), but details at the time of writing were not yet known.[37]

On the more 'development' side of the bank, the BPDC will participate alongside Costa Rica's other public universal banks in contributing to and administering a government-led ₡900 billion (€1.5 billion) National Development Fund (FONADE) programme, announced in mid-May 2020.[38] The source of capital will come from

[36] Available at www.crhoy.com/economia/mas-de-23-mil-personas-gestionaron-retiro-del-fcl-en-el-popular/. Accessed 15 May 2020.

[37] See www.mtss.go.cr/elministerio/despacho/covid-19-mtss/plan_proteger/bono_proteger.html. Accessed 15 May 2020.

[38] Available at https://qcostarica.com/%C2%A2900-billion-fund-to-revive-the-economy/. Accessed 15 May 2020.

within the country's public banks themselves, as agreed to by the banks, but the government will explicitly back the credits given. The programme is to support the reopening of businesses by providing the necessary working capital. Each public bank determines its own credit specifications, but the programme is structured around easing credit record requirements, reducing interest rates, providing sector-specific state guarantees to the public banks, and offering up to a two-year grace period on repayments (although a 'symbolic' payment is required every 180 days). The state guarantees are offered through the Costa Rican Banca Para el Desarrollo (a unique Costa Rican-style development bank), which received an injection of ₡200 billion (€325 million) from the National Development Fund (FONADE).

The BPDC's official response to issues of bank worker and workplace safety appear to stand out among the six cases discussed. Unlike the other banks, the BPDC details, extensively and transparently, its actions across all of its corporate arms.[39] For example, the Popular Insurance arm established a 'Crisis Committee' to update, manage, and coordinate actions around Covid-19 regulations and requirements. Across the conglomerate, the BPDC has intensified cleaning routines in the commercial and administrative offices. Through its networks and client base, the BPDC disseminated Ministry of Health information on proper health and sanitation procedures (handwashing, cough and sneeze protocol, new ways of greeting). The BPDC committed to providing bank staff with appropriate and sufficient personal protective equipment and hygiene material, including masks and gloves where required. In common areas, the bank has placed posters on preventive measures and provided antibacterial gel dispensers. Large meetings have been suspended, telework promoted, official trips abroad suspended, and early detection of risk personnel in certain areas provided. The BPDC even states that it has provided webinars on staff mental health and on dealing with the personal impact of the pandemic on bank

---

[39] See www.bancopopular.fi.cr/Paginas/default.aspx. Accessed 15 May 2020.

workers. Other banks may well be undertaking similar measures, but none have been as transparent as the BPDC.

8.3.6 Kreditanstalt für Wiederaufbau (KfW)

The German development bank, the KfW (see Chapter 6), like the China Development Bank, has undertaken extensive government-led intervention programmes. On 11 March 2020 German Chancellor Angela Merkel declared that the German government would do whatever was necessary to confront the economic impact of the pandemic. Within a couple of weeks, the KfW assumed a central role in delivering on that promise within the framework of Germany's Economic Stabilisation Fund.[40] Following a 23 March 2020 Cabinet meeting, Federal Minister for Economic Affairs and Energy Peter Altmaier stated[41]:

> It is now important to help companies quickly and without red tape. An important element here is to provide access to liquidity. The improved financing conditions set out in the KfW Special Programme 2020 will help to significantly support the economy in this respect. Applications will be processed quickly and without undue bureaucracy. Payments will be made as quickly as possible because we know that, for many enterprises, every week counts.

In the lead up to the 23 March meeting, Finance Minister Scholz had announced that the government would loan the KfW €100 billion and empower it to provide 'unlimited' loans to struggling businesses. Any additional and necessary future guarantees backing KfW lending would be forthcoming as needed.[42] As in India, the unleashing of KfW financial capacity would be magnified, financially and geographically,

---

[40] See www.bundesfinanzministerium.de/Web/EN/Meta/QuickAccess/quickaccess .html. Accessed 14 May 2020.

[41] See www.bundesfinanzministerium.de/Web/EN/Meta/QuickAccess/quickaccess .html. Accessed 14 May 2020.

[42] 'Germany Tears Up Fiscal Rule Book to Counter Coronavirus Pandemic', FT.com, 21 March 2020. Available at www.ft.com/content/dacd2ac6-6b5f-11ea-89df-41bea055720b. Accessed 22 March 2020.

via Germany's nationwide system of regional and municipal public development banks, alongside the powerful, nationwide public savings banking system, the Sparkasse. Speaking on 23 March 2020, Dr Günther Bräunig, Chairman of the Board of Managing Directors at KfW, signalled the historical importance of the KfW's amassed historical expertise and capacity:

> The banks and KfW have prepared intensively for today. Never before have we been able to put a full programme together this quickly. The federal government will assume close to full liability and the loan margins are extremely low.[43]

The KfW and its government owners, moreover, would demonstrate responsiveness to evolving societal demands amidst crisis. Serious questions were raised early on regarding the limited effect of the KfW 80 per cent, and even 90 per cent, guarantees of loans offered by other banks. By 3 April 2020 the government updated the KfW offer. A new 'KfW Instant Loan' with a 100 per cent guarantee was created, releasing the banks holding Covid-19-related loans from any ultimate liability (Mertens et al. 2020, 6).

As of 14 May 2020, the KfW had acquired four core programmes geared towards coronavirus aid.[44] First, there is the KfW Special Programme, which targets investment and working capital for medium-sized enterprises and large companies. The KfW participates in syndicate financing, taking a risk share of at least €25 million and assuming up to 80 per cent of the risk but no more than 50 per cent of the total debt. Second, there is the KfW instant loans for medium-sized enterprises (noted earlier). A key feature here is that it is, indeed, *instant* credit, granted on the fulfilment of some basic specific conditions of the firm (of medium-size, more than ten employees, active since at least 1 January 2019, in good financial standing before

---

[43] See www.bundesfinanzministerium.de/Web/EN/Meta/QuickAccess/quickaccess .html. Accessed 14 May 2020.

[44] Available at www.kfw.de/KfW-Group/Newsroom/Latest-News/KfW-Corona-Hilfe-Unternehmen.html. Accessed 14 May 2020.

31 December 2019), and with specified credit limits according to size. Ten-year loans are granted at 3 per cent interest. As noted, the credit issuing bank is released from 100 per cent liability by KfW, itself backed by a Federal government guarantee. This enables a rapid granting of funds. Third, the KfW Entrepreneur Loan, which is for investments and working capital for companies older than five years. KfW assumes 80 per cent of large company and up to 90 per cent SME risks for the credit granting bank. It has a very high limit of up to €100 million per company. Fourth, there is the related KfW loan for young companies and a Start-Up Loan. As in the other programmes, eligible companies get access to investment and working capital as KfW assumes part of the bank's risk (80 per cent for large companies and up to 90 per cent for SMEs) for loans up to €100 million.

While details are less specific, the German government provided further support for the country's cultural industry through the KfW. The KfW Development Bank has worked to maintain operations abroad, albeit limited. In Columbia, the KfW is financing national partner banks; in Burkina Faso, KfW supported the West African Health Organization; in Democratic Republic of Congo, KfW Development Bank is financing scarce operating resources such as chlorine to help maintain the water supply. In the case of the KfW, the announced pandemic-related programmes are more distinctively geared towards private sector support (although in its normal operations, the KfW has significant public sector funding programmes, especially with municipalities). At the time of writing, it is unclear why specific public support programmes are not named, although, this may well have to do with the German government's national coordinated response and the fact that many smaller German development banks directly support the public sector and municipalities' financial requirements.

Amidst unprecedented crisis, these public banks have functioned through the public sphere to make time and resources available for the public and private sectors in attempts to protect public health, maintain employment, and stabilise the economy. Little of these efforts can be reasonably captured by mainstream market failure logics or additionality prescripts. Much of their capacity to respond has hinged on collaboration and cooperation, not competition, among different types of public banks and financial institutions, including developmental, commercial, and universal public banks as well as government treasuries, central banks, pension funds, and so on. Public banks therein have been innovative and pro-active. While important top-down government-led initiatives have been channelled through the public banks, so too have individual public banks designed their own responses to meet the needs of their communities.

There will be a need to assess the Covid-19 responses of public banks as time passes. Who has benefited and why? That public banks can be *made* to quickly respond at times of need and to do so both independently and in collaboration with government initiatives and other public sector entities is evident. The difference with private banks is not, however, a function of public ownership. The shielding of the public sphere makes difference possible, if not inevitable. No doubt contradictions in what public banks have done and will yet do will appear. I cannot imagine it to be otherwise; dynamic and contested entities as public banks are within class-divided capitalism. Yet as we emerge from the Covid-19 pandemic and aim to 'build forward better' there is an unprecedented opportunity to command of public banks a more democratised future and pro-public orientation bent towards realising a green and just transition for all. Public banks *can be made to* decarbonise, definancialise, and democratise the economy for the common good. Indeed, they already are. They can yet be *made* better.

References

AAAA (2015) 'Third International Conference on Financing for Development'. Addis Ababa Action Agenda, 13–16 July 2015. Available at www.un.org/esa/ffd/wp-content/uploads/2015/08/AAAA_Outcome.pdf. Accessed 23 January 2020.

AADFI (2020) *The Impact of the Covid-19 on AADFI Member DFIs*. Abidjan, Côte d'Ivoire: Association of African Development Finance Institutions (AADFI). Available at https://adfi-ci.org/news.php. Accessed 17 August 2020.

Aalbers, M. B. and Pollard, J. (2016) 'Geographies of Money, Finance and Crisis'. In Daniels, P., Bradshaw, M., Shaw, D., Sidaway, J. and Hall, T. (eds.), *An Introduction to Human Geography*, 5th ed. Harlow: Pearson, pp. 365–78.

Abraham, F. and Schmukler, S. L. (2017) 'A New Role for Development Banks?'. Research & Policy Briefs, No. 10. Washington, DC: World Bank Group. Available at http://documents.worldbank.org/curated/en/415631509024932431/A-new-role-for-development-banks. Accessed 25 July 2019.

ADFIAP (2009) *Developing a Regional Water Financing Strategy for Development Financing Institutions in Asia*. Makati City, Philippines: Association of Development Financing Institutions in Asia and the Pacific (ADFIAP). Available at www.adfiap.org/wp-content/uploads/2009/08/ADFIAP-Water-Report-August-2009.pdf. Accessed 7 November 2019.

Adkin, L. E. (1994) 'Environmental Politics, Political Economy, and Social Democracy in Canada'. *Studies in Political Economy*, 45(Fall): 130–69.

Adkin, L. E. (2019) 'Technology Innovation as a Response to Climate Change: The Case of the Climate Change Emissions Management Corporation of Alberta'. *Review of Policy Research*, 36(5): 603–34.

Aghion, B. A. (1999) 'Development Banking'. *Journal of Development Economics*, 58(1): 83–100.

AGPB (2014) *Promotional Banks in Germany: Acting in the Public Interest*. Berlin: Association of German Public Banks (Bundesverband Öffentlicher Banken Deutschlands, VÖB).

Aitken, R. (2013) 'The Financialization of Micro-Credit'. *Development and Change*, 44(3): 473–99.

Akyüz, Y. (2013) *The Financial Crisis and the Global South: A Development Perspective*. London: Pluto Press.

Akyüz, Y. (2017) 'Inequality, Financialization and Stagnation'. South Centre Research Paper, No. 73, February. Geneva: South Centre. Available at www .southcentre.int/wp-content/uploads/2017/02/RP73_Inequality-Financialization-and-Stagnation_EN.pdf. Accessed 10 June 2020.

Alavi, H. (1982) 'State and Class under Peripheral Capitalism'. In Alavi, H. and Shanin, T. (eds.), *Introduction to the Sociology of Developing Societies*. London: Macmillan Press, pp. 289–307.

Albo, G. (2005) 'Contesting the "New Capitalism"'. In Coates, D. (ed.), *Varieties of Capitalism, Varieties of Approaches*. New York: Palgrave Macmillan, pp. 63–82.

ALIDE (2020) *Responses of Latin American Development Banks to the Economic Crisis Precipitated by Covid-19*, 1st ed. San Isidro, Peru: Asociación Latinoamericana de Instituciones Financieras para el Desarrollo (ALIDE). Available at www.alide.org.pe/wp-content/uploads/2020/06/RESPONSES-DB .pdf. Accessed 17 August 2020.

Altvater, E. (1997) 'Financial Crises on the Threshold of the 21st Century'. In Panitch, L. V. (ed.), *Socialist Register 1997: Ruthless Criticism of All That Exists*. London: The Merlin Press, pp. 48–74.

Amalorpavanathan, R. (2017a) 'A Catalytic Agent to Prevent Market Failures and to Address Financial Scarcity and the Opportunity for Public Private Partnership'. Global Symposium on Development Financial Institutions: 'Balancing Sustainability and Social Mandate: Development Financial Institutions in a New World', 19–20 September 2017, Kuala Lumpur, Malaysia. Available at www.worldbank.org/en/events/2017/09/19/global-dfi-symposium#3. Accessed 13 April 2020.

Amalorpavanathan, R. (2017b) 'Sustainable Development Financing'. In Global Symposium on Development Financial Institutions: 'Balancing Sustainability and Social Mandate: Development Financial Institutions in a New World', 19–20 September 2017, Kuala Lumpur, Malaysia. Available at www.worldbank.org/en/events/2017/09/19/global-dfi-symposium#3. Accessed 13 April 2020.

Andrews, M. A. (2005) 'State-Owned Banks, Stability, Privatization, and Growth: Practical Policy Decisions in a World without Empirical Proof'. IMF Working Paper, WP/05/10. Washington, DC: International Monetary Fund.

Andrianova, S. (2012) 'Public Banks and Financial Stability'. *Economic Letters*, 116(1): 86–88.

Andrianova, S., Demetriades, P. and Shortland, A. (2012) 'Government Ownership of Banks, Institutions and Economic Growth'. *Economica*, 9(315): 449–69.

Angel, J. (2017) 'Towards an Energy Politics In-Against-and-Beyond the State: Berlin's Struggle for Energy Democracy'. *Antipode*, 49(3): 557–76.

Anielski, M. and Ascah, B. (2018) *Alberta's Public Bank: How ATB Can Help Shape the New Economy*. Edmonton, Canada: Parkland Institute.

Arnsperger, C. and Varoufakis, Y. (2006) 'What Is Neoclassical Economics? The Three Axioms Responsible for Its Theoretical Oeuvre, Practical Irrelevance and, Thus, Discursive Power'. *Panoeconomicus*, 53(1): 5–18.

Arora, R. I. and Wondemu, K. (2018) 'Do Public Sector Banks Promote Regional Growth? Evidence from an Emerging Economy'. *Review of Urban & Regional Development Studies*, 30(1): 66–87.

Atkinson, A. B. and Piketty, T. (eds.) (2010) *Top Incomes: A Global Perspective*. Oxford: Oxford University Press.

Attridge, S. and Engen, L. (2019) *Blended Finance in the Poorest Countries: The Need for a Better Approach*. London: Overseas Development Institute. Available at www.odi.org/sites/odi.org.uk/files/resource-documents/12666 .pdf. Accessed 28 August 2019.

Aysan, A. F. and Ceyhan, S. P. (2010) 'Efficiency of Banking in Turkey before and after the Crises'. *Banks and Bank Systems*, 5(2): 179–98.

Babb, S. and Kentikelenis, A. (2018) 'International Financial Institutions as Agents of Neoliberalism'. In Cahill, D., Cooper, M., Konings, M. and Primrose, D. (eds.), *The SAGE Handbook of Neoliberalism*. Thousand Oaks, CA: Sage, pp. 16–27.

Bach, D. (2017) 'The Financing of Energy Efficient Refurbishment: KfW's Offer for Municipalities'. Presentation to the Forum Annuel du CFFDD: Accélérer la rénovation énergétique des bâtiments, Brussels, 16 March 2017. Available at www.frdo-cfdd.be/sites/default/files/content/download/files/dominik_bach_kfw .pdf. Accessed 3 March 2020.

Badré, B. (2018) *Can Finance Save the World? Regaining Power over Money to Serve the Common Good*. Oakland, CA: Berrett-Koehler Publishers.

Balassa, B. (1982) 'Structural Adjustment Policies in Developing Economies'. *World Development*, 10(1): 23–38.

Ban, C. and Bohle, D. (2020) 'Definancialization, Financial Repression and Policy Continuity in East-Central Europe'. *Review of International Political Economy*. DOI: 10.1080/09692290.2020.1799841.

Banco Popular y de Desarrollo Comunal (BPDC) (2010) 'Pautas y orientaciones generales, sus valores y principios'. Available at www.bancopopular.fi .cr/AsambleaTrabajadores/Documents/Pautas%20y%20Orientaciones.pdf. Accessed 25 March 2019.

Banco Popular y de Desarrollo Comunal (BPDC) (2012) *Reporte de Sostenibilidad Conglomerado Financiero Banco Popular*. San José, Costa Rica: BPDC.

Banco Popular y de Desarrollo Comunal (BPDC) (2015) *Reporte de Sostenibilidad Conglomerado Financiero Banco Popular*. San José, Costa Rica: BPDC.

Banco Popular y de Desarrollo Comunal (BPDC) (2017) *Reporte de Sostenibilidad Conglomerado Financiero Banco Popular*. San José, Costa Rica: BPDC.

BankTrack (2019) 'Banking on Climate Change – 2019 Fossil Fuel Finance Report Card'. BankTrack, Honor the Earth, Indigenous Environmental Network, Oil Change International, Rainforest Action Network, Sierra Club. Available at www.banktrack.org/publications. Accessed 3 March 2020.

Barth, J. R., Caprio, G. and Levine, R. (2006) *Rethinking Bank Regulation: Till Angels Govern*. Cambridge: Cambridge University Press.

Barone, B. and Spratt, S. (2015) 'Development Banks from the BRICS'. Institute of Development Studies Evidence Report, No. 111. Brighton: IDS. Available at www.ids.ac.uk/publications/development-banks-from-the-brics/.   Accessed 23 January 2018.

Barrowclough, D. and Gottschalk, R. (2018) 'Solidarity and the South: Supporting the New Landscape of Long-Term Development Finance'. UNCTAD Research Paper, No. 24, UNCTAD/SER.RP/2018/6. Geneva: United Nations Conference on Trade and Development (UNCTAD). Available at https://unctad.org/en/pages/PublicationWebflyer.aspx?publicationid=2233. Accessed 29 June 2020.

Basu, L. (2019) 'The "Washington Consensus" Is dead. But What Should Replace It?' *openDemocracy*, 13 April 2019. Available at www.opendemocracy.net. Accessed 13 June 2019.

Bateman, M. (2010) *Why Doesn't Microfinance Work? The Destructive Rise of Local Neoliberalism*. London: Zed Books.

Bateman, M. (2012) 'How Lending to the Poor Began, Grew, and Almost Destroyed a Generation in India'. *Development and Change*, 43(6): 1385–402. DOI: 10.1111/j.1467-7660.2012.01804.x.

Bateman, M. (2013) 'Financing Local Economic Development: In Search of the Optimal Local Financial System'. In ÖFSE (Hg.) *Österreichische Entwicklungspolitik, Analysen, Berichte, Informationen mit dem Schwerpunktthema "Private Sector Development – Ein neuer Businessplan für Entwicklung?."* Wien, pp. 43–52.

Bateman, M. (2017) 'Small Loans, Big Problems: The Rise and Fall of Microcredit as International Development Policy'. *Development and Change*, virtual issue. DOI: 10.1111/dech.12349.

Bateman, M., Duvendack, M. and Loubere, N. (2019) 'Is Fintech the New Panacea for Poverty Alleviation and Local Development? Contesting Suri and Jack's M-Pesa Findings Published in Science'. *Review of African Political Economy*, 46(161): 480–95.

Bator, F. M. (1958) 'The Anatomy of Market Failure'. *Quarterly Journal of Economics*, 72(3): 351–79.

Bauwens, M., Kostakis, V. Troncoso, S. and Utratel, A. M. (2017) *Commons Transition and P2P: A Primer*. Amsterdam: The Transnational Institute. Available at www.tni.org/files/publication-downloads/commons_transition_and_p2p_primer_v9.pdf. Accessed 7 July 2019.

Bayliss, K. and Fine, B. (eds.) (2008) *Privatization and Alternative Public Sector Reform in Sub-Saharan Africa: Delivering on Electricity and Water*. New York: Palgrave Macmillan.

Beaud, M. (2001) *A History of Capitalism, 1500–2000*, trans. T. Dickman and A. Lefebvre. New York: Monthly Review Press.

Beitel, K. (2016) *The Municipal Public Bank: Regulatory Compliance, Capitalization, Liquidity, and Risk*. New York: Roosevelt Institute. Available at https://rooseveltinstitute.org/wp-content/uploads/2016/07/RI-Municipal-Bank-Regulatory-Compliance-Capitalization-Liquidity-Risk-201607.pdf. Accessed 19 June 2019.

Bengtsson, E. (2008a) 'A History of Scandinavian Socially Responsible Investing'. *Journal of Business Ethics*, 82(4): 969–83.

Bengtsson, E. (2008b) 'Socially Responsible Investing in Scandinavia – A Comparative Analysis'. *Sustainable Development*, 16(3): 155–68.

Bennett, D. and Sharpe, K. (1980) 'The State as Banker and Entrepreneur: The Last-Resort Character of the Mexican State's Economic Intervention, 1917–76'. *Comparative Politics*, 12(2): 165–89.

Berry, C. and Macfarlane, L. (2018) 'A New Public Banking Ecosystem: A Report to the Labour Party'. Commissioned by the Communication Workers Union and the Democracy Collaborative. Available at http://labour.org.uk/wp-content/uploads/2019/03/Building-a-new-public-banking-ecosystem.pdf. Accessed 3 September 2019.

Bertay, A. C., Demirgüç-Kunt, A. and Huizinga. H. (2015) 'Bank Ownership and Credit over the Business Cycle: Is Lending by State Banks Less Procyclical?'. *Journal of Banking & Finance*, 50: 326–39.

Bhattacharya, A., Meltzer, J. P., Oppenheim, J., Qureshi, Z. and Stern, N. (2016) *Delivering on Sustainable Infrastructure for Better Development and Better Climate*. Washington, DC: New Climate Economy. Available at https://newclimateeconomy.report/2016/. Accessed 5 August 2019.

Bircan, Ç. and Saka, O. (2018) 'Lending Cycles and Real Outcomes: Costs of Political Misalignment'. LSE 'Europe in Question' Discussion Paper Series. LEQS Paper No. 139/2018. Basel, Switzerland: London School of Economics.

BIS (2017) *87th Annual Report 2016–17*. Basel: Bank for International Settlements (BIS).

Block, F. (2014) 'Democratizing Finance'. *Politics & Society*, 42(1): 3–28.

BND (1970–2019) *Annual Report*. Bismarck, ND: Bank of North Dakota. Available at https://bnd.nd.gov/annual-report/. Accessed 1 April 2020.

Booth, J. A. (1998) *Costa Rica: Quest for Democracy*. Boulder, CO: Westview Press.

Botey, L. E. C. (n.d.) 'From Discipline to Responsibilization: Assessment of Credit Applicants, the Case of a Workers' Bank in Latin America'. Working Paper, Department Accounting & Management Control. Paris: HEC PARIS. Available at https://studies2.hec.fr/jahia/webdav/site/hec/shared/sites/cuenca-botey/acces_anonyme/PaperCSFC_CuencaBotey.pdf. Accessed 25 March 2019.

Boyd, R. and Ngo, T.-W. (2005) 'Emancipating the Political Economy of Asia from the Growth Paradigm'. In Boyd, R. and Ngo, T.-W. (eds.), *Asian States: Beyond the Developmental Perspective*. London: RoutledgeCurzon, pp. 1–18.

Bracking, S. (2012) 'How do Investors Value Environmental Harm/Care? Private Equity Funds, Development Finance Institutions and the Partial Financialization of Nature-based Industries'. *Development and Change*, 43(1): 271–93.

Bracking, S. (2016) *The Financialisation of Power: How Financiers Rule Africa*. New York: Routledge.

Brei, M. and Schclarek, A. (2013) 'Public Bank Lending in Times of Crisis'. *Journal of Financial Stability*, 9(4): 820–30.

Brown, E. (2013) *The Public Banking Solution: From Austerity to Prosperity*. Baton Rouge, LA: Third Millennium Press.

Brown, E. (2019) *Banking on the People: Democratizing Money in the Digital Age*. Washington, DC: The Democracy Collaborative.

Buchanan, J. M. (1999) 'Politics without Romance'. In *The Collected Works of James M. Buchanan, Volume 1: The Logical Foundations of Constitutional Liberty*. Indianapolis, IN: Liberty Fund, pp. 45–59.

Butzbach, O. (2012) 'European Savings Banks and the Future of Public Banking in Advanced Economies: The Cases of France, Germany, Italy and Spain'. *Public Banking Institute Journal*, 1(1): 34–78.

Butzbach, O. (2016) 'The Evolution of Organizational Diversity in Banking: Savings Banks' Consolidation and Sector Coordination in France and Italy, 1980–2012'. *Organization Studies*, 37(4): 565–89.

Butzbach, O. and von Mettenheim, K. (eds.) (2014) *Alternative Banking and Financial Crisis*. London: Pickering & Chatto.

Butzbach, O. and von Mettenheim, K. (eds.) (2015) 'Alternative Banking and Theory'. *Accounting, Economics, and Law: A Convivium*, 5(2): 105–71.

Butzbach, O., Rotondo, G. and Desiato, T. (2020) 'Can Banks Be Owned?' *Accounting, Economics, and Law: A Convivium*, 10(1): 20170004. DOI: 10.1515/ael-2017-0004.

Calomiris, C. W. and Haber, S. (2014) *Fragile by Design: Banking Crises, Scarce Credit, and Political Bargains*. Princeton, NJ: Princeton University Press.

Cammack, P. (2003) 'The Governance of Global Capitalism: A New Materialist Perspective'. *Historical Materialism*, 11(2): 37–59.

Caprio, G. and Fiechter, J. L., Litan, R. E. and Pomerleano, M. (eds.) (2004) *The Future of State-Owned Financial Institutions*. Washington, DC: Brookings Institution Press.

Carroll, T., Gonzalez-Vicente, R. and Jarvis, D. S. L. (2019) 'Capital, Conflict and Convergence: A Political Understanding of Neoliberalism and Its Relationship to Capitalist Transformation'. *Globalizations*, 16(6): 778–803.

Carroll, W. K. (1989) 'Neoliberalism and the Recomposition of Finance Capital in Canada'. *Capital & Class*, 13: 81–113.

Castree, N. and Christophers, B. (2015) 'Banking Spatially on the Future: Capital Switching, Infrastructure, and the Ecological Fix'. *Annals of the Association of American Geographers*, 105(2): 378–86.

CBI (2018) *The Green Bond Market in the Nordics*. London: Climate Bonds Initiative.

CBRC (2014) 'Notice of the China Banking Regulatory Commission on Key Performance Indicators of Green Credit Implementation'. CBRC General Office, No. 186. China Banking Regulatory Commission. Available at www.cbrc.gov.cn/EngdocView.do?docID=C5EAF470E0B34E56B2546476132CCC56. Accessed 24 February 2018.

CDB (2013–19) *Sustainability Report*. Beijing: China Development Bank.

Chakrabarti, R. (2012) 'State Bank of India: The Opportunities and Challenges of Being a State-Owned Bank in India'. In Yi-chong, Xu (ed.), *The Political Economy of State-Owned Enterprises in China and India*. Houndsmills, Basingstoke: Routledge Macmillan, pp. 247–72.

Chakravarty, S. P. and Williams, J. (2006) 'How Significant Is the Alleged Unfair Advantage Enjoyed by State-Owned Banks in Germany?', *Cambridge Journal of Economics*, 30(2): 219–26.

Chang, D. O. (2013) 'Labour and the "Developmental State": A Critique of the Developmental State Theory of Labour'. In Fine, B., Saraswati, J. and Tavasci, D. (eds.), *Beyond Developmental State: Industrial Policy into the Twenty-First Century*. London: Pluto Press, pp. 85–109.

Chavez, D. (2015) *The Meaning, Relevance and Scope of Energy Democracy*. Amsterdam: Transnational Institute. Available at www.tni.org/en/article/the-meaning-relevance-and-scope-of-energy-democracy. Accessed 10 June 2019.

Chen, M. (2019) 'State Actors, Market Games: Credit Guarantees and the Funding of China Development Bank'. *New Political Economy*, 25(3): 453–68.

Cheneval, F. and de Soto, H. (eds.) (2006) *Realizing Property Rights*. Zürich, Switzerland: Rüffer & Rub.

Chesnais, F. (2016) *Finance Capital Today: Corporations and Banks in the Lasting Global Slump*. Boston: Brill.

Chiu, B. and Lewis, M. K. (2006) *Reforming China's State-Owned Enterprises and Banks*. Cheltenham: Edward Elgar.

Christophers, B. (2015) 'The Limits to Financialization'. *Dialogues in Human Geography*, 5(2): 183–200.

Christophers, B. (2018) 'Financialisation as Monopoly Profit: The Case of US Banking'. *Antipode*, 50(4): 864–90.

Clark, D. (2016) *The Global Financial Crisis and Austerity: A Basic Introduction*. Bristol: Bristol University Press.

Clark, G. (2000) *Pension Fund Capitalism*. Oxford: Oxford University Press.

Clarke, G. R. G., Cull, R. and Shirley, M. M. (2005) 'Bank Privatization in Developing Countries: A Summary of Lessons and Findings'. *Journal of Banking & Finance*, 29: 1905–30.

Clement, K. (2004) 'Structural Fund Programmes as Instruments for Sustainable Regional Development a Review of Nordic Effectiveness'. *Innovation: The European Journal of Social Science Research*, 17(1): 43–60.

Clifton, J. Díaz Fuentes, D. and Gómez, A. L. (2018) 'The European Investment Bank: Development, Integration, Investment?, *Journal of Common Market Studies*, 56(4): 733–50.

Clifton, J. Díaz Fuentes, D. and Howarth, D. (eds.) (forthcoming 2021a) *Regional Development Banks in the World Economy*. Oxford: Oxford University Press.

Clifton, J. Díaz Fuentes, D., García, C. and Gómez, A. L. (forthcoming 2021b) 'Is a European "Hidden Investment State" Emerging in Spain? The Role of *Instituto de Crédito Oficial*'. In D. Mertens, D. Thiemann, M. and Volberding, P. (eds.), *The Reinvention of Development Banking in the European Union*. Oxford: Oxford University Press.

Climate Bonds Initiative (2018) *Bond and Climate Change: The State of the Market 2018*, September 2018. Available at www.climatebonds.net/files/reports/cbi_sotm_2018_final_01k-web.pdf. Accessed 7 June 2019.

Coady, D., Parry, I., Nghia-Piotr, L. and Shang, B. (2019) 'Global Fossil Fuel Subsidies Remain Large: An Update Based on Country-Level Estimates'. Working Paper No. 19/89, Washington, DC: International Monetary Fund. Available at www.imf.org/. Accessed 3 March 2020.

Coates, D. (2014) 'Studying Comparative Capitalisms by Going Left and by Going Deeper'. *Capital & Class*, 38(1): 18–30.

Cochran, I. and Pauthier, A. (2020) *Public Financial Institutions Can Help Make the Post-Covid Response "Just and Green"*. Paris: Institute for Climate Economics (I4CE). Available at www.i4ce.org/public-financial-institutions-can-help-make-the-post-covid-response-just-and-green/. Accessed 13 July 2020.

Cochran, I., Hubert, R., Marchal, V. and Youngman, R. (2014) 'Public Financial Institutions and the Low-Carbon Transition: Five Case Studies on Low-Carbon Infrastructure and Project Investment'. OECD Environment Working Papers, No. 72. Paris: OECD. Available at http://dx.doi.org/10.1787/5jxt3rhpgn9t-en. Accessed 10 June 2018.

Cochran, I., Eschalier, C. and Deheza, M. (2015) 'Mainstreaming Low-Carbon Climate-Resilient Growth Pathways into Investment Decision-Making Lessons from Development Financial Institutions on Approaches and Tools'. Background Paper prepared for IDFC Climate Finance Forum. Available at www .i4ce.org. Accessed 18 June 2019.

Cogen, M. (2015) *An Introduction to European Intergovernmental Organisations*. Abingdon: Routledge.

Colburn, F. D. and Cruz, S. A. (2018) 'Latin America's Shifting Politics: The Fading of Costa Rica's Old Parties'. *Journal of Democracy*, 29(4): 43–53.

Congdon, T. (2012) 'Central Banks'. In Toporowski, J. and Michell, J. (eds.), *Handbook of Critical Issues in Finance*. Cheltenham: Edward Elgar, pp. 43–48.

Cornett, M. M., Guo, L., Khaksari, S. and Tehranian, H. (2010) 'The Impact of State Ownership on Performance Differences in Privately-Owned versus State-Owned Banks: An International Comparison'. *Journal of Financial Intermediation*, 19: 74–94.

Cortés, C. (2014) *Conquistas Sociales en Costa Rica*. San José, Costa Rica: Grupo Nacional.

CPI (2017) *Global Landscape of Climate Finance 2017*. London: Climate Policy Initiative. Available at www.climatepolicyinitiative.org. Accessed 22 September 2019.

CPI (2018) *Global Climate Finance: An Updated View 2018*. London: Climate Policy Initiative. Available at www.climatepolicyinitiative.org. Accessed 3 October 2019.

CPI (2019) *Global Landscape of Climate Finance 2019*. London: Climate Policy Initiative. Available at www.climatepolicyinitiative.org. Accessed 2 March 2020.

Cull, R., Martinez Peria, M. S. and Verrier, J. (2017) 'Bank Ownership: Trends and Implications'. IMF Working Paper, WP/17/60. Washington, DC: International Monetary Fund. Available at www.imf.org/en/Publications/WP/Issues/2017/03/22/Bank-Ownership-Trends-and-Implications-44753. Accessed 10 June 2019.

Culpeper, R. (2012) 'Financial Sector Policy and Development in the Wake of the Global Crisis: The Role of National Development Banks'. *Third World Quarterly*, 33(3): 383–403.

Cumbers, A. (2012) *Reclaiming Public Ownership: Making Space for Economic Democracy*. London: Zed Books.

Cumbers, A. and McMaster, R. (2012) 'Revisiting Public Ownership: Knowledge, Democracy and Participation in Economic Decision Making'. *Review of Radical Political Economics*, 44(3): 358–73.

Cypher, J. M. (1989) 'The Debt Crisis as "Opportunity": Strategies to Revive U.S. Hegemony'. *Latin American Perspectives*, 16(1): 52–78.

de Brunhoff, S. (2003) 'Financial and Industrial Capital: A New Class Coalition'. In Saad-Filho, A. (ed.), *Anti-Capitalism: A Marxist Introduction*. London: Pluto Press, pp. 142–51.

De Luna-Martínez, J. and Vicente, C. L. (2012) *Global Survey of Development Banks*. Washington, DC: World Bank Group.

De Luna-Martínez, J., Vicente, C. L., Arshad, A. B., Tatucu, R. and Song, J. (2018) *2017 Survey of National Development Banks*. Washington, DC: World Bank Group.

del Ángel-Mobarak, G. A., Bazdrech Parada, C. and Suarez Parada, F. (eds.) (2005) *Cuando el Estado se Hizo Banquero: Consequencias de la Nacionalizacion*. Colecion Lecturas de El Trimestre Economico. Mexico City: Fondo de Cultura Economica.

Deeg, R. E. (1999) *Finance Capitalism Unveiled: Banks and the German Political Economy*. Ann Arbor: University of Michigan Press.

Deeg, R. E. (1998) 'What Makes German Banks Different'. *Small Business Economics*, 10(2): 93–101.

Demirgüç-Kunt, A. and Servén, L. (2010) 'Are All the Sacred Cows Dead? Implications of the Financial Crisis for Macro- and Financial Policies'. *The World Bank Research Observer*, 25(1): 91–124.

DGTZ (2005) *Reforming Agricultural Development Banks*. Eschborn, Germany: Deutsche Gesellschaft für Technische Zusammenarbeit.

Di John, J. (2016) 'What Is the Role of National Development Banks in Late Industrialisation?'. Issues Papers on Structural Transformation and Industrial Policy, No. 010-2016. Ethiopian Development Research Institute (EDRI). Available at www.edri.org.et/index.php/2014-03-30-05-55-02/other-publications/15-issue-papers/94-paper-10-what-is-the-role-of-national-development-banks-in-late-industrialisation. Accessed 10 June 2019.

Dinç, I. S. (2005) 'Politicians and Banks: Political Influences on Government-Owned Banks in Emerging Markets'. *Journal of Financial Economics*, 77: 453–79.

Doctor, M. (2015) 'Assessing the Changing Roles of the Brazilian Development Bank'. *Bulletin of Latin American Research*, 34(2): 197–213.

Dos Santos, P. L. (2009) 'On the Content of Banking in Contemporary Capitalism'. *Historical Materialism*, 17(2): 180–213.

Duffy-Tumasz, A. (2009) 'Paying Back Comes First: Why Repayment Means More Than Business in Rural Senegal'. *Gender & Development*, 17(2): 243–54.

Duménil, G. and Lévy, D. (2004) 'The Economics of US Imperialism at the Turn of the 21st Century'. *Review of International Political Economy*, 11(4): 657–76.

Duménil, G. and Lévy, D. (2013) *The Crisis of Neoliberalism*. Cambridge, MA: Harvard University Press.

Durrani, A. and Rosmin, M. and Volz, U. (2020) 'The Role of Central Banks in Scaling Up Sustainable Finance – What Do Monetary Authorities in the Asia-Pacific Region Think?'. *Journal of Sustainable Finance and Investment*, 10(2): 92–112.

Duvendack, M., Palmer-Jones, R., Copestake, J. G., Hooper, L., Loke, Y. and Rao, N. (2011) *What Is the Evidence of the Impact of Microfinance on the Well-Being of Poor People?* London: EPPI-Centre, Social Science Research Unit, Institute of Education, University of London.

Dymski, G. (2009) 'Racial Exclusion and the Political Economy of the Subprime Crisis'. *Historical Materialism*, 17(2): 149–79.

Edelman, M. (1999) *Peasants against Globalization: Rural Social Movements in Costa Rica*. Redwood City, CA: Stanford University Press.

EAPB (2018) *Annual Report 2018*. Brussels: European Association of Public Banks. Available at www.eapb.eu/our-work/publications.html. Accessed 1 July 2019.

EAPB (2020) *Statement on the Role of Public Banks in the Context of the COVID 19 Crisis*. Brussels: European Association of Public Banks. Available at https://eapb.eu/. Accessed 2 August 2020.

Eccles, N. (2013) 'Sustainable Investment, Dickens, Malthus and Marx'. *Journal of Sustainable Finance and Investment*, 3(4): 287–302.

EPSC (2017) 'Financing Sustainability: Triggering Investments for the Clean Economy'. EPSC Strategic Notes, Issue 25, 8 June 2017, Brussels: European Political Strategy Centre, European Commission. Available at https://ec.europa.eu/epsc/sites/epsc/files/strategic_note_issue_25.pdf. Accessed 10 June 2019.

Epstein, G. A. (2005) *Financialization and the World Economy*. Cheltenham: Edward Elgar.

Epstein, G. A. (2010) 'The David Gordon Memorial Lecture: Finance without Financiers: Prospects for Radical Change In Financial Governance'. *Review of Radical Political Economics*, 42(3): 293–306.

Epstein, G. A. (2015) 'Development Central Banking: A Review of Issues and Experiences'. Working Paper, No. 182. Geneva: International Labour Organization. Available at www.ilo.org/employment/Whatwedo/Publications/working-papers/WCMS_377808/lang–en/index.htm. Accessed 10 October 2019.

Erdoğdu, M. M. (2004) 'South Korean State Capacity: From Development to Crisis Management'. In Jomo, K. S. (ed.), *After the Storm: Crises, Recovery and Sustaining Development in Four Asian Economies*. Singapore University Press, pp. 260–302.

Ervine, K. (2013) 'Carbon Markets, Debt and Uneven Development'. *Third World Quarterly*, 34(4): 653–70.

Ervine, K. (2018) *Carbon*. Cambridge: Polity Press.

Eurodad et al. (2018) *History RePPPeated: How Public Private Partnerships are failing*. Brussels: EURODAD in cooperation with Heinrich-Böll-Stiftung. Available at https://eurodad.org/HistoryRePPPeated. Accessed 13 July 2019.

Fama, E. F. (1970) 'Efficient Capital Markets: A Review of Theory and Empirical Work'. *Journal of Finance* 25(2): 383–417.

Feagin, J. R., Orum, A. M. and Sjoberg, G. (eds.) (1991) *A Case for the Case Study*. Chapel Hill, NC: UNC Press Books.

Felber, C. (2015) *Change Everything: Creating an Economy for the Common Good*. London: Zed Books.

Felloni, G. (2005) *Genoa and the History of Finance: A Series of Firsts!* Genoa: Banco di San Giorgio.

Ferguson, J. (2009) 'The Uses of Neoliberalism'. *Antipode*, 41(S1): 166–84.

Ferrari, A., Mare, D. S. and Skamnelos, I. (2017) 'State Ownership of Financial Institutions in Europe and Central Asia'. Policy Research Working Paper No. 8288. Washington, DC: World Bank. Available at https://openknowledge.worldbank.org/handle/10986/29079. Accessed 10 June 2019.

FiC (2020) *Finance in Common: The First Global Summit of Public Development Banks*. Conference Booklet. Available at https://wfdfi.net/2020/04/29/finance-in-common-2020-booklet-featuring-information-about-the-summit-and-public-development-banks/. Accessed 24 July 2020.

Finance Watch (2016) *Representation of the Public Interest in Banking*. Brussels: Finance Watch.

Fine, B. (2008) 'Privatization's Shaky Theoretical Foundations'. In Bayliss, K. and Fine, B. (eds.), *Privatization and Alternative Public Sector Reform in Sub-Saharan Africa: Delivering on Electricity and Water*. New York: Palgrave Macmillan, pp. 13–30.

Fine, B. (2010) 'Locating Financialisation'. *Historical Materialism*, 18(2): 97–116.

Fine, B. and Saad-Filho, A. (2004) *Marx's Capital*, 4th ed. London: Pluto Press.

Fine, B. and Saad-Filho, A. (2017) 'Thirteen Things You Need to Know About Neoliberalism'. *Critical Sociology*. 43 (4–5): 685–706.

Fishback, P. (2007) 'The New Deal'. In Fiscback, P. (ed.), *Government and the American Economy: A New History*. Chicago: University of Chicago Press, pp. 384–431.

FoEUS (2017) *Investing in a Green Belt and Road? Assessing the Implementation of China's Green Credit Guidelines Abroad*. Washington, DC: Friends of the Earth United States.

Foster, J. B. (2008) 'The Financialization of Capital and the Crisis'. *Monthly Review*, 11: 1–19.

Fraser, N. (1990) 'Rethinking the Public Sphere: A Contribution to the Critique of Actually Existing Democracy'. *Social Text*, 25/26: 56–80.

Friedman, M. (1962) *Capitalism and Freedom*. Chicago: University of Chicago Press.

Frigerio, M. and Vandone, D. (2020) 'European Development Banks and the Political Cycle'. *European Journal of Political Economy*, 62(March). DOI: 10.1016/j.ejpoleco.2019.101852.

Gallagher, K. P., Irwin, A. and Koleski, K. (2012) 'The New Banks in Town: Chinese Finance in Latin America'. *Inter-American Dialogue*, March 2012, pp. 1–40.

Garcia-Arias, J. (2015) 'International Financialization and the Systemic Approach to International Financing for Development'. *Global Policy*, 6(1): 24–33.

George, A. and Bennett, A. (2005) *Case Studies and Theory Development in the Social Sciences*. BCSIA Studies in International Security. Cambridge, MA: The MIT Press.

Gerber, J.-F. (2020) 'Degrowth and Critical Agrarian Studies'. *The Journal of Peasant Studies*, 47(2): 235–64. DOI: 10.1080/03066150.2019.1695601.

Gerschenkron, A. (1962) *Economic Backwardness in Historical Perspective: A Book of Essays*. Cambridge: Belknap Press of Harvard University Press.

Gestrin, C. (2018) 'Eco-cooperation with Russia Vital for Baltics Despite Sanctions'. *EU Observer*, 6 March 2018. Available at https://euobserver.com/opinion/141179 Accessed 28 April 2018.

Ghosh, J. (2005) 'The Economic and Social Effects of Financial Liberalization: A Primer for Developing Countries'. DESA Working Paper, No. 4 ST/ESA/2005/DWP/4. New York: United Nations Department of Economic and Social Affairs (UN DESA). Available at www.un.org/esa/desa/papers/2005/wp4_2005.pdf?utm_source=OldRedirect&utm_medium=redirect&utm_campaign=OldRedirect. Accessed 10 June 2017.

Ghosh, J. (2013) 'Microfinance and the Challenge of Financial Inclusion for Development'. *Cambridge Journal of Economics*, 37(6): 1203–19.

Ghosh, J. (2019) 'The Uses and Abuses of Inequality'. *Journal of Human Development and Capabilities*, 20(2): 181–96.

Goda, T., Onaran, Ö. and Stockhammer, E. (2016) 'Income Inequality and Wealth Concentration in the Recent Crisis'. *Development and Change*, 48(1): 3–27.

Gokkon, B. (2018) 'Environmentalists Are Raising Concerns over China's Belt and Road Initiative'. *Pacific Standard*. Available at https://psmag.com/environ ment/environmental-concerns-over-chinese-infrastructure-projects. Accessed 5 March 2020.

Goss, J. and Pacheco, D. (1999) 'Comparative Globalisation and the State in Costa Rica and Thailand'. *Journal of Contemporary Asia*, 29(4): 516–35.

Grabel, I. (2011) 'Not Your Grandfather's IMF: Global Crisis, "Productive Incoherence" and Developmental Policy Space'. *Cambridge Journal of Economics*, 35: 805–30.

Graeber, D. (2011) *Debt: The First 5,000 Years*. New York: Melville House.

Gransow, B. (2015) 'Chinese Infrastructure Investment in Latin America – An Assessment of Strategies, Actors and Risks'. *Journal of Chinese Political Science*, 20(3): 267–87.

Greiling, D. and Grüb, B. (2015) 'Towards Citizen Accountability of Local Public Enterprises'. *Annals of Public and Cooperative Economics*, 86(4): 641–55.

Griffith-Jones, S. (2015) 'The Positive Role of Good Development Banks'. Third International Conference on Financing for Development, Addis Ababa. Available at www.un.org/esa/ffd/ffd3/blog/positive-role-development-banks .html. Accessed 10 June 2018.

Griffith-Jones, S. (2016) 'National Development Banks and Sustainable Infrastructure; the Case of KfW'. Global Economic Governance Initiative, No. 6. 07/2016. Available at www.bu.edu/gegi. Accessed 10 December 2018.

Griffith-Jones, S. and Ocampo, J. A. (eds.) (2018) *The Future of National Development Banks*. Oxford: Oxford University Press.

Griffith-Jones, S. and te Velde, D. W. (2020) 'Development Finance Institutions and the Coronavirus Crisis'. ODI Briefing Papers. London: Overseas Development Institute. Available at www.odi.org/publications/16844-development-finance-institutions-and-coronavirus-crisis. Accessed 8 May 2020.

Griffith-Jones, S., Tyson, J. and Calice, P. (2011) 'The European Investment Bank and SMEs: Key Lessons for Latin America and the Caribbean'. Financiamiento del Desarrollo, No. 236. Santiago, Chile: UN CEPAL.

Griffith-Jones, S., Ocampo, J. A., Rezende, F., Schclarek, A. and Brei, M. (2018) 'The Future of National Development Banks'. In Griffith-Jones, S. and Ocampo, J. A. (eds.), *The Future of National Development Banks*. Cambridge: Cambridge University Press, pp. 1–36.

Griffith-Jones, S., Marodon, R. and Ocampo, J. A. (2020) 'Mobilizing Development Banks to Fight COVID-19'. *Project Syndicate*, 8 April 2020. Available at www.project-syndicate.org/commentary/mobilizing-development-banks-to-fight-covid19-by-stephany-griffith-jones-et-al-2020-04. Accessed 12 May 2020.

Guillén Romo, H. (2005) *México frente a la Mundialización Neoliberal*. Mexico City: Ediciones Era.

Gumede, W., Govender, M. and Motshidi, K. (2011) 'The Role of South Africa's State-Owned Development Finance Institutions in Building a Democratic Developmental State'. Development Planning Division. Working Paper Series 29. Johannesburg, South Africa: Development Bank of Southern Africa. Available at www.dbsa.org/. Accessed 2 April 2019.

Guo, L. Qu, Y., Wu, C. and Gui, S. (2018) 'Evaluating Green Growth Practices: Empirical Evidence from China'. *Sustainable Development*, 26(3): 302–19.

Haas, T. and Sander, H. (2016) 'Shortcomings and Perspectives of the German Energiewende'. *Socialism and Democracy*, 30(2): 121–43.

Haber, S. (2005) 'Mexico's Experiments with Bank Privatization and Liberalization, 1991–2003'. *Journal of Banking and Finance*, 29: 2325–53.

Habermas, J. (1991[1962]). *The Structural Transformation of the Public Sphere: An Inquiry into a Category of Bourgeois Society*. Boston: MIT Press.

Hall, P. and Soskice, D. (eds.) (2001) *Varieties of Capitalism: The Institutional Foundations of Comparative Advantage*. New York: Oxford University Press.

Hall, P. and Soskice, D. (2009) 'An Introduction to Varieties of Capitalism'. In Hancké, B. (ed.), *Debating Varieties of Capitalism: A Reader*. Oxford: Oxford University Press.

Hanieh, A. (2011) *Capitalism and Class in the Gulf Arab States*. New York: Palgrave Macmillan.

Hanieh, A. (2013) *Lineages of Revolt: Issues of Contemporary Capitalism in the Middle East*. Chicago, IL: Haymarket Books.

Hanieh, A. (2018) *Money, Markets, and Monarchies: The Gulf Cooperation Council and the Political Economy of the Contemporary Middle East*. Cambridge: Cambridge University Press.

Hanna, T. M. (2018a) *Our Common Wealth: The Return of Public Ownership in the United States*. Manchester: Manchester University Press.

Hanna, T. M. (2018b) *The Crisis Next Time: Planning for Public Ownership as an Alternative to Corporate Bank Bailouts*. Washington, DC: The Democracy Collaborative. Available at https://thenextsystem.org/learn/stories/crisis-next-time-planning-public-ownership-alternative-corporate-bank-bailouts. Accessed 31 March 2020.

Hanna, T. M. (2018c) 'The Next Economic Settlement: The Return of Public Ownership'. *Renewal: A Journal of Labour Politics*, 26: 17–32.

Harmes, A. (2001) *Unseen Power: How Mutual Funds Threaten the Political and Economic Wealth of Nations*. Toronto: Stoddart.

Hart-Landsberg, M. and Burkett, P. (2005) *China and Socialism: Market Reforms and Class Struggle*. New York: Monthly Review Press.

Harvey, D. (1999[1982]). *The Limits to Capital*. New York: Verso.

Harvey, D. (2005) *A Brief History of Neoliberalism*. New York: Oxford University Press.

Harvey, D. (2010) *The Enigma of Capital and the Crises of Capitalism*. London: Profile Books.

Harvey, D. (2012) *Rebel Cities: From the Right to the City to the Urban Revolution*. London: Verso.

Harvey, D. (2015) 'Nation State – God on Earth?' *Challenging Capitalist Modernity II: Dissecting Capitalist Modernity – Building Democratic Confederalism*. Proceedings of the Conference Held at the University of Hamburg, 3–5 April 2015.

Hau, H. and Thum, M. (2009) 'Subprime Crisis and Board (In-)Competence: Private vs. Public Banks in Germany'. CESifo Working Paper Series, No. 2640, ECGI – Finance Working Paper No. 247/2009. Munich, Germany: CESifo GmbH. Available at www.cesifo.org/en/publikationen/2009/working-paper/subprime-crisis-and-board-competence-private-vs-public-banks. Accessed 20 June 2017.

Hawkins, J. and Mihaljek, D. (2001) 'The Banking Industry in the Emerging Market Economies: Competition, Consolidation and Systemic Stability – An Overview'. *BIS Papers*, 4: 1–44.

Hayek, F. A. (1984[1967]) 'Principles of a Liberal Social Order'. In Nishiyama, C. and Leube, K. (eds.), *The Essence of Hayek*. Stanford: Hoover Institution Press, pp. 363–81.

Herndon, T. and Paul, M. (2018) 'A Public Banking Option: As a Mode of Regulation for Household Financial Services in the United States'. Joint Report of The Roosevelt Institute and the Samuel DuBois Cook Center on Social Equity. Available at http://rooseveltinstitute.org/public-banking-option/. Accessed 18 April 2019.

Hickel, J. (2019) 'The Contradiction of the Sustainable Development Goals: Growth versus Ecology on a Finite Planet'. *Sustainable Development*, 27(5): 873–84.

Hickel, J. and Kallis, G. (2019) 'Is Green Growth Possible?'. *New Political Economy*, 25(4): 469–86.

Hilferding, R. (2006[1910]) *Finance Capital: A Study of the Latest Phase of Capitalist Development*, trans. M. Watnick and S. Gordon. London: Routledge.

Ho, P. (2013) 'In Defense of Endogenous, Spontaneously Ordered Development: Institutional Functionalism and Chinese Property Rights'. *Journal of Peasant Studies*, 40(6): 1087–118.

Ho, P. (2014) 'The 'Credibility Thesis' and Its Application to Property Rights: (In) secure Land Tenure and Social Welfare in China'. *Land Use Policy*, 40: 13–27.

Ho, P. (2016) 'An Endogenous Theory of Property Rights: Opening the Black Box of Institutions'. *The Journal of Peasant Studies*, 43(6): 1121–44.

Ho, P. (2017) *Unmaking China's Development: The Function and Credibility of Institutions*. Cambridge: Cambridge University Press.

Ho, P. (2020) 'The Credibility of (In)formality: Or, the Irrelevance of Institutional Form in Judging Performance'. *Cities*, 99(April). DOI: 10.1016/j.cities.2020.102609.

Ho, S. and Marois, T. (2019) 'China's Asset Management Companies as State Spatial–Temporal Strategy'. *The China Quarterly*, 239: 728–51.

Hubert, R. and Cochran. I. (2013) *Public Finance Institutions & the Low-Carbon Transition Case Study: KfW Bankengruppe*. CDC Climate Research Case Study Supplement. Available at www.i4ce.org/wp-core/wp-content/uploads/2015/10/14-09_cdc_climat_study_pfis_-_uk_gib.pdf. Accessed 16 February 2020.

Hudson, M. (2018) *... and forgive them their debts: Lending, Foreclosure, and Redemption from Bronze Age to the Jubilee Year*. Dresden, Germany: ILSET-Verlag.

Hui, E. (2016) 'The Labour Law System, Capitalist Hegemony and Class Politics in China'. *The China Quarterly*, 226: 431–55.

Humphrey, C. (2016) 'The Invisible Hand: Financial Pressures and Organizational Convergence in Multilateral Development Banks'. *Journal of Development Studies*, 52(1): 92–112.

I4CE (2017) *Landscape of Climate Finance in France*. Paris: Institute for Climate Economics. Available at www.i4ce.org/wp-core/wp-content/uploads/2017/12/1212-I4CE2772-Decideurs-VA-web.pdf. Accessed 1 July 2019.

I4CE (2018) *Landscape of Climate Finance in France*. Paris: Institute for Climate Economics. Available at www.i4ce.org/wp-core/wp-content/uploads/2018/11/I4CE-Landscape-of-climate-finance-2018-EN-summary-vf.pdf. Accessed 1 July 2019.

IMF (2020) *Fiscal Monitor: Policies to Support People during the COVID-19 Pandemic*. Washington, DC: International Monetary Fund.

IMF/World Bank (2015) *From Billions to Trillions: Transforming Development Finance Post-2015 Financing for Development: Multilateral Development Finance*. Development Committee, Joint Ministerial Committee of the Boards of Governors of the Bank and the Fund on the Transfer of Real Resources to Developing Countries. DC2015–0002. Available at www.worldbank.org. Accessed 10 June 2018.

Industrial Commission of North Dakota (2011) *State to Offer Loans to Political Subdivisions Impacted by Weather*. 16 June 2011. Available at www.nd.gov/ndic/ic-press/pfa-disaster.pdf. Accessed 7 April 2020.

IPCC (2018) *Global Warming of 1.5°C. An IPCC Special Report on the Impacts of Global Warming of 1.5°C above Pre-industrial Levels and Related Global Greenhouse Gas Emission Pathways, in the Context of Strengthening the Global Response to the Threat of Climate Change, Sustainable Development, and Efforts to Eradicate Poverty.* Geneva: Intergovernmental Panel on Climate Change. Available at www.ipcc.ch/sr15/. Accessed 4 October 2019.

Itoh, M. and Lapavitsas, C. (1999) *Political Economy of Money and Finance.* London: Macmillan Press.

Jessop, B. (1990) *State Theory: Putting the Capitalist State in Its Place.* Cambridge: Polity Press.

Jessop, B. (2016) 'Territory, Politics, Governance and Multispatial Metagovernance'. *Territory, Politics, Governance,* 4(1): 8–32.

Jiabao, W. (2011) *China's Twelfth Five Year Plan (2011–2015).* Available at https://cbi.typepad.com/china_direct/2011/05/chinas-twelfth-five-new-plan-the-full-english-version.html. Accessed 10 December 2019.

Johnson, C. (1982) *Miti and the Japanese Miracle: The Growth of Industrial Policy: 1925–1975.* Stanford: Stanford University Press.

Jones, L. and Zeng, J. (2019) 'Understanding China's "Belt and Road Initiative": Beyond "Grand Strategy" to a State Transformation Analysis'. *Third World Quarterly,* 40(8): 1415–39.

Jonung, L. (2008) 'Lessons from Financial Liberalisation in Scandinavia'. *Comparative Economic Studies,* 50(4): 564–98.

Ju, X. and Lo, D. (2012) 'The Cost and Benefit of Banking Regulations and Controls, Chinese Style'. *PSL Quarterly Review,* 66(263): 385–402.

Kabeer, N. (2005) 'Is Microfinance a Magic Bullet' for Women's Empowerment? Analysis of Findings from South Asia'. *Economic and Political Weekly,* 4709–18.

Kapsos, S. and Bourmpoula, E. (2013) 'Employment and Economic Class in the Developing World'. ILO Research Paper, No. 6. Geneva: International Labour Office. Available at www.ilo.org/wcmsp5/groups/public/—dgreports/—inst/documents/publication/wcms_216451.pdf. Accessed 10 June 2018.

Karacimen, E. (2014) 'Financialization in Turkey: The Case of Consumer Debt'. *Journal of Balkan and Near Eastern Studies,* 16(2): 161–80.

Karmel, S. M. (1994) 'Emerging Securities Markets in China: Capitalism with Chinese Characteristics'. *The China Quarterly,* 140(December): 1105–20.

Karwowski, E. (2019) 'Towards (De-)financialisation: The Role of the State'. *Cambridge Journal of Economics,* 43(4): 1001–27.

Karwowski, E. and Centurion-Vicencio, M. (2018) 'Financialising the State: Recent Developments in Fiscal and Monetary Policy'. Financial Geography Working Paper No. 11, ffhalshs-01713028. Oxford: FinGeo.

Kattel, R. and Mazzucato, M. (2018) 'Mission-Oriented Innovation Policy and Dynamic Capabilities in the Public Sector'. *Industrial and Corporate Change*, 27(5): 787–801.

Keynes, J. M. (1926) *The End of Laissez-Faire*. London: I. and V. Woolf.

KfW (2015) *Annual Report 2014*. Frankfurt, Germany: KfW Group. Available at www.kfw.de. Accessed 2 February 2018.

KfW (2017) *KfW at a Glance: Facts and Figures*. Updated March 2017. Frankfurt, Germany: KfW Group. Available at www.kfw.de. Accessed 2 February 2018.

KfW (2019a) *KfW at a Glance Facts and Figures*. Updated April 2019. Frankfurt, Germany: KfW Group. Available at www.kfw.de. Accessed 3 May 2019.

KfW (2019b) *KfW Presents Itself*. Updated April 2019. Frankfurt, Germany: KfW Group. Available at www.kfw.de. Accessed 22 June 2019.

Kishimoto, S. and Petitjean, O. (eds.) (2017) *Reclaiming Public Services: How Cities and Citizens Are Turning Back Privatisation*. Amsterdam: Transnational Institute–TNI.

Kishimoto, S., Steinfort, L. and Petitjean, O. (eds.) (2020) *The Future Is Public towards Democratic Ownership of Public Services*. Amsterdam: Transnational Institute–TNI. Available at www.tni.org/files/publication-down loads/futureispublic_online_def_14_july.pdf. Accessed 31 July 2020.

Kodrzycki, Y. K. and Elmatad, T. (2011) 'The Bank of North Dakota: A Model for Massachusetts and Other States?' New England Public Policy Center Research Report, No. 11–12. Boston: Federal Reserve Bank of Boston.

Konings, M. (2018) *Capital and Time: For a New Critique of Neoliberal Reason*. Stanford: Stanford University Press.

Körner, T. and Schnabel, I. (2011) 'Public Ownership of Banks and Economic Growth: The Impact of Country Heterogeneity'. *Economics of Transition*, 19(3): 407–41.

Kulikoff, A. (2000) *From British Peasants to Colonial American Farmers*. University of North Carolina Press.

Kumari, A. and Sharma, A. K. (2017) 'Infrastructure Financing and Development: A Bibliometric Review'. *International Journal of Critical Infrastructure Protection*, 16: 49–65.

La Porta, R., Lopez-de-Silanes, F. and Shleifer, A. (2002) 'Government Ownership of Banks'. *The Journal of Finance*, 57(1): 265–301.

Laeven, L. and Valencia, F. (2013) 'Systemic Banking Crises Database'. *IMF Economic Review*, 61(2): 225–70.

Lapavitsas, C. (2011) 'Theorizing Financialization'. *Work, Employment and Society*, 25(4): 611–26.

Lauber, V. and Jacobsson, S. (2016) 'The Politics and Economics of Constructing, Contesting and Restricting Socio-political Space for Renewables – The German

Renewable Energy Act'. *Environmental Innovation and Societal Transitions*, 18: 147–63.

Lal, D. (2000) *The Poverty of 'Development Economics'*. London: MIT Press.

Langley, P. (2008) *The Everyday Life of Global Finance: Saving and Borrowing in Anglo-America*. Oxford: Oxford University Press.

Lapavitsas, C. (2009) 'Financialised Capitalism: Crisis and Financial Expropriation'. *Historical Materialism*, 17(2): 114–48.

Lapavitsas, C. (2010) 'Systemic Failure of Private Banking: A Case for Public Banks'. In Arestis, P. and Sawyer, M. (eds.), *21st Century Keynesian Economics*. Houndsmills: Palgrave Macmillan, pp. 162–99.

Lapavitsas, C. (2011) 'Theorizing Financialization'. *Work, Employment and Society*, 25(4): 611–26.

Lapavitsas, C. (2013) *Profiting without Producing: How Finance Exploits Us All*. London: Verso.

Lapavitsas, C. and Mendieta-Munoz, I. (2016) 'The Profits of Financialization'. *Monthly* Review, 68(3): 49–62.

Lawrence, M. (2014) *Definancialisation: A Democratic Reform of Finance*. London: Institute for Public Policy Research.

Lazonick, W. and Shin, J.-S. (2020) *Predatory Value Extraction: How the Looting of the Business Corporation Became the US Norm and How Sustainable Prosperity Can Be Restored*. Oxford: Oxford University Press.

Leder Macek, S. (2019) *White Paper: Public Banking in the Northeast and Midwest States*. The Northeast-Midwest Institute. Available at www.nemw.org. Accessed 20 February 2020.

Lefeber, L. and Vietorisz, T. (2007) 'The Meaning of Social Efficiency'. *Review of Political Economy*, 19(2): 139–64.

Lefebvre, H. (2016[1972]) *Marxist Thought and the City*, trans. R. Bononno and foreword by S. Elden. Minneapolis: University of Minnesota Press.

Lehoucq, F. E. (1990) 'Class Conflict. Political Crisis and the Breakdown of Democratic Practices in Costa Rica: Reassessing the Origins of the 1948 Civil War'. Papers in International Political Economy. Duke University Program in Political Economy.

Lehoucq, F. E. (1996) 'The Institutional Foundations of Democratic Cooperation in Costa Rica'. *Journal of Latin American Studies*, 28(2): 329–55.

Lerche, J. (2013) 'The Agrarian Question in Neoliberal India: Agrarian Transition Bypassed?'. *Journal of Agrarian Change*. 13(3): 382–404.

Lessambo, F. I. (2015) *International Financial Institutions and Their Challenge*. New York: Palgrave Macmillan.

Lessambo, F. I. (2019) *The U.S. Banking System: Laws, Regulations, and Risk Management*. Cham, Switzerland: Springer Nature.

Leys, C. (1996) *The Rise and Fall of Development Theory*. Bloomington, IN: Indiana University Press.

Levy Yeyati, E., Micco, A. and Panizza, U. (2007) 'A Reappraisal of State-Owned Banks'. *Economia*, 7(2): 209–47.

Li, Y. and Gallagher, K. P. (2019) 'The Environmental Impact of China-financed Coal-fired Power Plants in South East Asia'. GCI Working Paper 007. Boston University's Global Development Policy Center. Available at www.bu.edu/gdp/files/2019/04/GCI-WP-7-Coal-Satellite-Li-Gallagher-2019-1.pdf. Accessed 2 February 2020.

Lo, D. and Zhang, Y. (2011) 'Making Sense of China's Economic Transformation'. *Review of Radical Political Economics*, 43(1): 33–55.

Lockwood, E. (2020) 'The International Political Economy of Global Inequality'. *Review of International Political Economy*. DOI: 10.1080/09692290.2020.1775106.

Lohmann, L. (2006) 'Carbon Trading – A Critical Conversation on Climate Change, Privatisation and Power'. *Development Dialogue*, 48: 73–100.

Macfarlane, L. and Brett, M. (2020) *Charting a Just & Sustainable Recovery for Scotland*. London: Common Wealth. Available at www.common-wealth.co.uk/reports/charting-a-just-and-sustainable-recovery-for-scotland. Accessed 27 August 2020.

Macfarlane, L. and Mazzucato, M. (2018) 'State Investment Banks and Patient Finance: An International Comparison'. UCL Institute for Innovation and Public Purpose, Working Paper Series (IIPP WP 2018–01). London: UCL IIPP. Available at www.ucl.ac.uk/bartlett/public-purpose/wp2018-01. Accessed 3 September 2019.

MacLean, K. (2012) 'Banking on Women's Labour: Responsibility, Risk, and Control in Village Banking in Bolivia'. *Journal of International Development*, 24: S100–11.

MacLean, N. (2017) *Democracy in Chains: The Deep History of the Radical Right's Stealth Plan for America*. London: Scribe.

Mader, P. (2013) 'Rise and Fall of Microfinance in India: The Andhra Pradesh Crisis in Perspective'. *Strategic Change*, 22(1–2): 47–66.

Magdoff, F. and Williams, C. (2017) *Creating and Ecological Society: Toward a Revolutionary Transformation*. New York: Monthly Review Press.

Malm, A. (2015) 'Exploding in the Air: Beyond the Carbon Trail of Neoliberal Globalisation'. In Pradella, L. and Marois, T. (eds.), *Polarizing Development: Alternatives to Neoliberalism and the Crisis*. London: Pluto Press, pp. 108–18.

Maltais, A. and Nykvist, B. (2020) 'Understanding the Role of Green Bonds in Advancing Sustainability'. *Journal of Sustainable Finance & Investment*. DOI: 10.1080/20430795.2020.1724864.

Mandel, E. (1968[1962]) *Marxist Economic Theory*, trans. B. Pearce. London: The Merlin Press.

Marcelin, I. and Mathur, I. (2015) 'Privatization, Financial Development, Property Rights and Growth'. *Journal of Banking & Finance*, 50: 528–46.

Marois, T. (2005) 'From Economic Crisis to a "State" of Crisis?: The Emergence of Neoliberalism in Costa Rica'. *Historical Materialism*, 13(3): 101–34.

Marois, T. (2008) 'The 1982 Mexican Bank Statization and Unintended Consequences for the Emergence of Neoliberalism'. *Canadian Journal of Political Science*, 41(1): 143–67.

Marois, T. (2011) 'Emerging Market Bank Rescues in an Era of Finance-led Neoliberalism: A Comparison of Mexico and Turkey'. *Review of International Political Economy*, 18(2): 168–96.

Marois, T. (2012) *States, Banks, and Crisis: Emerging Finance Capitalism in Mexico and Turkey*. Cheltenham: Edward Elgar.

Marois, T. (2013) *State-Owned Banks and Development: Dispelling Mainstream Myths*. Kingston, Canada: Municipal Services Project.

Marois, T. (2014) 'Historical Precedents, Contemporary Manifestations: Crisis and the Socialization of Financial Risk in Neoliberal Mexico'. *Review of Radical Political Economics*, 46(3): 308–30.

Marois, T. (2015) 'Banking on Alternatives to Neoliberal Development'. In Pradella, L. and Marois, T. (eds.), *Polarizing Development: Alternatives to Neoliberalism and the Crisis*. London: Pluto Press, pp. 27–38.

Marois, T. (2016) 'State-Owned Banks and Development: Dispelling Mainstream Myths'. In Erdoğdu, M. and Christiansen, B. (eds.), *Handbook of Research on Comparative Economic Development Perspectives on Europe and the MENA Region*. Hershey, PA: IGI Global, pp. 52–72.

Marois, T. (2017) *How Public Banks Can Help Finance a Green and Just Energy Transformation*. Amsterdam: Transnational Institute.

Marois, T. (2018) *Towards a Green Public Bank in the Public Interest*. Geneva: UNRISD (United Nations Research Institute for Social Development). Available at www.unrisd.org. Accessed 14 July 2019.

Marois, T. (2019a) 'Public Banking on the Future We Want'. In Steinfort, L. and Kishimoto, S., (eds.), *Public Finance for the Future We Want*. Amsterdam: Transnational Institute, pp. 150–56.

Marois, T. (2019b) 'The Transformation of the State Financial Apparatus in Turkey since 2001'. In Yalman, G. L. and Marois, T. and Güngen, A. R. (eds.), *The Political Economy of Financial Transformation in Turkey*. Abingdon: Routledge.

Marois, T. (2021) A Dynamic Theory of Public Banks (and why it matters). UCL Institute for Innovation and Public Purpose (IIPP) Working Paper Series. No. 6. London: UCL IIPP.

Marois, T. and Güngen, A. R. (2016a) 'Credibility and Class in the Evolution of Public Banks: The Case of Turkey'. *Journal of Peasant Studies*, 43(6): 1285–309.

Marois, T. and Güngen, A. R. (2016b) '(Re)Making Public Banks: The Case of Turkey'. In McDonald, D. (ed.), *Making Public in a Privatized World: The Struggle for Essential Services*. London: Zed Books.

Marois, T. and Güngen, A. R. (2019a) 'The Neoliberal Restructuring of Banking in Turkey since 2001'. In Yalman, G. L., Marois, T. and Güngen, A. R. (eds.), *The Political Economy of Financial Transformation in Turkey*. Abingdon: Routledge.

Marois, T. and Güngen, A. R. (2019b) *A US green Investment Bank for All: Democratized Finance for a Just Transition*. Washington, DC: Next System Project/Democracy Collaborative.

Marois, T. and Muñoz-Martínez, H. (2016) 'Navigating the Aftermath of Crisis and Risk in Mexico and Turkey'. *Research in Political Economy*, 31: 165–94.

Martens, J. (2017) 'Reclaiming the Public (Policy) Space for the SDGs: Privatization, Partnerships, Corporate Capture and the Implementation of the 2030 Agenda'. *Spotlight on Sustainable Development 2017: Reclaiming Policies for the Public*. Report by the Civil Society Reflection Group on the 2030 Agenda for Sustainable Development, pp. 10–18.

Martin, M. F. (2012) 'China's Banking System: Issues for Congress'. Congressional Research Service, 7–5700. Available at www.crs.gov. Accessed 10 June 2018.

Martin, R. (2002) *Financialization of Daily Life*. Philadelphia: Temple University Press.

Maxfield, S. (1992) 'The International Political Economy of Bank Nationalization: Mexico in Comparative Perspective'. *Latin American Research Review*, 27(1): 75–103.

Maxfield, S., Winecoff, W. K. and Young, K. L. (2017) 'An Empirical Investigation of the Financialization Convergence Hypothesis'. *Review of International Political Economy*, 24(6): 1004–29.

Mazzucato, M. (2013) 'Financing Innovation: Creative Destruction vs Destructive Creation'. *Industrial and Corporate Change*, 22: 851–67.

Mazzucato, M. (2015[2013]) *The Entrepreneurial State*, rev. ed. London: Anthem Press.

Mazzucato, M. (2018) *The Value of Everything: Making and Taking in the Global Economy*. London: Penguin-Allen Lane.

Mazzucato, M. and McPherson, M. (2018) 'The Green New Deal: A Bold Mission-Oriented Approach'. IIPP Policy Brief (December). London: Institute for Innovation and Public Purpose.

Mazzucato, M. and Mikheeva, O. (2020) 'The EIB and the new EU missions framework'. *UCL Institute for Innovation and Public Purpose IIPP Policy Report*. WP 2020-17. London: IIPP. Available at: https://www.ucl.ac.uk/bartlett/public-purpose/wp2020-17. Accessed 20 December 2020

Mazzucato, M. and Penna, C. C. R. (2016) 'Beyond Market Failures: The Market Creating and Shaping Roles of State Investment Banks'. *Journal of Economic Policy Reform*, 19(4): 305–26.

Mazzucato, M. and Penna, C. C. R. (2018) 'National Development Banks and Mission-Oriented Finance for Innovation'. In Griffith-Jones, S. and Ocampo, J. A. (eds.), *The Future of National Development Banks*. Cambridge: Cambridge University Press, pp. 255–77.

Mazzucato, M. and Semieniuk, G. (2017) 'Public Financing of Innovation: New Questions'. *Oxford Review of Economic Policy*, 33(1): 24–48.

Mazzucato, M. and Semieniuk, G. (2018) 'Financing Renewable Energy: Who Is Financing What and Why It Matters'. *Technological Forecasting & Social Change*, 127: 8–22.

McDonald, D. (ed.) (2014) *Rethinking Corporatization and Public Services in the Global South*. Zed Books: London.

McDonald, D. (2015) 'Defend, Militate, Alternate: Public Options in a Privatized World'. In Pradella, L. and Marois, T. (eds.), *Polarizing Development: Alternatives to Neoliberalism and the Crisis*. London: Pluto Press, pp. 119–30.

McDonald, D. (2016a) 'To Corporatize or Not to Corporatize (And If so How)?'. *Utilities Policy*, 40: 107–14.

McDonald, D. (ed.) (2016b) *Making Public in a Privatized World: The Struggle for Essential Services*. London: Zed Books.

McDonald, D. (2018) 'Innovation and New Public Water'. *Journal of Economic Policy Reform*, 23(1): 67–82.

McDonald, D. and Ruiters, G. (eds.) (2012) *Alternatives to Privatization: Public Options for Essential Services in the Global South*. Abingdon: Routledge.

McDonald, D. A., Marois, T. and Barrowclough, D. V. (eds.) (2020) *Public Banks and Covid-19: Combatting the Pandemic with Public Finance*. Municipal Services Project (Kingston), UNCTAD (Geneva), and Eurodad (Brussels). Available at https://publicbankscovid19.org/. Accessed 1 December 2020.

McNally, D. (2015) 'Crisis, Austerity and Resistance in the United States'. In Pradella, L. and Marois, T. (eds.), *Polarizing Development: Alternatives to Neoliberalism and the Crisis*. London: Pluto Press, pp. 260–70.

McNally, D. (2020) *Blood and Money: War, Slavery, Finance, and Empire*. Chicago: Haymarket Books.

Megginson, W. L. (2005a) *The Financial Economics of Privatization*. New York: Oxford University Press.

Megginson, W. L. (2005b) 'The Economics of Bank Privatization'. *Journal of Banking and Finance*, 29: 1931–80.

Megginson, W. L. (2015) 'Introduction'. The PB [Privatization Barometer] Report 2014/15. Milano, Italy: Fondazione Eni Enrico Mattei, pp. 2–4.

Meiksins Wood, E. (2002) *The Origin of Capitalism: A Longer View*. London: Verso.

Mertens, D., Rubio, E. and Thiemann, M. (2020) 'COVID-19 and the Mobilisation of Public Development Banks in the EU'. EU Budget Policy Paper, No. 252. Paris: Jacques Delors Institute. Available at https://institutdelors.eu/en/publications/covid-19-and-the-mobilisation-of-public-development-banks-in-the-eu/. Accessed 1 May 2020.

Meyer, C. B. (2001) 'A Case in Case Study Methodology'. *Field Methods*, 13(4): 329–52.

Mezzadri, A. (2017) *The Sweatshop Regime: Labouring Bodies, Exploitation and Garments Made in India*. Cambridge: Cambridge University Press.

Michaelowa, A., Shishlov, I., Brescia, D. (2019) 'Evolution of International Carbon Markets: Lessons for the Paris Agreement'. *Wiley Interdisciplinary Reviews: Climate Change*, 10(6): 1–24.

Milanovic, B. (2012) 'Global Income Inequality in Numbers: In History and Now'. World Bank Policy Research Working Paper, No. 6259. Available at https://openknowledge.worldbank.org/handle/10986/12117?locale-attribute=en. Accessed 10 June 2018.

Minsky, H. P. (2008[1986]) *Stabilizing an Unstable Economy*. London: McGraw-Hill.

Minsky, H. P., Papadimitriou, D. B., Phillips, R. J. and Wray, L. R. (1993) 'Community Development Banking: A Proposal to Establish a Nationwide System of Community Development Banks'. Public Policy Brief, No. 3. The Jerome Levy Economics Institute of Bard College.

Mishel, L. and Bivens, J. (2013) 'The Pay of Corporate Executives and Financial Professionals as Evidence of Rents in Top 1 Percent Incomes'. Working Paper No. 296. Economic Policy Institute. Available at www.epi.org/publication/pay-corporate-executives-financial-professionals/. Accessed 10 June 2018.

Mishkin, F. S. (2009) 'Why We Shouldn't Turn Our Backs on Financial Globalization'. *IMF Staff Papers*, 56(1): 139–70.

Mitchell, S. (2012) 'Public Banks: Bank of North Dakota'. Institute for Local Self-Reliance. Available at https://ilsr.org/rule/bank-of-north-dakota-2/. Accessed 5 April 2020.

Miyamura, S. (2016) 'Rethinking Labour Market Institutions in Indian Industry: Forms, Functions and Socio-Historical Contexts'. *The Journal of Peasant Studies*, 43(6): 1262–84.

Mohanty, C. T. and Miraglia, S. (2012) 'Gendering Justice, Building Alternative Futures'. In McDonald, D. A. and Ruiters, G. (eds.), *Alternatives to Privatization: Public Options for Essential Services in the Global South*. Cape Town, South Africa: HSRC Press, pp. 99–132.

Montgomery, A. (1960) 'From a Northern Customs Union to EFTA'. *Scandinavian Economic History Review*, 8(1): 45–70.

Morgan, J. and Olsen. W. (2011) 'Aspiration Problems for the Indian Rural Poor: Research on Self-Help Groups and Micro-Finance'. *Capital & Class*, 35(2): 189–212.

Moslener, U., Thiemann, M. and Volberding, P. (2018) 'National Development Banks as Active Financiers: The Case of KfW'. In Griffith-Jones, S. and Ocampo, J. A. (eds.), *The Future of National Development Banks*. Cambridge: Cambridge University Press, pp. 63–85.

Mühlenkamp, H. (2015) 'From State to Market Revisited: A Reassessment of the Empirical Evidence on the Efficiency of Public (and Privately-Owned)'. *Annals of Public and Cooperative Economics*, 86(4): 535–57.

Mukhopadhyay, B. G. (2016) *NABARD's Experience in Climate Finance*. Bonn, Germany: United Nations Framework Convention on Climate Change. Available at https://unfccc.int/files/adaptation/application/pdf/asia_6.1c_ nabard_experience_in_climate_finance.pdf. Accessed 7 April 2020.

Muñoz-Martínez, H. and Marois, T. (2014) 'Capital Fixity and Mobility in Response to the 2008–09 Crisis: Variegated Neoliberalism in Mexico and Turkey'. *Environment and Planning D: Society and Space*, 32(6): 1102–19.

Murray, A. and Spronk, S. (2019) 'Blended Financing, Canadian Foreign Aid Policy, and Alternatives'. *Studies in Political Economy*, 100(3): 270–86. DOI: 10.1080/ 07078552.2019.1682781.

Myrdal, G. (1963[1957]). *Economic Theory and Under-Developed Regions*. London: Gerald Duckworth.

NABARD (1983) *Annual Report 1982–83*. Mumbai, India: National Bank for Agriculture and Rural Development.

NABARD (1984) *Annual Report 1983–84*. Mumbai, India: National Bank for Agriculture and Rural Development.

NABARD (2000) *Annual Report 1999–2000*. Mumbai, India: National Bank for Agriculture and Rural Development.

NABARD (2005) *Annual Report 2004–2005*. Mumbai, India: National Bank for Agriculture and Rural Development.

NABARD (2014) *Annual Report 2013–14*. Mumbai, India: National Bank for Agriculture and Rural Development.

NABARD (2017) *Annual Report 2016–17*. Mumbai, India: National Bank for Agriculture and Rural Development.

NABARD (2018) *Annual Report 2017–18*. Mumbai, India: National Bank for Agriculture and Rural Development.

NABARD (2019) *Annual Report 2018–19*. Mumbai, India: National Bank for Agriculture and Rural Development.

NABARD (2000) *Annual Report 1999–2000*. Mumbai, India: National Bank for Agriculture and Rural Development.

Nash, G. D. (1959) 'Herbert Hoover and the Origins of the Reconstruction Finance Corporation'. *The Mississippi Valley Historical Review*, 46(3): 455–68.

Naqvi, N. (2019) 'Renationalizing Finance for Development: Policy Space and Public Economic Control in Bolivia'. *Review of International Political Economy*. DOI: 10.1080/09692290.2019.1696870.

Naqvi, N., Henow, A. and Chang, H. J. (2018) 'Kicking away the Financial Ladder? German Development Banking under Economic Globalisation'. *Review of International Political Economy*, 25(5): 672–98.

NCM (2017) *Nordic Action on Climate Change*. Copenhagen, Denmark: Nordic Council of Ministers.

Neuhann, D. and Saidi, F. (2018) 'Do Universal Banks Finance Riskier but More Productive Firms?'. *Journal of Financial Economics*, 128(1): 66–85.

Newell, P. (2011) 'The Governance of Energy Finance: The Public, the Private and the Hybrid'. *Global Policy*, 2(S1): 94–105.

Newell, P. and Paterson, M. (2010) *Climate Capitalism: Global Warming and the Transformation of the Global Economy*. Cambridge: Cambridge University Press.

Newsham, A. and Bhagwat, S. (2016) *Conservation and Development*. Abingdon: Routledge.

NIB (2012) *Sustainability Policy and Guidelines*. Helsinki, Finland: Nordic Investment Bank.

NIB (2015) *Annual Report 2014*. Helsinki, Finland: Nordic Investment Bank.

NIB (2016) *Annual Report 2015*. Helsinki, Finland: Nordic Investment Bank.

NIB (2017) *Annual Report 2016*. Helsinki, Finland: Nordic Investment Bank.

NIB (2018a) *Annual Report 2017*. Helsinki, Finland: Nordic Investment Bank.

NIB (2018b) *Financial Report 2017*. Helsinki, Finland: Nordic Investment Bank.

NIB (2018c) *Mission, Strategy and Values of the Nordic Investment Bank*. Helsinki, Finland: Nordic Investment Bank.

NIB (2019) *NIB Activity Report 2018*. Helsinki, Finland: Nordic Investment Bank.

Nightingale, A. J., Eriksen, S., Taylor, M., Forsyth, T., Pelling, M., Newsham, A., et al. (2020) 'Beyond Technical Fixes: Climate Solutions and the Great Derangement'. *Climate and Development*, 12(4): 343–52.

Nipper. J. (2002) 'The Transformation of Urban East Germany since the 'Wende': From a Socialist City to a … ?'. *Hommes et Terres du Nord*, 4: 63–74.

Noronha, R. (2013) '"The Most Revolutionary Law Ever Approved": Social Conflict and State Economic Intervention during the Portuguese Revolution (1974–1975)'. In Trindade, L. (ed.), *The Making of Modern Portugal*. Newcastle: Cambridge Scholars Publishing, pp. 290–310.

O'Connor, J. (2009[1979]) *The Fiscal Crisis of the State*. London: Transaction Publishers.

Orbis (2018) Orbis. Bureau van Dijk. [Online]. Available at www.bvdinfo.com/. Accessed 13 October 2018.

Orbis (2020) Orbis. Bureau van Dijk. [Online]. Available at www.bvdinfo.com/. Accessed: 20 April 2020.

OECD (2017a) 'Green Investment Banks: Innovative Public Financial Institutions Scaling up Private, Low-Carbon Investment'. OECD Environment Policy Paper No. 6. Paris: OECD. Available at www.oecd-ilibrary.org/environment/green-investment-banks_e3c2526c-en. Accessed 10 June 2019.

OECD (2017b) *Investing in Climate, Investing in Growth*. Paris: OECD. Available at http://dx.doi.org/10.1787/9789264273528-en. Accessed 20 January 20120.

OECD (2020) *The Impact of the Coronavirus (COVID-19) Crisis on Development Finance*. Paris: OECD. Available at https://read.oecd-ilibrary.org/view/?ref=134_134569-xn1go1i113&title=The-impact-of-the-coronavirus-(COVID-19)-crisis-on-development-finance. Accessed 13 July 2020.

Oğuz, Ş. (2013) 'The Developmental State as an Institutional Construct: A Historical and Theoretical Critique'. *Review of Public Administration*, 7(4): 97–120.

Oliver, P., Clark, A., Meattle, C. and Buchner, B. (2018) *Global Climate Finance: An Updated View*. London: Climate Policy Initiative. Available at www.climatepolicyinitiative.org. Accessed 1 July 2019.

Olson, J. (1988) *Saving Capitalism: The Reconstruction Finance Corporation and the New Deal, 1933–1940*. Princeton, NJ: Princeton University Press.

OMFIF (2017) *Global Public Investor 2017*. London: Official Monetary and Financial Institutions Forum.

OMFIF (2019) *Global Public Investor 2019*. London: Official Monetary and Financial Institutions Forum.

Onaran, O., Stockhammer, E. and Grafl, L. (2011) 'Financialisation, Income Distribution and Aggregate Demand in the USA'. *Cambridge Journal of Economics*, 35(4): 637–61.

Öniş, Z. (1991) 'The Logic of the Developmental State'. *Comparative Politics*, 24(1): 109–26.

Orhangazi, Ö. (2008a) *Financialization and the US Economy*. Cheltenham: Edward Elgar.

Orhangazi, Ö. (2008b) 'Financialisation and Capital Accumulation in the Non-financial Corporate Sector: A Theoretical and Empirical Investigation on the US Economy: 1973–2003'. *Cambridge Journal of Economics*, 32(6): 863–86.

Ostry, J. D., Loungani, P. and Furceri, D. (2016) 'Neoliberalism Oversold?'. *Finance & Development*, June: 38–41.

Öztürk, H., Gultekin-Karakas, D. and Hısarcıklılar, M. (2010) 'The Role of Development Banking in Promoting Industrialization in Turkey'. *Région et Développement*, 32: 153–78.

Palermo, G. (2019) 'Power: A Marxist View: Coercion and Exploitation in the Capitalist Mode of Production'. *Cambridge Journal of Economics*, 43(5): 1353–75.

Pan, J. (2016) *China's Environmental Governing and Ecological Civilization*. Berlin: Springer-Verlag.

Panitch, L. and Gindin, S. (2012) *The Making of Global Capitalism: The Political Economy of American Empire*. London: Verso.

Parsons, T. (1971) *The System of Modern Societies*. Englewood Cliffs, NJ: Prentice-Hall.

Paul, F. C. (2018) 'Deep Entanglements: History, Space and (Energy) Struggle in the German Energiewende'. *Geoforum*, 91(May): 1–9.

Peck, J. and Theodore, N. (2007) 'Variegated Capitalism'. *Progress in Human Geography*, 31(6): 731–72.

Peck, J. and Theodore, N. (2012) 'Follow the Policy: A Distended Case Approach'. *Environment and Planning A: Economy and Space*, 44(1): 21–30.

Peetz, E. (2019) 'Water – The Overlooked Crisis'. *KfW Development Bank, Perspectives on Development Finance*, No. 1, March 13.

Pellandini-Simányi, L., Hammer, F. and Vargha, Z. (2015) 'The Financialization of Everyday Life or the Domestication of Finance?'. *Cultural Studies*, 29(5–6): 733–59.

Périlleux, A. and Nyssens, M. (2017) 'Understanding Cooperative Finance as a New Common'. *Annals of Public and Cooperative Economics*, 88(2):155–77.

Polanyi, K. (2001[1944]) *The Great Transformation: The Political and Economic Origins of Our Time*, 2nd ed. Boston: Beacon Press.

Pollard, J. (2012) 'Gendering Capital: Financial Crisis, Financialization and (an Agenda for) Economic Geography'. *Progress in Human Geography*, 37(3): 403–23.

Poulantzas, N. (2000[1978]) *State, Power, Socialism*. New York: Verso Classics.

Povel, F. and Heidebrecht, J. (2015) 'Why and How Development Banks Should Contribute to Finance the Sustainable Development Goals'. www.un.org/esa/ffd/ffd3/blog/why-and-how-development-banks-should-contribute-to-finance-sdgs.html

Pradella, L. (2015) 'Beyond Impoverishment: Western Europe in the World Economy'. In Pradella, L. and Marois, T. (eds.), *Polarizing Development: Alternatives to Neoliberalism and the Crisis*. London: Pluto Press, pp. 15–26.

Pradella, L. and Marois, T. (eds.) (2015) *Polarizing Development: Alternatives to Neoliberalism and the Crisis*. London: Pluto Press.

Premchander, S. and Chidambaranatham, M. (2007) 'One Step Forward or Two Steps Back? Proposed Amendments to NABARD'. *Economic and Political Weekly*, 42(12): 1006–08.

Pringle, T. (2011) *Trade Unions in China: The Challenge of Labour Unrest*. London: Routledge.

Pringle, T. (2015) 'Labour as an Agent of Change: The Case of China'. In Pradella, L. and Marois, T. (eds.), *Polarizing Development: Alternatives to Neoliberalism and the Crisis*. London: Pluto Press, pp. 192–202.

Przeworski, A. (2004) 'The Last Instance: Are Institutions the Primary Cause of Economic Development?'. *European Archives of Sociology*, 45(2): 165–88.

PSA (2014) *Down the Rabbit Hole What the Bankers Aren't Telling You!* New Delhi: Programme for Social Action. Available at www.psa-india.net/publica tions. Accessed 7 July 2019.

Radcliffe, S. A. (2015) 'Development Alternatives'. *Development and Change*, 46(4): 855–74.

Radice, H. (2004) 'Comparing National Capitalisms'. In Perraton, J. and Clift, B. (eds.), *Where Are National Capitalisms Now?* New York: Palgrave Macmillan.

Rajeev, M., Vani, B. P. and Veerashekharappa (2020) 'Group Lending through an SHG Bank-Linkage Programme in India: Transaction Costs and Social Benefits'. *Development in Practice*, 30(2): 168–81.

Randefelt, R. (2002) 'What Is NIB Doing for the Barents Sea Environment'. Prospects for NIB financing of environmental projects in the Arctic region. Presentation on behalf of Nordic Investment Bank. Downloaded from the Arctic Council Open Access Repository: https://oaarchive.arctic-council.org/. Accessed 10 June 2019.

Rao, P. S. (2012) 'NABARD and RBI: A 30-Year Legacy Being Upturned'. *Economic & Political Weekly*. XLVII(38): 27–30.

Rappaport, G. D. (1996) *Stability and Change in Revolutionary Pennsylvania: Banking, Politics, and Social Structure*. University Park, PA: Pennsylvania State University Press.

Ray, R., Gallagher, K., Lopez, A. and Sanborn, C. (2015) *China in Latin America: Lessons from South-South Cooperation and Sustainable Development*. Boston: Boston University's Global Economic Governance Initiative.

Ray, R., Gallagher, K. P. and Sanborn, C. A. (eds.) (2020) *Development Banks and Sustainability in the Andean Amazon*. Abingdon: Routledge.

Redclift, M. R. (1987) *Sustainable Development: Exploring the Contradictions*. London: Routledge.

Redclift, M. R. (2005) 'Sustainable Development (1987–2005): An Oxymoron Comes of Age'. *Sustainable Development*, 13(4): 212–27.

Redclift, M. R. (2017) 'Sustainable Development in the Age of Contradictions'. *Development and Change*, 49(3): 695–707.

Reiche, D. (2008) 'Sovereign Wealth Funds as a New Instrument of Climate Protection Policy? Study of Norway as a Pioneer of Ethical Guidelines for Investment Policy'. No. 173e, Wuppertal Institute for Climate, Environment and Energy.

Ribeiro de Mendonça, A. R. and Deos, S. (2017) 'Beyond the Market Failure Argument: Public Banks as Stability Anchors'. In Scherrer, C. (ed.), *Public Banks in the Age of Financialization*. Cheltenham: Edward Elgar, pp. 13–28.

Roberds, W. and Velde, F. R. (2014) 'Early Public Banks'. Working Paper 2014–03. Federal Reserve Bank of Chicago. Available at www.econstor.eu/handle/10419/96660. Accessed 10 June 2018.

Roberts, A. (2015) 'Gender, Financial Deepening and the Production of Embodied Finance: Towards a Critical Feminist Analysis'. *Global Society*, 29(1): 107–27.

Robinson, W. I. (2003) *Transnational Conflicts: Central America, Social Change, and Globalization*. New York: Verso.

Rodríguez, J. and Santiso, J. (2007) 'Banking on Development: Private Banks and Aid Donors in Developing Countries'. OECD Development Centre Working Papers, No. 263. Paris: OECD. Available at https://ideas.repec.org/p/oec/devaaa/263-en.html. Accessed 10 June 2016.

Rodrik, D. (2008) 'Second-Best Institutions'. *American Economic Review*, 98(2): 100–04.

Romero, M. J. (2017) *Public Development Banks: Towards a Better Model*. Brussels: Eurodad. Available at www.eurodad.org/Public-Development-Banks-towards-a-better-model. Accessed 14 July 2019.

Röper, N. (2018) 'German Finance Capitalism: The Paradigm Shift Underlying Financial Diversification'. *New Political Economy*, 23(3): 366–90.

Rostow, W. W. (1971) *The Stages of Economics Growth: A Non-Communist Manifesto*. London: Cambridge University Press.

Rudolph, H. (2009) 'State Financial Institutions: Mandates, Governance, and Beyond'. World Bank Policy Research Working Paper 5141. Washington, DC: The World Bank. Available at https://elibrary.worldbank.org/doi/abs/10.1596/1813-9450-5141. Accessed 10 June 2018.

S&P (2019) *Ratings Direct: Bank of North Dakota*. New York: Standard & Poor's Financial Services.

Sanderson, H. and Forsythe, M. (2013) *China's Superbank*. Singapore: John Wiley & Sons.

Sawyer, M. (2016) 'Confronting Financialisation'. In Arestis, P. and Sawyer, M. (eds.), *Financial Liberalisation*. International Papers in Political Economy. Houndsmills: Palgrave Macmillan, pp. 43–85.

Sawyer, M. (2017) 'The Processes of Financialisation and Economic Performance'. *Economic and Political Studies*, 5(1): 5–20.

Scherrer, C. (ed.) (2017) *Public Banks in the Age of Financialization: A Comparative Perspective*. Cheltenham: Edward Elgar.

Schmidt. H.-I. (2003) 'Pushed to the Front: The Foreign Assistance Policy of the Federal Republic of Germany, 1958–1971'. *Contemporary European History*, 12(4): 473–507.

Schmit, M., Gheeraert, L., Denuit, T. and Warny, C. (2011) *Public Financial Institutions in Europe*. Brussels: European Association of Public Banks.

Schneiberg, M. (2013) 'Lost in Transposition? (A Cautionary Tale): The Bank of North Dakota and Prospects for Reform in American Banking'. In Lounsbury, M. and Boxenbaum, E. (eds.), *Research in the Sociology of Organizations*, vol. 39A. Bingley: Emerald Group.

Scholtens, B. and Sievänen, R. (2013) 'Drivers of Socially Responsible Investing: A Case Study of Four Nordic Countries'. *Journal of Business Ethics*, 115(3): 605–16.

Schrooten, M. (2019) 'Book Review: *Public Banks in the Age of Financialization: A Comparative Perspective*, Christoph Scherrer'. *Australian Journal of Public Administration*, 78(1): 131–33.

Schweizer, P.-J., Renn, O., Köck, W., Bovet, J., Benighaus, C., Scheel, O. and Schröter, R. (2016) 'Public Participation for Infrastructure Planning in the Context of the German "Energiewende"'. *Utilities Policy*. 43(Part B): 206–09.

Scott, D. (2007) *Strengthening the Governance and Performance of State-Owned Financial Institutions*. Washington, DC: The World Bank.

Seabrooke, L. (2006) 'The Bank for International Settlements'. *New Political Economy*, 11(1): 141–49.

Selwyn, B. (2014) *The Global Development Crisis*. Cambridge: Polity Press.

SFPBTF (2018) *Final Report to the Santa Fe City Council*. Santa Fe Public Bank Task Force, 17 April 2018. Available at www.santafenm.gov/public_bank_task_force. Accessed 23 May 2018.

Sgambati, S. (2019) 'The Art of Leverage: A Study of Bank Power, Money-Making and Debt Finance'. *Review of International Political Economy*, 26(2): 287–312.

Sharma, M. (2010) *Management of Financial Institutions: With Emphasis on Bank and Risk Management*. New Delhi: PHI Learning.

Shetty, S. L. (2009) 'Agricultural Credit and Indebtedness: Ground Realities and Policy Perspectives'. In Reddy, D. N. and Mishra, S. (eds.), *Agrarian Crisis in India*. New Delhi: Oxford University Press, pp. 61–86.

Shih, V. (2004) 'Dealing with Non-Performing Loans: Political Constraints and Financial Policies in China'. *The China Quarterly*, 180: 922–44.

Shirley, M. M. (1999) 'Bureaucrats in Business: The Roles of Privatization versus Corporatization in State-Owned Enterprise Reform'. *World Development*, 27(1): 115–36.

Shishlov, I., Nicol, M. and Cochron, I. (2018) *Green Bonds Research Program Work Package 2*. Paris: Institute for Climate Economics (I4CE).

Shleifer, A. (1998) 'State versus Private Ownership'. *Journal of Economic Perspectives*, 12(4): 133–50.

Shleifer, A. and Vishny, R. W. (1994) 'Politicians and Firms'. *Quarterly Journal of Economics*, 109: 995–1025.

Shleifer, A. and Vishny, R. W. (1997) 'A Survey of Corporate Governance'. *Journal of Finance*, 52: 737–83.

Shonfield, A. (1969[1965]). *Modern Capitalism: The Changing Balance of Public and Private Power*. New York: Oxford University Press.

Sidki, M. and Boll, D. (2019) 'What Do Citizens Think about Public Enterprise? Subjective Survey Data on the Legitimacy of the Economic Activities of the German Public Sector'. *Annals of Public and Cooperative Economics*, 90(4): 615–39.

Sipilä, J. (2016) Speech at the Nordic Investment Bank's 40th Anniversary Seminar, by Prime Minister of Finland Juha Sipilä, Copenhagen, 02 November 2016. www.nib.int Accessed 27 April 2018.

SIWI (2018) *Water Pollution Data in the Baltic Sea Basin – A Local to Regional Approach*. Stockholm, Sweden: Stockholm International Water Institute. Available at www.siwi.org. Accessed 16 March 2020.

Skidelsky, R., Martin, F. and Westerlind Wigstrom, C. (2011) *Blueprint for a British Investment Bank*. London: Centre for Global Studies.

Soederberg, S. (2010) *Corporate Power and Ownership in Contemporary Capitalism. The Politics of Resistance and Domination*. Abingdon: Routledge.

Soederberg, S. (2013a) 'Universalising Financial Inclusion and the Securitisation of Development'. *Third World Quarterly*, 34(4): 593–612.

Soederberg, S. (2013b) 'The US Debtfare State and the Credit Card Industry: Forging Spaces of Dispossession'. *Antipode*, 45(2): 493–512.

Soederberg, S. (2014) *Debtfare States and the Poverty Industry: Money, Discipline, and the Surplus Population*. Abingdon: Routledge.

Spratt, S. (2009) *Development Finance: Debates, Dogmas, and New Directions*. London: Routledge.

Spratt, S. (2015) 'Financing Green Transformations'. In Scoones, I., Leach, M. and Newell, P. (eds.), *The Politics of Green Transformations*. Abingdon: Taylor & Francis, pp. 153–69.

Spratt, S. and Ryan-Collins, L. (2012) 'Development Finance Institutions and Infrastructure: A Systematic Review of Evidence for Development Additionality'. A Report Commissioned by the Private Infrastructure Development Group.

Spronk, S. (2010) 'Water and Sanitation Utilities in the Global South: Re-centering the Debate on "Efficiency"'. *Review of Radical Political Economics*, 42(2): 156–74.

Spronk, S. and Miraglia, S. (2015) 'Neoliberalism, Social Reproduction and Women's Resistance: Lessons from Cambodia and Venezuela'. In Pradella, L. and Marois, T. (eds.), *Polarizing Development: Alternatives to Neoliberalism and the Crisis*. London: Pluto Press, pp. 98–107.

Spufford, P. (2014) 'Provision of Stable Moneys by Florence and Venice, and North Italian Financial Innovations in the Renaissance Period'. *Explaining Monetary and Financial Innovation Financial and Monetary Policy Studies*, 39: 227–51.

Stallings, B. (2006) *Finance for Development: Latin America in Comparative Perspective*. Washington, DC: The Brookings Institution.

Standard and Poors (2017) *Ratings Direct: Nordic Investment Bank*. Stockholm: Standard & Poor's Financial Services.

Stavrides, S. (2016) *Common Space: The City as Commons*. London: Zed Books.

Stockhammer, E. (2012) 'Financialization, Income Distribution and the Crisis'. *Investigación Económica*, 71(279): 39–70.

Strange, S. (1994[1988]) *States and Markets*, 2nd ed. Pinter Publishers: London.

Steinfort, L. and Kishimoto, S. (eds.) (2019) *Public Finance for the Future We Want*. Amsterdam: Transnational Institute. Available at www.tni.org/en/publicfi nance. Accessed 2 June 2019.

Stern, N. (2007) *The Economics of Climate Change*. Cambridge: Cambridge University Press.

Stiglitz, J. (1994) 'The Role of the State in Financial Markets'. Proceedings of the World Bank Annual Conference on Development Economics 1993. Washington, DC: World Bank. pp. 19–61.

Studart, R. and Gallagher, K. P. (2016) 'Infrastructure for Sustainable Development: The Role of National Development Banks'. GEGI Policy Brief 007. Boston: Global Economic Governance Initiative–GEGI.

Sullivan, S. (2013) 'Banking Nature? The Spectacular Financialisation of Environmental Conservation'. *Antipode*, 45: 198–217.

Storm, S. (2018) 'Financialization and Economic Development: A Debate on the Social Efficiency of Modern Finance'. *Development and Change*, 49(2): 302–29.

Sweeney, R. (2019) 'Transformation of Banking Reconsidered: How Feasible Is "De-financialisation"?'. *Cambridge Journal of Economics*, 43(4): 1053–71.

Sweeney, S. and Treat, J. (2017) 'Preparing a Public Pathway Confronting the Investment Crisis in Renewable Energy'. Trade Unions for Energy Democracy (TUED) Working Paper, No. 10. New York: Trade Unions for Energy Democracy. Available at http://unionsforenergydemocracy.org/resources/tued-publications/tued-working-paper-10-preparing-a-public-pathway/. Accessed 16 July 2020.

Sweezy, P. M. (1997) 'More (or Less) on Globalization'. *Monthly Review*, 49(4): 3.

Summers, T. (2016) 'China's "New Silk Roads": Sub-national Regions and Networks of Global Political Economy'. *Third World Quarterly*, 37(9): 1628–43.

Taylor, M. (2012) 'The Antinomies of "Financial Inclusion": Debt, Distress and the Workings of Indian Microfinance'. *Journal of Agrarian Change*, 12(4): 601–10.

Taylor, M. (2014) *The Political Ecology of Climate Change Adaptation: Livelihoods, Agrarian Change and the Conflicts of Development*. London: Routledge Press.

Taylor, M. (2017) 'From Tigers to Cats: The Rise and Crisis of Microfinance in Rural India'. In Bateman, M. and Maclean, K. (eds.), *Seduced and Betrayed: Exposing the Contemporary Microfinance Phenomenon*. Albuquerque: University of New Mexico Press.

Ten Brink, T. (2013) 'Paradoxes of Prosperity in China's New Capitalism'. *Journal of Current Chinese Affairs*, 42(4): 17–44.

Thayer, T. (1953) 'The Land-Bank System in the American Colonies'. *The Journal of Economic History*, 13(2): 145–59.

Thirlwall, A. P. (2011) *Economics of Development: Theory and Evidence*, 9th ed. Houndmills: Palgrave Macmillan.

Tilly, R. (1998) 'Universal Banking in Historical Perspective'. *Journal of Institutional and Theoretical Economics*, 154(1): 7–32.

Tiwari, M. (2013) 'The Global Financial Crisis and Self-Help Groups in Rural India: Are There Lessons from Their Micro Savings Model?'. *Development in Practice*, 23(2): 278–91.

Tomaskovic-Devey, D., Lin, K.-H., Meyers, N. (2015) 'Did Financialization Reduce Economic Growth?'. *Socio-Economic Review*, 13(3): 525–48.

Tooze, A. (2018) *Crashed: How a Decade of Financial Crises Changed the World*. New York: Viking.

Toporowski, J. (1994) 'Banks and Financial Institutions'. In Arestis, P. and Sawyer, M. (eds.), *The Elgar Companion to Radical Political Economy*. Brookfield, VT: Edward Elgar, pp. 20–4.

Tricarico, A. (2015) *Reclaiming Public Banks: A Thought Provoking Exercise*. Brussels: CounterBalance. Available atwww.eurodad.org/files/pdf/1546411-reclaiming-public-banks-a-thought-provoking-exercise.pdf. Accessed 18 June 2019.

Tukic, N. and Burgess, M. (2016) 'China's Role in Africa's Water Sector: Mapping the Terrain'. *Waterlines*, 35(1): 18–36.

Tullock, G., Seldon, A. and Brady, G. L. (2002) *Government Failure: A Primer on Public Choice*. Washington, DC: Cato Institute.

Turner, G., Tan, N. and Sadeghian, D. (2012) 'The Chinese Banking System'. *RBA: Bulletin*, (September Quarter): 1–13.

UNCTAD (2018) *Scaling up Finance for the Sustainable Development Goals: Experimenting with Models of Multilateral Development Banking*. Geneva: United Nations Conference on Trade and Development.

UNCTAD (2019) *Trade and Development Report 2019: Financing a Global Green New Deal*. Geneva: United Nations Conference on Trade and Development.

UNEP (2015) *The Financial System We Need*. Nairobi, Kenya: United Nations Environment Programme.

UN IATF (2017–19) *Financing for Sustainable Development Report*. New York: United Nations Inter-agency Task Force on Financing for Development.

UN Water (2015) *The United Nations World Water Development Report 2015: Water for a Sustainable World*. Paris: UNESCO.

van der Zwan, N. (2014) 'State of the Art: Making Sense of Financialisation'. *Socio-Economic Review*, 12(1): 99–129.

Vanberg, V. J. (2005) 'Market and State: The Perspective of Constitutional Political Economy'. *Journal of Institutional Economics*, 1(1): 23–49.

Vanaerschot, F. (2019) 'Democratizing Nationalized Banks'. In Steinfort, L. and Kishimoto, S. (eds.), *Public Finance for the Future We Want*. Amsterdam: Transnational Institute, pp. 136–49.

Vergara-Camus, L. (2014) 'Sugarcane Ethanol: The Hen of the Golden Eggs? Agrarian Capital and the State under Lula's Presidency'. In Spronk, S. and Webber, J. (eds.), *Crisis and Contradiction: Marxist Perspectives on Latin America in the Global Economy*. Leiden: Brill Academic Publishers, pp. 211–35.

VÖB (2014) *Promotional Banks in Germany: Acting in the Public Interest*. Berlin: Association of German Public Banks (Bundesverband Öffentlicher Banken Deutschlands, VÖB).

Volz, U., Böhnke, J., Eidt, V., Knierim, K., Richert, K. and Roeber, G.-M. (2015) *Financing the Green Transformation – How to Make Green Finance Work in Indonesia*. Houndmills: Palgrave Macmillan.

von Braunmühl, C. (1978) 'On the Analysis of the Bourgeois Nation State within the World Market Context. An Attempt to Develop a Methodological and Theoretical Approach'. In Holloway, J. and Picciotto, S. (eds.), *State and Capital: A Marxist Debate*. London: Edward Arnold, pp. 160–77.

von Mettenheim, K. (2010) *Federal Banking in Brazil*. London: Pickering & Chatto.

von Mettenheim, K. (2012) 'Public Banks: Competitive Advantages and Policy Alternatives, *Public Banking Institute Journal*, 1(1): 2–34.

von Mettenheim, K. and Butzbach, O. (2012) 'Alternative Bank: Theory and Evidence from Europe'. *Brazilian Journal of Political Economy*, 32(4): 580–96.

von Mettenheim, K. and Butzbach, O. (2014) 'Alternative Banking History'. In von Mettenheim, K. and Butzbach, O. (eds.), *Alternative Banking and Financial Crisis*. London: Pickering & Chatto, pp. 11–28.

von Mettenheim, K. and Butzbach, O. (2017) 'Back to the Future of Alternative Banks and Patient Capital'. In Scherrer, C. (ed.), *Public Banks in the Age of Financialization: A Comparative Perspective*. Cheltenham: Edward Elgar, pp. 29–50.

von Mettenheim, K. and Del Tedesco Lins, M. A. (eds.) (2008) *Government Banking: New Perspectives on Sustainable Development and Social Inclusion From Europe and South America*. Rio de Janeiro and Berlin: Konrad Adenauer Foundation.

von Weizsäcker, E. U., Young, O. R. and Finger, M. (eds.) (2005) *Limits to Privatization: How to Avoid too Much of a Good Thing: A Report to the Club of Rome*. London: Earthscan.

Wade, R. H. (2002) 'US Hegemony and the World Bank: The Fight over People and Ideas'. *Review of International Political Economy*, 9(2): 201–29.

Wainwright, H. (2014) *The Tragedy of the Private, The Potential of the Public*. Published by Public Services International (Ferney-Voltaire, France) and the Transnational Institute (Amsterdam, Netherlands). Available at www.world-psi.org/en/tragedy-private-potential-public. Accessed 7 July 2019.

Wainwright, H. (2020) 'Transforming the State: Towards Democracy-Driven Public Ownership'. In Kishimoto, S., Steinfort, L. and Petitjean, O. (eds.), *The Future is Public towards Democratic Ownership of Public Services*. Amsterdam: Transnational Institute. Available at www.tni.org/files/publication-down loads/futureispublic_online_def_14_july.pdf. Accessed 31 July 2020.

Walby, S. (2013) 'Finance versus Democracy? Theorizing Finance in Society'. *Work, Employment, Society*, 27: 489–507.

Walter, C. and Howie, F. (2012) *Red Capitalism: The Fragile Financial Foundation of China's Extraordinary Rise*. Singapore: John Wiley & Sons.

Wang, H. (2017) 'New Multilateral Development Banks: Opportunities and Challenges for Global Governance'. *Global Policy*, 8(1): 113–18.

Wang, M. L., Wang, W., Shen, Y. D., Cun, F. L. and He, Z. (2020) 'Causal Relationships between Carbon Dioxide Emissions and Economic Factors: Evidence from China'. *Sustainable Development*, 28(1): 73–82.

Wang, Y. (2016) 'The Sustainable Infrastructure Finance of China Development Bank: Composition, Experience and Policy Implications'. Global Economic

Governance Initiative Working Paper, No. 5, 07/2016. Boston: Boston University Global Economic Governance Initiative. Available at www.bu.edu/ pardeeschool/files/2016/07/Wang.New_.Final_.pdf. Accessed 10 June 2018.

Wang, Z., He, H. and Fan, M. (2014) 'The Ecological Civilization Debate in China: The Role of Ecological Marxism and Constructive Postmodernism-Beyond the Predicament of Legislation'. *Monthly Review*, 66(6): 37–59.

Warner, M. E. (2015) 'Profiting from Public Values: The Case of Social Impact Bonds'. In Bryson, J., Crosby, B. and Bloomberg, L. (eds.), *Creating Public Value in Practice*, New York: CRC Press/Taylor and Francis, pp. 143–60.

Whitener, B. (2019) *Crisis Cultures: The Rise of Finance in Mexico and Brazil*. University of Pittsburgh Press.

Wilson, B. M. (1998) *Costa Rica: Politics, Economics, and Democracy*. Boulder, CO: Lynne Rienner Publishers.

Weber, H. (2004) 'The New Economy and Social Risk: Banking on the Poor'. *Review of International Political Economy*, 11(2): 356–86.

Weber, O. (2014) 'The Financial Sector's Impact on Sustainable Development'. *Journal of Sustainable Finance & Investment*, 4(1): 1–8.

Weber, O. and Saravade, V. (2019) 'Green Bonds: Current Development and Their Future'. Centre for International Governance Innovation Papers, No. 210, January. Waterloo, Canada: Centre for International Governance Innovation.

WEF (2006) *Building on the Monterrey Consensus: The Untapped Potential of Development Finance Institutions to Catalyse Private Investment*. Financing for Development Initiative. Geneva: World Economic Forum. Available at https:// sustainabledevelopment.un.org/getWSDoc.php?id=3030. Accessed 28 May 2019.

Wen, J. (2011) *Report on the Work of the Government*, delivered at the Fourth Session of the Eleventh National People's Congress, 5 March. Beijing.

Whiteside, H. (2017) 'The Canada Infrastructure Bank: Private Finance as Poor Alternative'. *Studies in Political Economy*, 98(2): 223–37.

Williamson, J. (1990) 'What Washington Means by Policy Reform'. In Williamson, J. (ed.), *Latin American Adjustment: How Much Has Happened?*. Washington: Institute for International Economics, pp. 7–20.

World Bank (2001) *Finance for Growth: Policy Choices in a Volatile World*. Washington, DC: The World Bank.

World Bank (2012a) *Global Financial Development Report 2013: Rethinking the Role of State in Finance*. Washington, DC: The World Bank.

World Bank (2012b) *Survey of National Development Banks*. Washington, DC: The World Bank.

World Bank (2012c) *Green Infrastructure Finance: Framework Report*. Washington, DC: The World Bank.

World Bank (2014) *Global Financial Development Report 2014: Financial Inclusion*. Washington, DC: The World Bank

World Bank (2018) *2017 Survey of National Development Banks*. Washington, DC: The World Bank.

World Bank/IMF (2015) 'From Billions to Trillions: Transforming Development Finance Post-2015 Financing for Development: Multilateral Development Finance'. Development Committee, Joint Ministerial Committee of the Boards of Governors of the Bank and the Fund on the Transfer of Real Resources to Developing Countries. DC2015–0002, 2 April 2015.

World Bank/IMF (2017) 'Maximizing Finance for Development: Leveraging the Private Sector for Growth and Sustainable Development'. World Bank Group and International Monetary Fund Development Committee, DC2017–0009. Available at http://siteresources.worldbank.org/DEVCOMMINT/Documentation/23758671/DC2017–0009_Maximizing_8–19.pdf. Accessed 20 May 2019.

World Economic Forum (WEF) (2020) *New Nature Economy Report II the Future of Nature and Business*. Geneva: WEF. Available at www3.weforum.org/docs/WEF_The_Future_Of_Nature_And_Business_2020.pdf. Accessed 10 September 2020.

Wright, E. O. (2010) *Envisioning Real Utopias*. London: Verso.

Wu, R. (2003) 'Segregation and Convergence: The Chinese Dilemma for Financial Services Sectors'. In Cass, D. Z., Williams, B. G. and Barker, G. (eds.), *China and the World Trading System – Entering the New Millennium*. Cambridge: Cambridge University Press, pp. 283–98.

Xu, J., Ren, X. and Wu, X. (2019) 'Mapping Development Finance Institutions Worldwide: Definitions, Rationales, and Varieties'. NSE Development Financing Research Report No. 1. Beijing: Peking University Institute of New Structural Economics.

Xu, Q. (2018) 'China Development Bank: Born Bankrupt, Born Shaper'. In Griffith-Jones, S. and Ocampo, J. A. (eds.), *The Future of National Development Banks*. Cambridge: Cambridge University Press, pp. 39–62.

Yalman, G. and Marois, T. and Güngen, A. R. (eds.) (2019) *The Political Economy of Financial Transformation in Turkey*. Abingdon: Routledge.

Yeung, G. (2009) 'Hybrid Property, Path Dependence, Market Segmentation and Financial Exclusion: The Case of the Banking Industry in China'. *Transactions of the Institute of British Geographers*. 34(2): 177–94.

Yin, R. K. (2014) *Case Study Research Design and Methods*, 5th ed. Thousand Oaks, CA: Sage.

Ysa, T., Giné, M., Esteve, M. and Sierra, V. (2012) 'Public Corporate Governance of State-Owned Enterprises: Evidence from the Spanish Banking Industry'. *Public Money & Management*, 32(4): 265–72.

Zaifer, A. (2020) 'Variegated Privatisation: Class, Capital Accumulation and State in Turkey's Privatisation Process in the 1980s and 1990s'. *Critical Sociology*, 46(1): 141–56.

Zhang, H. (2020) 'Regulating Green Bond in China: Definition Divergence and Implications for Policy Making'. *Journal of Sustainable Finance & Investment*, 10(2): 141–56.

Ziraat Bank (2010) *2009 Annual Report*. Ankara, Turkey: Ziraat Bank.

Index